The Republican Party
in the US Senate 1974–1984

For my parents

The Republican Party in the US Senate

1974–1984: party change and institutional development

CHRISTOPHER J. BAILEY

Manchester University Press

Distributed exclusively in the USA and Canada by
St. Martin's Press, New York

Copyright © Christopher J. Bailey 1988

Published by
Manchester University Press, Oxford Road, Manchester M13 9PL, UK

Distributed exclusively in the USA and Canada by
St. Martin's Press, Inc., 175 Fifth Avenue, New York, NY 10010, USA

British Library cataloguing in publication data

Bailey, Christopher J.
  The Republican Party in the US Senate 1974–1984:
  party change and institutional development.
  1. United States. *Congress, Senate*–History
  2. Republican Party *(U.S.)*–History
  I. Title
  324.2734   JK2356
ISBN 0 7190 2582 6 *hardback*   ⊂ ⊂

Library of Congress cataloging in publication data applied for

6003664076

Printed in Great Britain by Billing & Sons Limited, Worcester
Typesetting: Heather Hems, Tower House, Queen Street, Gillingham, Dorset

Contents

Acknowledgements

I am indebted to many people, both in the United Kingdom and the United States, for the help they gave me with this book. First and foremost I should like to thank Gillian Peele for her constant help and encouragement. I also benefited greatly from the advice of the late Philip Williams who was always ready to share his vast store of knowledge. On a visit to Washington D.C. in October 1983 I was fortunate enough to meet Austin Ranney, James Reichley, Michael Malbin, Thomas Mann, Norman Ornstein, Steven Smith, and Roger Davidson. I should like to take this opportunity to thank them for giving me some of their valuable time, and for allowing me to use their contacts on Capitol Hill. I must also thank Roger Davidson for supplying me with detailed statistics and information on congressional activity. Of course, any errors of fact or interpretation remaining in the book are mine alone.

On a more personal note, I should like to thank my friends and colleagues who made the whole project much more enjoyable. In particular I should like to express my gratitude to Kathy and Tom Imbemba for their incredible hospitality and generosity in looking after me in Washington D.C., and to Bill Nave for showing me the sights of New York. Closer to home I should like to thank Mark Thackeray, Philip Stephens, Michael Bloom, Peter Crook, and Bernie Watts of Exeter College, Oxford, for providing me with many distractions from my work. I must also thank my new colleagues in the Department of American Studies at the University of Keele for making me feel welcome and providing a pleasant environment to complete this book. Special thanks go to Mrs Karen Harrison and Mrs Maureen Simkin for typing the manuscript with considerable speed and precision.

Finally, I should like to thank Mandy, my wife, for her constant support and forbearance during the past few years.

June 1987   C. J. B.
University of Keele

1 Introduction

Traditional studies of the US Congress have strangely neglected the impact that the political parties have on the congressional process. The discussion of the organisation and activities of the parties in these works has generally been incidental to an approach which concentrated on the institutional role of Congress, and the affect of this role on its membership. More recent research, however, has tended to move away from this line of inquiry, and instead has started to look at the effect that the individual may have on the structure of an institution.[1] In particular, the career goals, experience and actions of Cpngress's membership have been shown to be pertinent to features such as the distribution of power and the nature of decision-making within the institution. A study of the Republican Party within the US Senate between 1974 and 1984 is peculiarly suited to this approach and provides a valuable means of understanding contemporary change within the institution. Not only have both the Republican Party and the Senate been understudied in recent years, but the dramatic changes within the GOP during this period as it recovered from the nadir of Watergate were to have an important affect on the chamber's procedures and structure.

The morale of the Republican Party in the Senate at the beginning of the 94th Congress (1975–6) was at its lowest since the New Deal election of 1936. Although the party's losses during the Watergate election of 1974 were far less than expected, and the GOP's total of thirty-eight seats in the Senate was greater than the Republicans had enjoyed for all but the last of the 1960s, there was a general feeling among Republican senators that President Ford's pardon of Richard Nixon had seriously damaged their party's electoral viability.[2] Typical was the concern expressed by Senator Howard Baker (R – Tenn) that President Ford's action 'may reopen a caustic and divisive debate in the country'.[3] To most observers the GOP looked destined to remain the minority party in the Senate for the foreseeable future, with the Republicans lacking both a sizeable constituency and a coherent public philosophy. Several conservative senators, including Jesse Helms (R - NC), James McClure (R - Idaho), Paul Laxalt (R - Nev), and Jake Garn (R - Utah), were even reported as having articulated the possibility of forming a new third party.[4] Six years later however, the Republicans took control of the Senate for the first time since the 83rd Congress (1953–4), and seemed poised to provide backing for President Reagan's planned assault on the programmes of the Great Society. Not only had they managed to increase their support among the electorate but they also appeared to have developed a set of policies which could be presented as a viable alternative to the public philosophy which had dominated American politics since the New Deal.

To a certain extent the revival in Republican strength in the Senate during the late 1970s was a consequence of a more general reaction against the philosophy of the Great Society and discontent with the Federal Government's attempts to regulate the economy. Evidence of a backlash against the social programmes of the 1960s and 1970s can be seen in the formation of a number of groups commonly associated with the New Right. Right-to-Life organisations such as the National Right to Life Committee, the National Pro-Life Political Action Committee, the Life Amendment Political Action Committee, and the American Life Lobby sprang up following the Supreme Court's ruling in the cases *Roe* v. *Wade* and *Doe* v. *Bolton* in 1973 that a woman had a constitutional right to an abortion during the first three months of a pregnancy.[5] These rulings, and subsequent decisions in the cases *Planned Parenthood of Missouri* v. *Danforth* (1976), *Maher* v. *Roe* (1977), *Bellotti* v. *Baird* (1979) and *Harris* v. *McRae* (1980) were opposed by the New Right not only because they were perceived as condoning 'baby killing' but also because they seemed to represent an example of the Supreme Court's construction of constitutional rights.[6] Religious groups such as Moral Majority, Christian Voice, and Religious Roundtable mobilised to oppose the Supreme Court's school prayer decisions and the spread of the permissive society. As one direct-mail letter from Christian Voice stated: 'My friend, our world is being turned upside down and inside out because we Christians have been sitting back and allowing God to be excluded from our schools, allowed our government to promote baby-killing with our tax dollars, supported the so-called "equal rights" for sexual perverts and much, much more. . .'[7] Other groups, both single-interest and more general organisations such as the National Conservative Political Action Committee and the Committee for the Survival of a Free Congress, were formed to oppose gun control, busing, the civil rights programmes of the Great Society which were perceived by many as favouring minorities, and their supporters in Congress.[8]

While the groups of the New Right mobilised to oppose the Civil rights measures of the 1960s and their supporters in Congress, and in particular liberal Democrats and Republicans in the Senate, the performance of the economy seemed to discredit Keynesian techniques of demand management. Between 1973 and 1981 economic output in the United States grew at a rate of 1·2 per cent per year compared with the average annual rate of 2·2 per cent between 1948 and 1973. Unemployment averaged more than 6 per cent during the 1970s after averaging less than 5 per cent in the 1950s and 1960s, and the rate of inflation reached double figures in 1979–80. With the economy performing so poorly, with many people feeling that the civil rights programmes of the 1960s had gone 'too far, too quickly', and with the foreign policy of the United States in disarray following the overthrow of the Shah of Iran and the Russian invasion of Afghanistan, there can be little doubt that the electorate's desire for change helped the Republican electoral resurgence during the late 1970s. In 1978 they gained three seats in the Senate, in 1980 they gained twelve seats to capture the Senate with the largest increase in the number of Republican senators in a presidential election year since 1868, and in 1982 maintained their position.[9]

In addition to benefiting from the new mood of the electorate, the Republicans also proved much more adept at taking advantage of the changing electoral environment of the late 1970s than the Democrats.[10] During this period a number of new developments in the techniques of electioneering combined with changes in the American electorate caused by an expansion in higher education and the lowering of the voting age following the passage of the 26th Amendment in 1971 to create a highly unstable electoral environment in which traditional party loyalties and labels meant increasingly less as determinants of voting behaviour. The weakening of partisanship in the electorate, exemplified by the growth in the number of 'independents' from about 25 per cent of the electorate in the 1950s to just under 40 per cent by the late 1970s, led to a far greater emphasis being placed upon the machinery of electioneering.[11] Organisation and the mastery of new campaign techniques thus assumed a far greater importance in determining the outcome of elections. Using devices such as television and direct mail the Republicans were able to transform the electorate's general desire for change into specific complaints against incumbent Democrats. As the Democratic Senator Daniel Moynihan stated: 'There were two things that hit us. First was money, money, money, money . . . Then there was . . . organisation and technology . . . We are so far behind that we . . . are in danger of becoming the permanent minority party.'[12]

The Republican gains in the Senate during the late 1970s should therefore be viewed as the result of their ability to take advantage of the new developments in electioneering and seize the initiative when dealing with the major issues facing the United States. This enabled Republican candidates to attract electoral support from groups such as white southerners and Roman Catholics which had previously tended to vote Democratic, and thus confound those observers who believed that the post-Watergate GOP was destined to contract on an ageing, white, Anglo-Saxon base.[13] Of more importance, however, was the fact that the increase in the number of Republican senators not only changed the nature of the GOP in the Senate but also affected the structure of the chamber itself.

The increased number of Republicans elected to the Senate during the late 1970s and early 1980s significantly altered the traditional composition of the party. Between 1974 and 1980 the size and influence of the once pre-eminent Mid-Atlantic, New England and Midwest sections of the party had declined considerably.[14] By 1980 the Republican Party in the Senate was dominated by its Southern and Western wings. In the 97th Congress (1981–2) 51 per cent of Republican senators came from states in the South, Rocky Mountain, and Pacific Coast regions of the United States. This percentage rose to 52·7 per cent in the 98th Congress (1983–4), giving the GOP a distinct 'sunbelt' complexion, and seeming to confirm the prediction made by Kevin Phillips in his book *The Emerging Republican Majority* that the South and West were areas of potential Republican strength.[15] A comparison with the regional distribution of Republican senators in the 83rd Congress reveals the extent of these changes. The GOP's majority in the 83rd Congress was based firmly on the traditional Republican strongholds of the Midwest, Mid-Atlantic, and New England states with senators from these regions constituting 50 per cent of the party's membership. By the 97th Congress senators from these regions made up only 26·3 per cent of the GOP's strength, a percentage which fell to 25·5 per cent in the 98th Congress.

The change in the regional distribution of Republican senators had an important impact on the nature of the GOP in the Senate.

As Kirkpatrick Sale has written:

> The Republican Party, formed a century ago to transform the South, has finally had to admit defeat; it is the South that has transformed the Republican Party . . . The most far-reaching change in any political party in recent times has come about from the single fact of the Republicans opening themselves to the new and increasingly powerful forces of the South and Southwest, and thereby relegating the previously dominant forces to the Northeast to a diminished position.[16]

Changes in its regional composition not only led to the Republican Party adopting different policies and priorities as it opened itself up to new social forces but equally importantly led to major generational changes in its membership.

Unlike most European parties the two main American parties have never been ideologically monolithic, but rather have tended to represent different regions and interest groups.[17] As a consequence of the fact that most senators are primarily motivated by constituency concerns and the need to construct a successful electoral coalition which will enable them to gain re-election, ideological divisions within the Senate tend to accommodate and reflect constituency pressures rising out of shared 'regional and economic interests, personal and what might be termed tribal loyalties, and agreements on political strategy'.[18] Any change in the regional composition of the parties, therefore, is likely to alter their ideological stance. In the Senate the increased strength of the Republican Party's Southern and Western wings, and the relative decline of its Midwestern, New England, and Mid-Atlantic sections, was reflected in the party's more pronounced conservatism on economic, social and foreign affairs issues. Many of the new Republican senators from the South and West represented a conservative tradition in the United States which dated from the Second World War and stood in stark contrast to the traditional conservatism of the Midwest as represented in the past by the likes of Senators Robert Taft and Everett Dirksen, and the more moderate approach generally undertaken by Northeastern Republicans such as Senator Jacob Javits (R – NY). Western conservatives such as Senator Barry Goldwater (R – Ariz) were no longer content with moderating the rate of change in society but wanted a return to an earlier condition of society where racial tensions, permissiveness, drug abuse and increases in crime were believed to be unknown.

While the changing geographical distribution of the Republican Party in the Senate had a major affect on the party's ideological make-up, strengthening the conservative elements of the party at the expense of the more moderate elements, the influx of Republicans from states in the South and West also served to accentuate certain generational changes that were taking place within the party's membership. During the late 1970s the qualities required for success in the electoral arena were considerably different from what they had been a decade earlier. Reforms such as the Federal Election Campaign Act (1971) and its amendments of 1974, 1976 and 1979, together with the increased use of television in Senate races, gave rise to what Gary Jacobson has described as the 'ascendent importance of individual candidates and campaigns'.[19] Increasingly the role of the political party in the campaign gave way to the technology of television-centred campaigns built on the findings of opinion polls, and run by media and public relations experts.[20] By the late 1970s most senatorial candidates were 'self-starters': putting together their own political organisations with help and finance from various Political Action Committees (PACs), and succeeding with little help, or even opposition from party officials. Gordon Humphrey in New Hampshire in 1978, Jeremiah Denton in Alabama in 1980, and Mary Buchanan in Colorado in 1980, even managed to defeat the official Republican nominees in their primary elections. Candidates for the Senate no longer had to gain the support of the party to ensure their election. Rather, electoral success was largely dependent upon a candidate's ability to take advantage of the new campaign techniques and speak to the ascendent interests within a state.

The skills required for electoral success, therefore, did not have to be learnt by serving a political apprenticeship, but instead, could be bought by hiring a political consultant. This meant that candidates for the Senate in the 1970s no longer needed much, if any, experience of elected office in order to succeed. Once again a comparison between the 83rd and 97th Congress illustrates this point well. In the 83rd Congress there were three Republican senators with no previous experience of elected office: John Marshall Butler (R – Md), Wallace F. Bennett (R – Utah), and William A. Partell (R – Conn).[21] The inclusion of John Marshall Butler in this list is particularly revealing as in many respects he can be regarded as the forerunner of the modern senatorial candidate. He was the first candidate for the Senate to use tele-vision as a campaign tool, and in a state where the Republican organisation was virtually nonexistent he developed his own organisation under the guidance of Jon M. Jonkel, a public relations expert from Chicago.[22] By the 97th Congress such practices were commonplace, and the number of Republican senators with no previous experience of elected office much greater. In 1981 the number of Republicans falling into this category was fifteen. Of these fifteen senators seven came from states in the South and West where the Republican Party organisation was generally weaker than in the Midwest, Mid-Atlantic, and New England states.

The developments in electioneering which led to changes in the level of previous political experience found among Republican senators also had an affect upon the party's age structure. With senators no longer needing to serve an 'apprenticeship' in a lower political office they were able to gain election to the Senate at an earlier age. The increasing use of television in election campaigns, moreover, placed a premium on those individuals who could use the medium well. This tended to favour 'younger' candidates who were able to portray themselves as youthful, fit, and dynamic. In the 83rd Congress most Republican senators were in the 56–65 years age group, and only fifteen senators, or 31·3 per cent of the party, were under the age of 56 years. In the 97th Congress most Republican senators were in the 46–55 years age group, and a total of thirty-seven senators, or 69·9 per cent of the party were under the age of 56 years.

The importance of these changes lies in the fact that it is the generational make-up of a party's membership, and the nature of the electoral environment, which largely determines its political *style*. Studies have shown that there is a distinct contrast in legislative style between party-initiated members and self-starters.[23] Party regulars, having worked their way up through the party apparatus, tend to be followers and compromisers, while the normally younger, less experienced, self-starters are usually more issue-orientated and publicity conscious. The new breed of Republican senators of the late 1970s were mainly self-starters and their behaviour tended to reflect the individualism of the organisations from which they came. They won their seats largely through their own efforts. They were self selected, put together their own political organisations, raised their own money, and developed their own campaigns. Not having needed the party to gain election they did not feel beholden to it once in the Senate.

Party coherence was also undermined by certain developments in electioneering during the late 1970s, in particular, the increasing sophistication of direct-mail techniques and the growing involvement of Political Action Committees in campaigns, which heightened the visibility of incumbents, and made it essential for officeholders to respond to the wishes, fears and prejudices of their constituents. As one such officeholder, Senator Dale Bumpers (D – Ark), stated: 'The Founding Fathers gave senators six year terms so they could be statesmen for at least four years and not respond to every whim and caprice. Now a senator in his first year knows that any vote could hurt him five years later. So senators behave like House members. They're running constantly.'[24] Senators thus had little need of the party to gain election, and once elected tended to place constituency concerns above all else. Paradoxically, therefore, the very developments in the electoral environment which had allowed the Republican Party to fashion a majority in 1980 also weakened the party's unity and undermined the authority of the party leadership.

The Constitution's only reference to leadership posts and responsibilities in the Senate are contained in two passages of Article I, Section 3. One clause provides that the vice-president 'shall be President of the Senate, but shall have no vote, unless they are equally divided'. The other provides that the 'Senate shall . . . choose . . . a President pro tempore, in the absence of the vice-president, or when he shall exercise the office of President of the United States'. In the years 1823–6, 1828, 1841, 1843 and 1863 the president pro tempore was authorised to appoint members of the Senate to standing committees, but generally senators have been reluctant to place substantial power in these positions, and neither post has ever equalled the significance of the Speaker of the House of Representatives. Senator Arthur Vandenberg (R – Mich) exerted considerable political influence as president pro tempore in the 80th Congress (1947–8), but this was largely a consequence of the fact that he was also Chairman of the Senate's Foreign Relations Committee. On certain occasions, however, rulings by the vice-president or president pro tempore on points of order have had an enormous impact on American public policy. For example, when a motion was made in 1948 to bring an anti-poll-tax bill to the Senate floor for consideration, Senator Richard Russell (D – Ga) made a point of order that a procedural motion was not a pending measure and, therefore, not subject to a vote of cloture to end debate. President *pro tempore* Arthur Vandenberg sustained Russell's point. In effect the decision nullified Rule 22, the standing rule which detailed the requirements of a vote of cloture because a motion to bring up a bill always had to precede a vote on the bill itself. Vandenberg's ruling effectively brought to an end the possibility of civil rights reform during the Truman Administration.[25]

Rather than being concentrated in the hands of the presiding officers, power in the Senate has tended to be entrusted to the majority and minority leaders. A lack of constitutional authority, and the fact that senators tend to regard themselves as un-regimented ambassadors from their states, however, has severely limited the power of the party leadership. Individual leaders such as John W. Kern (D – Ind) between 1911 and 1917, Joseph T. Robinson (D – Ark) between 1933 and 1937, and Lyndon B. Johnson (D – Texas) between 1955 and 1961, have managed to exert considerable authority, but such power has been personal rather than institutional. Johnson gave the following summary of the office of majority leader: 'There is no patronage; no power to discipline; no authority to fire senators like a President can fire members of his cabinet . . . the only real power available to the leader is the power of persuasion.'[26] The Texan's skill as a leader lay in a willingness to use the full resources of his office for the purpose of persuasion in what became known as the 'Johnson Treatment'.[27]

There have been occasions, therefore, when leaders such as Johnson have been able to use their authority to shape the setting of the institution in which they served. During the 1970s, however, the authority of the party leadership was weakened by competing influences and power centres. The emergence of new election laws placed a premium on the ability of the individual candidate to develop his own organisation, and generated demands for congress-ional reform which altered the distribution of power within the Senate. Reforms such as the Legislative Reorganisation Act (1970) which introduced a new set of limitations on committee assign-ments and opened committee hearings to the public, S.Res 9 (1975) which opened committee mark-ups, S.Res 12 (1975) which opened conference committees, S.Res 60 (1975) which provided more staff for junior senators, and S.Res 4 (1977) which authorised the first overhaul of the Senate's committee system since the Legislative Reorganisation Act (1946), worked to weaken the authority of both the party and committee leadership in the Senate. Moreover, in addition to undermining the authority of the Senate's leadership, these reforms also had the unintended effect of reinforcing the importance of constituency politics in the chamber. By opening up the proceedings of the Senate they facilitated greater scrutiny of the voting records of individual senators by special interest groups.

The factors limiting the power of the party leaders in the

Senate provide a useful illustration of how the nature of an institution influences the structure of the political parties operating at that level. The role of the Senate as the institution which represents the interests of the state in the federal government has led to the development of parties in which power has tended to be decentralised. Senators have usually regarded themselves as the representatives of their states, encapsulating what James Madison described as the 'constitutional recognition of the portion of sovereignty remaining in the individual states'.[28] Consequently there has been a tendency to resist attempts at centralising party leadership as most senators have argued that such centralisation would compromise their independence and hence their perceived role as ambassadors from their states.

Although it is clear that the institutional role of the Senate, its design as a small conservative body and guardian of the interests of the states, tends to generate a *general* structure which emphasises informality and a lack of strong leadership, it is also apparent that the *specific* manner in which power is distributed within the chamber is dependent upon the nature of its membership. The Constitution suggests that all senators are equal, yet obviously, both the committee and the party systems work to distribute power in ways which increase the power of committee chairmen and party leaders, with the actual degree of centralisation being dependent upon factors such as the prevailing electoral environment and the requirements of policy-making. As these factors are likely to vary, implicit in this analysis is the idea that the structure of the Senate should not be viewed as static, but rather, should be interpreted as the result of a dynamic interaction between the institution and its membership. Not only does the institution influence the structure of the parties but the parties also have an affect on the institution.

The dramatic changes within the Republican Party between 1974 and 1984 had an important effect on the rules and procedures of the Senate. During the late 1970s the turnover rate of senators increased considerably. In the elections of 1974 85·2 per cent of those senators seeking re-election were successful, but by 1980 this percentage had fallen to 55·2 per cent. These high turnover rates meant that the ratio of junior to senior Republican senators increased from 1:2·07 in the 94th Congress to 1:0·511 in the 97th Congress. The importance of these figures lies in the fact that, as Thomas Mann had pointed out, 'elections shape the internal politics of Congress by setting the overall level of membership stability'.[29] A low degree of turnover is highly compatible with the seniority system, and generates a fairly stable environment within the institution as the few junior members are willing to wait their turn to assume the advantages of incumbency. A high turnover rate, however, generates an unsettled environment where a large cadre of junior members begins to question the benefits of the seniority system, and calls for changes in the chamber's rules and procedures.

In addition to providing a bulwark against any effort to centralise power once more within the party, the high turnover rates of the late 1970s also meant that there were fewer experienced senators available to educate those freshmen lacking in political experience. This point was made by one Senate aide who explained: 'We usually changed three or four members at a time. The newcomers were absorbed by the comity, the tradition, the club. But now they set the rules of the body. It's no longer the club it used to be.'[30] Lacking a deep understanding of the institution in which they served, and conscious of the need to satisfy constituency interests, many of the new Republican senators used the Senate's norms and rules to further their own aims in a manner which subverted the traditional use of those procedures. Senate Jake Garn (R – Utah) summed up this attitude when he stated: 'If I'm against a bill in committee, I try to keep it there. If I can slow down a mark-up, or find some tactic to keep it off the floor, I'll do it . . . I don't particularly have loyalty to tradition.'[31] The use of the filibuster in particular was extended beyond previous practice by senators such as Garn, Jesse Helms, Orrin Hatch (R – Utah), and James McClure (R – Idaho). Whereas in the past the filibuster had been used sparingly, usually by senior senators concerned with such major issues as the New Deal or civil rights, by the 1970s they were being undertaken by junior senators over issues of a far more transient nature. There were only two filibusters between 1955 and 1960 but there were an average of 11·4 per Congress between 1971 and 1980.[32] As Senator Patrick Leahy (D – Vt) somewhat scathingly remarked: 'The obstructionists were often the giants of the Senate. It wasn't someone trying to get ten seconds on the evening news.'[33]

Concomitant with this increase in the number of filibusters was an increase in the number of votes taken to cut off debate, or invoke cloture, in the Senate's terminology. There were two cloture votes between 1950 and 1960 but 111 between 1970 and 1980. More such votes occurred during the last six weeks of 1984 than during the first ten years following Rule 22's adoption in 1917.[34] Indeed, given a growing concern about the need to expedite floor business in the Senate, sponsors of legislation routinely filed a cloture petition immediately a bill was sent to the floor for consideration. This development was criticised by Senator Dan Quayle (R – Ind) who remarked: 'The Senate has cloturitis. We invoke it here, there, and everywhere.'[35]

During the late 1970s and early 1980s the Senate thus became increasingly anarchic as individual senators asserted their own independence at the expense of collective action. The power of committee and party leaders, already weakened by the reforms of the early 1970s, was reduced further as obstruction and an unwillingness to compromise became the hallmark of an institution whose members were generally ready to do anything in order to achieve their own goals, no matter what the larger cost. One additional problem faced by the Republican Party was that their success in the 1980 elections propelled many inexperienced senators into positions of authority, and a significant number found it difficult to adapt to their new responsibilities. The result was often legislative deadlock with bills tied up for weeks by obstinate senators or groups of senators. This situation led many observers to question the Senate's ability to function with Senator Quayle even claiming that 'We are witnessing the disintegration of the US Senate'.[36]

In most Western democracies the concern shown by Senator Quayle over the future of a second chamber would be of little importance as chambers such as the British House of Lords generally wield little real power. However, while other second chambers have tended to cede power and leadership either to their respective lower chambers or executives, the US Senate has managed to maintain its power, deriving its authority from the Constitution and the fact that it is the sole representative of the American states in the Federal Government. Apart from the right to initiate money bills the Senate has the same legislative powers as the House of Representatives, and in addition performs specific executive and judicial functions. Article I, Section 3 of the Constitution gives the Senate the sole power to try all impeachments, and Article II, Section 2 states that the Senate's consent is required for certain presidential appointments and to ratify treaties. Far from relinquishing these powers senators have steadfastly defended them, and during the early 1970s even tried to assert their authority through measures such as The Case Act (1972), The War Powers Resolution (1973), and the Congressional Budget and Impoundment Act (1974). The latter was particularly important because its provisions gave the Senate a far more prominent role in the budget process than it had hitherto enjoyed. Not only did the Act create a Senate Budget Committee but the decision to place no restrictions on tenure meant that its membership became more knowledgeable about budgetary matters than their House Budget counterparts, who were only allowed to serve on the committee for six years in any one decade.

The US Senate is thus an immensely powerful institution, with major responsibilities in both foreign and domestic affairs. A suggestion that the chamber is unable to meet its responsibilities because of the conflicting demands of its membership will therefore have important implications for American government. The purpose of this book is to examine this interaction between the Senate and its membership by focusing on the activities of the Republican Party between 1974 and 1984. By looking at the background, aims and actions of Republican senators in a period when the GOP in particular, and the American political system in general, was in a state of flux, not only will the manner in which individuals affect the institution be made clear but some conclusions about the modern Senate's role in the federal system and its ability to meet its responsibilities in the post-Watergate era may also be drawn. In fact, stating this interaction between institution and party is essential to any understanding of both the Senate and the Republican Party's operations within the chamber. Moreover, given the Senate's importance such a study will also provide a useful preface to an understanding of the workings of American government in general.

2 The interaction between party and institution

Observers of the American party system have long recognised the decentralised nature of both the Democratic and Republican Parties. Austin Ranney has argued that it is 'the judgement of most political scientists that the net result of party development from 1824 to the 1950s was to make American parties the least centralised in the world'.[1] There have never been *national* party machines, and until the early 1970s even the delegates at the quadrennial national party conventions were chosen through procedures determined by the states.[2] It would therefore be a mistake to describe the organisation of the American parties in the terms which are used to describe most European parties. In his classic work *Politics, Parties and Pressure Groups* V. O. Key suggested that the organisation of the two main American parties may most accurately be described as 'a system of layers of organisation'.[3] More recently Samuel J. Eldersveld has coined the term 'stratarchy' to describe the nature of the party organisations.[4] Comparing the American parties with their European counterparts, Eldersveld claimed that the Republican and Democratic Parties were characterised by the fact that their organisation was along layers or strata of control rather than being hierarchically structured with a centralised leadership. Not only was each stratum of the American political party relatively autonomous in its own sphere but at each level or echelon of the party there were specialised organs to perform functions at that level.

American political parties should thus be regarded as multi-level phenomena and any detailed study of them must make a distinction between their different institutional contexts. Traditional histories of the Republican Party such as George H. Mayer's *The Republican Party 1854–1964* and Malcolm Moos's *The Republicans: a History of their Party*, for example, are useful in providing a general outline of the party's development but are limited by their approach to the subject matter.[5] By failing to take account of the various institutional levels at which the party operates, whether local, state, congressional, or presidential, such works do not show the extent to which each level of the party is both shaped by, and helps shape, its institutional context. Stating this interaction between institution and party is, in fact, essential to an understanding of both for only then is it possible to comprehend the activity of a party at a specific level or, indeed, explain why institutional change occurs.

The institutional context

When the Founding Fathers met in Philadelphia in 1787 to devise the new constitution they were faced with the problem of having no model for the law-making body of a Federal State and, as a result, much of the debate at the Convention concerned the role of the states in the new system. From the outset it was generally agreed that the legislature should consist of two chambers. Both the Randolph and Pinckney Plans, laid before the Convention on the first day after it had adopted rules for its proceedings, provided for a two-chambered legislature. James Madison recorded that a resolution 'that the national legislature ought to consist of two branches' was passed 'without debate or dissent'.[6] The need for two legislative chambers was never challenged. Twleve of the thirteen states already had bicameral legislatures, and Madison took this as evidence that 'an attachment to more than one branch in the legislature' was, along with 'an attachment to republican government', one of the two points on which 'the mind of the people of America . . . was well settled'.[7]

The real problem was that of representation. The small states, led by Oliver Ellsworth of Connecticut, demanded equal representation in the Congress as the price of union. The larger states argued, just as cogently, that the states should be represented according to population. At this stage the Convention threatened to break down, and was only saved by the presentation of a compromise on 5 July 1787. This suggested that the lower house should have one representative for every 30,000 inhabitants, but that in the second chamber the states should be equally represented. This compromise was debated for ten days, with some commentators suggesting that it might be necessary to annex Delaware to Pennsylvania, and divide New Jersey between New York and Pennsylvania in order to avoid domination by the small states. On 16 July 1787, however, the whole compromise was adopted with Connecticut, New Jersey, Delaware, Maryland and North Carolina voting for the motion; Pennsylvania, Virginia,

South Carolina and Georgia voting against; while Massachusetts's four votes were equally divided. Thus, as George Haynes in his extensive study of the Senate noted, 'the principle of equal representation of the states found its way into the Constitution ... by the votes of less than a majority of the states present at the Convention'.[8]

The very fact that the Senate was created as the result of a political compromise has had an important impact upon its development. As James Madison remarked:

> The equality of representation in the Senate . . . being evidently the result of compromise between the opposite pretensions of the large and small states does not call for much discussion . . . It is superfluous to try, by the standard of theory, a part of the Constitution which is allowed on all hands to be the result, not of theory but of a spirit of amity, and that mutual difference and concession which the peculiarity of our political situation rendered indispensable.[9]

It is clear that the Founding Fathers had no clearly *defined* role for the Senate to play in their new system of government. Some expected it to become an advisory council to the president; others, with Shay's rebellion fresh in their minds, regarded it as a guardian of the 'rich and well born'; while others believed that it would serve primarily as a protector of the states. The fact that the chamber was given certain judicial and executive functions reflects this confusion. Article I, Section 3 of the Constitution gave the Senate the sole power to try all impeachments, and Article II, Section 2 gave it a foreign policy role: requiring the Senate's ratification of treaties and its consent to the appointment of ambassadors and other presidential appointments. What in fact was being created was a legislative body unique in the basis of its representation, in its relationship to the executive and to the other branches of government. It was designed as a small body, associated with the president much like an executive council, acting as a judge in the trial of impeachment, serving as a check upon the House of Representatives and, most importantly, protecting 'all states against encroachment by the new centralised power—the Federal Government'.[10]

The link between the Senate's role as a protector of the small states and its role as a check on the House of Representatives is clearly shown by the decision to have senators selected by the state legislatures. Madison argued that this arrangement was 'recommended by the double advantage of favoring a select appointment, and of giving to the state governments such an agency in the formation of the federal government as must secure the authority of the states'.[11] Implicit in these remarks is the belief that the Senate should act as a conservative check upon the popularly elected House of Representatives. In Federalist Paper No. 63 Madison made this point firmly:

> there are particular moments in public affairs when the people stimulated by some irregular passion, or some illicit advantage, or misled by the artful misrepresentation of interested men, may call for measures which they themselves will afterwards be the most ready to lament and condemn. In these critical moments, how salutary will be the interference of some temperate and respectable body of citizens, in order to check the misguided career, and to suspend the blow motivated by the people against themselves until reason, justice, and truth can regain their authority over the public mind.[12]

The framers of the Constitution wanted to create a government, but at the same time, they mistrusted the power of government. To protect individual liberty they believed that it was necessary to control the power of government: first through the electoral process, and second, by dividing authority among and within political institutions. As Madison points out: 'In framing a government which is to be administered by men over men, the great difficulty lies in this: you must first enable the government to control the governed; and in the next place oblige it to control itself. A dependence on the people is, no doubt, the primary control on the government; but experience has taught mankind the necessity of auxiliary precautions.'[13] Bicameralism should be viewed as one of these auxiliary precautions. The framers of the Constitution clearly believed that the two chambers of the legislature should behave so as to check one another. By the very act of dividing power they believed that they had created two 'different bodies of men who might watch and check one another'.[14] The Senate was conceived as providing a restraining, stabilising counterweight to the popularly elected House of Representatives.

By setting up two distinct and different bodies in the legislative branch the Founding Fathers made it necessary that the Senate and the House of Representatives should take separate action. As Richard F. Fenno has pointed out: 'The framers based their predictions of House and Senate behaviour on a set of assumptions about the importance of the structural differences they had prescribed. The superior "coolness", "system", and "wisdom" of the Senate, for example, were assumed to flow from its smaller size, the longer term of its members, and their selection by state legislatures.'[15] Although these predictions of senatorial behaviour proved to be inaccurate the structural differences between the House of Representatives and the Senate have led to certain behavioural differences between the two chambers, particularly in their distribution of power.

The Senate's design as a small, continuous body, and its role as 'an instrument for preserving that residual sovereignty' left to the individual states, tends to generate a general power structure that stresses informality and flexibility.[16] As a small institution the Senate can afford to be more relaxed in its procedures than the much larger House of Representatives, and as each senator is regarded as an ambassador from a 'sovereign' state he is usually accorded more deference than a representative from a small district within a state.[17] The flexibility of the Senate's procedures can be seen in the fact that much of the chamber's business is expedited by unanimous consent agreements rather than being governed by the elaborate processes detailed in its rules.[18] Unanimous consent agreements are usually initiated by the majority leader, or another member of the leadership, who will consult with the minority leader and other interested senators in an effort to work out an agreement on controlling debate and reaching a final resolution of the issue. As a single objection blocks a unanimous consent agreement, care is taken to protect the right of all senators and to assure that those who wish to speak, or offer amendments, will have an opportunity to do so.

A concern for the rights of individual senators is evident in the relative openness of the Senate's amending process. Unlike the House of Representatives where the Rules Committee usually determines the precise nature of the amending process for each piece of legislation, in the Senate a bill becomes open to almost unlimited amendment as soon as it is taken up for consideration.[19] Moreover, except in the cases of general appropriations bills which are governed by Standing Rule 26, concurrent budget resolutions, the procedure for which was laid down by the Congressional Budget and Impoundment Act (1974), bills on which cloture has been invoked, and measures regulated by unanimous consent agreements, such amendments need not be germane.[20] 'Amendments may be made so as totally to alter the nature of the proposition' wrote Thomas Jefferson in the parliamentary manual he prepared during his service as president of the Senate (1797–1801).[21] This right is very important and has been steadfastly defended. In 1974, for example, Senators John O.

Pastore (D – RI) and Lloyd Bentsen (D – Texas) introduced S.Res 257 (1974) which would have prohibited consideration of non-germane floor amendments to any bill which the Senate by a two-thirds vote decided should not be encumbered with unrelated provisions, but found little support for the measure. Non-germane amendments, or riders, are in fact a very potent legislative weapon in certain circumstances. As the President of the United States is empowered to veto entire bills only, and does not possess an 'item veto' which would enable him to veto portions of bills, riders have often been used to bypass presidential opposition to a measure. They have also been used to bypass unsympathetic committees in the Senate. In 1960, for example, majority leader Lyndon B. Johnson (D – Texas) circumvented a hostile Judiciary Committee by offering a civil rights bill as an amendment to an obscure piece of legislation aiding a school district in Missouri. Perhaps the most common use of non-germane amendments, however, has been to advance the agendas of special interest groups. The most blatant example of this type of action is the introduction of what has become known as a 'Christmas Tree Bill' at the end of almost every congressional session. A Christmas Tree Bill is usually a minor House-passed measure on to which the Senate has attached a variety of non-germane special-interest amendments.

The flexibility of the Senate's amending process reflects the deference accorded to individual senators as the representatives of their states, and as such is mirrored in the chamber's tradition of unlimited debate. Indeed, as Richard R. Beeman has shown, the tradition of unlimited debate in the Senate originally developed out of the norms of courtesy and respect afforded to each senator.[22] Moreover, although an ability to delay legislation is important in all legislatures, it is only in the Senate that the capacity to do so has remained practically unhindered.[23] The Senate provided the means to cut off debate in 1917 with the adoption of Standing Rule 22 following a particularly controversial filibuster against a proposal by President Woodrow Wilson to arm US merchant ships in order to give them some protection against German submarines, but efforts to ease the requirements for cloture have generally been resisted. From 1917 when it was established until 1975 Rule 22 provided that a filibuster could only be ended by a two-thirds majority vote. For most of that period this meant two-thirds of the senators voting and present, but between 1949 and 1959 the rule was strengthened to require a two-thirds vote of the sentire Senate membership. In 1975, following a decade of accusations by liberal Democrats that the policy preferences of the majority were being obstructed by the actions of a small minority, the rule was relaxed with the passage of S.Res 4 (1975) which reduced the vote needed to approve a cloture resolution to a three-fifths majority of the Senate's membership. During the debate over S.Res 4 (1975) the majority leader, Senator Mike Mansfield (D – Mont), indicated just how important the tradition of extended debate was to the Senate when he expressed his fears that the motion would 'destroy . . . the very uniqueness of this body; to relegate it to the status of any other legislative body and to diminish the Senate as an institution of this government'.[24] The right to extended debate was regarded as a unique characteristic of the Senate, intimately bound up with the role of senators as ambassadors from their states, and consequently something to be protected.

One particularly interesting aspect of the debate over S.Res 4 (1975), which provides an extremely good example of how the Senate's constitutional design has a *direct* effect on its procedures, concerned the question of whether the Senate should be viewed as a continuous body. Was the Senate, because one-third of its membership was elected every two years, a continuous body that should operate under existing rules, or should it be able to adopt new rules at the beginning of each Congress without being subject to existing rules? The importance of this question lies in the fact that if the Senate was considered to be a continuous body then proposed rule changes could be filibustered, and a vote of two-thirds of the membership would be required to invoke cloture. If, on the other hand, the Senate was considered to be a new body after every election, then a filibuster could be stopped by a majority vote at the beginning of a new Congress, thereby making it easier for proposed changes in the rules to be voted on and adopted. In 1957 Vice-President Richard Nixon, as presiding officer in the Senate, had offered an advisory opinion supporting the argument that the chamber should be viewed as a new body after each election, but in 1959 the Senate seemed to settle the matter when it added language to Standing Rule 32 to specify that: 'The rules of the Senate shall continue from one Congress to the next unless they are changed as provided in these rules.'[25] This interpretation was upheld throughout the 1960s, with the Senate overturning a formal rule made in 1969 by Vice-President Hubert Humphrey that a simple majority was enough to invoke cloture on debate over rule changes. By 1975, however, changes in the chamber's membership and a growing feeling that the filibuster was undermining the Senate's legislative effectiveness led to support for a ruling by Vice-President Nelson Rockefeller, based on the language of Article I, Section 5 of the Constitution, that the Senate could change its procedural rules by a majority vote. In a vote of 51 to 42 the Senate backed Rockefeller's ruling and thus facilitated the adoption of S.Res 4 (1975).

Institutional arrangements such as the right to extended debate and the openness of its amending process serve to delineate the environment in which the political parties must operate. The respect given to individual senators, for example, has tended to frustrate attempts to centralise power within the parties, and lends support to Randall B. Ripley's observation that the structure of the Senate 'gravitates towards individualism'.[26] Yet within the constraints of this institutional framework the actual distribution of power at any given time has varied considerably. Although the Founding Fathers believed that all senators should be regarded as equals, with Madison arguing that all the states 'ought to have an *equal* share in the common councils', both the party and committee systems work to distribute power in ways which impinge upon the rights of individual senators.[27] The fact that most of the Senate's business is carried out in committees has tended to increase the power of the committee chairmen, and the need to organise the chamber has had the effect of enhancing the power of the party leader. The actual extent that power is centralised in the committees and party will depend upon the requirements of the Senate's membership, and ultimately, whether individual senators are likely to benefit from such centralisation.

The distribution of power

The distribution of power within an institution such as the Senate should be viewed as the result of a complex interaction between the institution and its membership. While the constitutional design of the Senate works to disperse power, the specific distribution of power within the chamber will depend upon the goals of the membership: their own ambitions and the demands placed upon them by their constituents for policy. Research by David Mayhew, Richard Fenno and Morris Fiorina has suggested that the primary goal of most incumbent politicians is to gain re-election, and although the focus of these studies was the House of Representatives this central thesis can be applied equally well to the Senate following the development of stable career patterns in the chamber during the late nineteenth century.[28] In its initial years the Senate experienced considerable difficulty in holding on to its members. In the words of Douglas Price, senators 'fled the capital—not yet located in Washington—almost as fast as was humanly possible'.[29] Five of the original twenty-six senators resigned before serving out their terms of office, and of the ninety-four senators who served between 1789 and 1801 thirty-three resigned before completing their terms.[30] Members frequently left the Senate for other opportunities, both governmental and private. Beginning in the second half of the nineteenth century, however, the average length of service began to increase as the growth of the federal government and the increased importance of the slavery question made a career in the Senate more attractive. As William Riker has pointed out: 'The prestige of the Senate had at first been little more than that of a high state office, but this was no longer the case from about 1850: from 1790 to 1849, 48 senators resigned to take state office; from about 1850 to 1949, only 8.'[31]

The increasing attractiveness of a career in the Senate had a number of important consequences with regard to the organisation and structure of the chamber. As senators began to value a career in the Senate, so they became increasingly concerned about their chance of being re-elected, and tended to organise their activities accordingly. In such circumstances the nature of the prevailing electoral environment will obviously have an important effect on a senator's behaviour. This observation was made by H. Douglas Price who argued that 'the conditions of entry into a legislative body and of survival through successive terms are a major factor in the behaviour of aspirants and incumbents'.[32] John Bibby and Roger Davidson reinforced this argument when they stated that 'The nature of the process of recruiting, nominating, and electing candidates for Congress obviously has a profound effect on the behaviour of legislators'.[33] In other words, by determining such factors as the overall level of membership stability, the requirements for electoral success and the type of senator gaining election, the nature of the prevailing electoral environment will influence the behaviour of senators, and hence the relationship between individual senators, committee chairmen, and party leaders. A low level of turnover tends to generate a fairly stable environment, and facilitates the development of procedures such as the seniority system. The requirements for electoral success will influence the activity of senators and their relationship with the party organisation. More specifically, the role of the political party in the election campaign will be a significant factor in determining the relationship between office-holder and party organisation. In particular, a candidate who has relied upon the party apparatus to further his election chances will be more likely to pay attention to the party's demands than a candidate who has gained election through his own efforts and consequently owes the party very little. Finally, the age and experience of senators will also influence their behaviour. Older, more experienced legislators are more likely to understand the complexities of the institution's procedures than their younger, more inexperienced colleagues who may well be lacking in the skills necessary for legislative success.

Within the parameters of a general structure generated by the Senate's constitutional design the specific institutional arrangements found in the chamber, such as the relative power of individual senators, committee chairmen and party leaders, should thus be viewed as primarily a product of the prevailing electoral environment. The nature of the electoral arena at the end of the nineteenth century, for example, tended to centralise power within the party organisation. As David Rothman has remarked: 'Senators at the end of the nineteenth century came to Washington after a long and systematic apprenticeship. First holding minor posts and then moving into more responsible positions they finally won seats in the chamber.'[34] In the 1870s, 62 per cent of senators were experienced politicians, having served over four years in national office, or over six years in important state office. By the 1890s 78 per cent of the Senate's membership shared these qualifications, and by the 1900s the chamber was the preserve of professional politicians who owed their positions and electoral success to the party organisation.[35] Not only did the state parties control the state legislatures which elected senators at this time, but the very fact that senators had to face a number of elections to lower political office before gaining election to the Senate gave them considerable experience of political life and meant that they were more likely to accept authority than contest it.[36] In these circumstances it is hardly surprising that the senatorial parties developed rapidly. During the 1890s both the Republican organisation of Senators William B. Allison (R – Iowa) and Nelson W. Aldrich (R – RI), and the Democratic organisation of Senator Arthur P. Gorman (D – Md), began to use the party caucus to control Committee assignments and the scheduling of business.[37] Gorman is particularly important because despite wielding less political influence than either Allison or Aldrich he contributed more to the development of the modern party organisation. Named as chairman of the Democratic caucus in

1889 he proceeded to assume all of the party's top leadership posts himself, including those of floor leader, chairman of the party's Steering Committee, and chairman of the Democratic Committee-on-Committees, and thus managed to institutionalise his position in a manner which evaded Allison and Aldrich. The practice of electing a single majority leader or minority leader who would serve an entire Congress was finally established in the period between 1911 and 1913.[38]

The authority of the party leadership in the Senate during the late nineteenth century was predicated upon the party's control of the electoral process. In the first two decades of the twentieth century, however, a number of reforms sponsored by the Progressive Movement served to change the rules of politics by undercutting the influence of the party apparatus in election campaigns. First, the passage of the Pendleton Act (1883), and the extension of its provisions for the selection by merit of civil servants by Presidents Benjamin Harrison (1888–92) and William Taft (1908–12), gradually undermined the party's control over patronage, and hence their control over the voters.[39] Reforms of this sort were important because as Milton Rakove has pointed out: 'An effective political party needs five things: offices, jobs, money, workers, and voters. Offices beget jobs and money; jobs and money beget workers; workers beget voters; and votes beget offices.'[40] Without patronage to dispense, the political machines which had controlled the state legislatures began to decline. Second, the growing use of the direct primary, first used in Wisconsin in 1903, meant that the parties lost their control over who appeared in their name on the ballot paper. As Austin Ranney has stated: 'The primary system freed forces driving toward the disintegration of party organisations and facilitated the construction of factions and cliques attached to the ambitions of individual leaders.'[41] Third, the ratification of the 17th Amendment (1913), which provided for the direct election of senators, further weakened the ability of the parties to influence the outcome of elections. By obliging senators to seek an electoral base that was often independent of partisan or patronage networks, party coherence was undermined. As early as 1922 one commentator was already showing that the result of the direct election of senators was much weaker parties in the Senate: 'The senator came to think more in terms of himself and his reelection, nearly always an impelling motive, and less in terms of party.'[42]

In the long term the adoption of the 17th Amendment undermined one important aspect of the Senate's constitutional role. The constitutional design of the chamber was clearly designed to remove the chamber from what the Founding Fathers viewed as the problems associated with responsive, democratic government. As Madison stated, 'Another advantage . . . of the Senate is the additional impediment it must prove against improper acts of legislation'.[43] As has been noted, the fact that senators were given six-year terms, were elected by state legislatures, and only one third of the membership came up for re-election at any one time, was meant to distance senators from the passions of the electorate. By requiring the direct election of senators the 17th Amendment removed the most important factor that distanced the Senate from the passions of the electorate. Although senators still served six-year terms, the requirement that they should face the voters made them responsive to their constituents' demands, and by the 1970s some commentators were even arguing that it was the Senate, not the House of Representatives, which tended to yield 'to the impulse of sudden and violent passions'.[44]

By eroding the role of the party in elections the immediate effect of the progressive reforms was to reduce the authority of the party leadership in the Senate. The reforms not only weakened the control that the party wielded over the outcome of elections, thereby diminishing the allegiance owed to the party leadership by senators, but the fact that senators no longer needed to serve a long apprenticeship in lower political office before gaining election to the Senate meant that the type of person entering the chamber began to change. The new senators were younger and less experienced than their predecessors and, as such, were more willing to challenge authority than the professional politicians they replaced. As a result, progressive senators such as Senator Robert M. La Follette (R – Wisc) gradually dismantled the apparatus of leadership that had been established by Allison, Aldrich and Gorman.[45] Just as their counterparts in the House of Representatives undermined the rule of Speaker Joseph G. Cannon in 1910 by stripping him of his power to assign members to committees, so senators weakened the authority of the party leadership in the Senate by determining that the assignment of members to committees and the appointment of committee chairmen should be done on the basis of seniority. Unable to control committee assignments, the party leadership found it increasingly difficult to enforce discipline. The adoption of the seniority principle served to strengthen the authority of the committee chairmen at the expense of the party leadership, and in the process dispersed power within the chamber.

Developments in the electoral environment at the beginning of the twentieth century, therefore, had a major effect on the structure of power in the Senate by bringing about a change in the relationship between individual senators, committee chairmen, and party leaders which persisted, almost unaltered, until the late 1950s. This point is important to acknowledge because many political scientists writing about the Senate during the 1950s misunderstood both the nature of the chamber's conservatism and the factors behind its distribution of power. Donald D. Matthews and William S. White, in particular, advanced the argument that the official rules of the chamber which rewarded seniority, and its norms of behaviour which stressed ideas such as the need for junior senators to serve an apprenticeship, respect their seniors, be courteous, and display a spirit of reciprocity, produced and sustained a conservative leadership which, in turn, controlled leadership recruitment by maintaining the same procedures and customs.[46] This was a view shared by Senator Joseph S. Clark (D – Penn) who in a famous speech on the Senate establishment made in 1965 declared that: 'The Senate establishment as I see it . . . is a self-perpetuating oligarchy with mild, but only mild tones of plutocracy . . . the two-thirds majority of the Democratic senators who are Kennedy men, and therefore liberals, and therefore want to get the country moving again . . . are represented sparsely, if at all, in the Senate establishment.'[47] On another occasion Senator Clark related how when he first arrived in the Senate in January 1957, he and five other freshmen Democrats were treated to a luncheon by the then majority leader Lyndon Johnson. They found at each place a copy of William White's book *Citadel.* The books were inscribed 'with all best wishes' not only by the author but also by Johnson who urged the senators 'to consider Mr White's book as a sort of *McGaffey's Reader* from which they could learn much about "the greatest deliberative body in the world" '. Johnson also counselled them to 'mold' themselves with the Senate's 'way of life'.[48] In this way the conservatism of the Senate during the 1950s and early 1960s was transformed by Matthews, White and Clark from a purely contemporary phenomenon into what seemed like a fundamental law of the institution.

Matthews, White and Clark were correct in their claims that both the Senate's formal rules and its norms of behaviour tended to concentrate power in the hands of a small number of senior senators.[49] The power of the standing committee chairmen during the 1950s, for example, was outlined by George Galloway in his book *The Legislative Process in Congress*:

> They arrange the agenda of the committee, appoint the subcommittees, and refer bills to them. They decide what pending measures shall be considered and when, call committee meetings, and decide whether or not to hold hearings and when. They approve lists of scheduled witnesses and authorise staff studies, and preside at committee meetings . . . They are in a position to expedite measures they favor and to retard or pigeon-hole those they dislike.[50]

Matthews, White and Clark were mistaken, however, in their belief that this specific distribution of power was a permanent feature of the institution. Leaving aside the fact that it was an electoral 'accident' which allowed conservative Southern Democrats to take advantage of the seniority principle, the formal rules and norms of the Senate during this period must, on the whole, be interpreted as reflecting the general needs of the institution. Not only was the conservatism of the Senate a reflection of the political views of its membership but the prominent role given to committees in the legislative process was itself enough to enhance the authority of committee chairmen, and the fairly stable *nature* of the electoral environment during this period facilitated the development of the seniority system. Although there were always a few maverick senators such as Senator Wayne Morse (R – Ore) who were ready to challenge the chamber's customs, the adoption of the 'Johnson Rule'—which ensured that all senators would be given a seat on one major committee before any senator was assigned to a second major committee—by the Democratic Steering Committee in 1953, and by the Republicans in 1959, generally meant that most junior senators were willing to wait until they would be in a position to enjoy the benefits of seniority.[51]

This situation began to change, however, following the Democratic landslide in the congressional elections of 1958 when the Democrats gained thirteen seats from the Republicans. Just as the authority that the party leadership had enjoyed during the late nineteenth century had eventually been undermined by changes in the electoral environment and subsequent membership changes, so the power structure of the 1950s was transformed by the influx of new members in 1958, and the more general developments in electioneering which took place during the 1960s and 1970s. In addition to the ideological differences that appeared between many of the new junior senators and their more senior colleagues, there were also important generational changes related to age, previous political experience and other personal qualities, between the older Democrats and what James Q. Wilson has labelled as the 'amateur Democrats'.[52]

The election of 1958 brought about dramatic changes in the regional composition of the Democratic Party with the election of a number of senators from regions such as the Midwest which had traditionally tended to vote Republican, and consequently lacked a strong Democratic organisation. Senators from these regions thus had different needs and requirements from those Democrats who came from states with a long Democratic tradition. The new members expected a full share of responsibility from the beginning, and needed to make their reputations quickly in order to survive. Their main demands, therefore, were for the reform of the seniority system, especially the notion that a junior senator had to serve a period of 'apprenticeship' before acceding to power, and for increased staff resources to enable them to devise legislation of their own.

The generation gap between junior and senior senators, which had resulted from the considerable changes in the regional composition of the Democratic Party following the elections of 1958, was further widened by shifts in the electoral climate during the 1960s and 1970s which heightened the value of the visibility, credit-taking, and staff resources associated with committee leadership posts for members of both parties. Indeed, rather than being generated by ideological differences between the junior and senior senators the demands for reform were primarily the result of the different backgrounds and needs of the new senators. During the early 1970s, for example, the pressure for reform came from both junior Democrats and Republicans, and the two leading Republican proponents of change, Senators Charles Mathias (R – Md) and Bill Brock (R – Tenn), had little in common ideologically as Brock was associated with the Nixon administration and Mathias belonged to the moderate wing of the party. As party organisations declined in significance politicians necessarily became individual entrepreneurs, relying upon their own resources to create winning electoral coalitions. Increasingly they developed their own candidate organisations, raised their own money, and with the aid of professional political consultants ran their own campaigns. In this environment 'the apprenticeship-seniority system accounted for little. What the new breed of senators required was the "quick fix": the early acquisition of the public platform and staff resources associated with committee leadership.'[53] Only then would they be able to persuade the electorate that they were worth re-electing, and raise the funds necessary to run their campaigns.

Pressure from junior senators gradually altered the distribution of power within the Senate during the late 1960s and early 1970s.[54] In an attempt to limit the power of the committee chairmen the Legislative Reorganisation Act (1970) contained provisions which introduced a new set of limitations on committee assignments. All committees were divided among three classes, and senators were required to serve on two committees in the first class and permitted to serve on one in each of the other classes.[55] Class A committees in 1980 were Agriculture, Appropriations, Armed Services, Banking, Commerce, Energy, Environment, Finance, Foreign Relations, Governmental Affairs, Judiciary, and Labor and Human Resources. Class B committees were Budget, Rules, Veterans' Affairs, Aging and Intelligence; while Class C committees were Indian Affairs, Ethics, and the Joint Committees on Taxation, Library and Printing. The 1970 Reorganisation Act also opened Senate committee hearings to the public unless the committee for reasons of national security or the existence of confidential information voted otherwise. In 1975 the Senate extended the same principle first to committee mark-ups with the adoption of S.Res 9 (1975), a measure which had been introduced by Senator Lawton Chiles (D – Fla) then in his first term of office, and then to conference committees with the passage of S.Res 12 (1975). The latter measure had been introduced by Senator William Roth (R – Del) who was also in his first term of office. Two junior senators, Senator Mike Gravel (D – Alaska), elected in 1968, and Senator Bill Brock, elected in 1970, were also responsible for engineering the passage of S.Res 60 (1975), a measure which provided additional staffing resources for junior senators. Explaining the need for such staff, Gravel highlighted the lack of information available to junior senators: 'When we go to the floor to vote, half, or more than half, the time we do not know what we are voting on until we ask the gentleman in the back of the room, or somebody at the front of the room and they tell us how to vote. They will give us a thumbnail sketch, on the substance of the issue, on something that had maybe twenty hours debate, in half a minute.'[56] S.Res 60 (1975) authorised junior senators to hire up to three committee staff aides to work directly for them on their committees. Previously committee staff members had been controlled by the chairmen. A further attempt at promoting a more equitable distribution of power in the chamber was made in 1976 by Senator Dale Bumpers (D – Ark) when he introduced

S.Res 417 (1976). This measure proposed limiting the number of chairmanships a senator could hold to either two subcommittees or one subcommittee and one full committee. Then in his second year in the Senate, having been elected in 1974, Bumpers claimed that S.Res 417 (1976) 'would provide for a more even distribution of positions of leadership in the Senate'.[57]

Before action could be taken on S.Res 417 (1976), however, its provisions were incorporated in S.Res 4 (1977) which authorised the first major overhaul of the Senate committee system since the Legislative Reorganisation Act (1946).[58] S.Res 4 (1977) abolished three standing committees and three joint committees, created a new Energy Committee, set a ceiling on the number of committees and subcommittees a senator could chair, gave minority members a larger share of committee staff, and directed that committee hearings and other business be computerised to avoid scheduling conflicts.[59] Although all these provisions were significant, perhaps the most important were those which placed limits on the number of committees a senator could chair. Rule 25, paragraph 4 of S.Res 4 (1977) allowed each senator to serve on only two major committees and one minor committee, and on three subcommittees of the major committees and two of minor committees. It also prohibited them from chairing more than one committee, and more than one subcommittee on each committee of which they were members. By limiting the number of chairmanships a senator could hold the reorganisation opened the way for greater participation by junior senators in the formal power structure of the Senate. In 1976 only two subcommittees had been chaired by freshmen, the relatively unimportant Buildings and Ground Subcommittee of the Public Works Committee, and the Banking Committee's subcommittee on Small Businesses. With the reorganisation in 1977 seven senators became chairmen of subcommittees during their first year in the Senate. In this respect S.Res 4 (1977) may be regarded as having a similar effect as the Hansen Plan in the House of Representatives. Named after Representative Julia Butler Hansen (D – Wash) the latter increased subcommittee autonomy in 1973 by requiring committees with more than fifteen members to establish at least four subcommittees.[60] Both the Hansen Plan and S.Res 4 (1977) institutionalised the role of subcommittees in the legislative process, and indirectly confirmed the redistribution of power that was occurring in both chambers by allocating responsibilities and resources more evenly. Senator Adlai Stevenson, chairman of the Temporary Select Committee to Study the Senate Committee System, whose recommendations had constituted most of S.Res 4 (1977), declared that the measure 'democratised the Senate'.[61]

In addition to generating changes in the distribution of power within the Senate the requirements of the new electoral environment of the 1960s and 1970s also caused changes in the *role* of the individual senator. The preoccupation with re-election meant that senators became concerned with an ever wider range of issues leading to a dramatic increase in the average number of committee assignments held by a senator. As Roger Davidson points out: 'Insistent constituency concerns are revealed in members' efforts to garner more committees and subcommittee assignments.'[62] In the 80th Congress (1947–8) the average number of standing committee and subcommittee assignments per senator was 5·46, but by the 93rd Congress (1973–4) this figure had risen to 12·04.[63] These expanding committee and subcommittee obligations left senators with little time to socialise with their colleagues, and undermined the chamber's function as a forum for debate.

As the workload of individual senators mushroomed during the late 1960s and early 1970s so the Senate sought to adapt by expounding its staff resources. Between 1967 and 1977 the number of personal staff employed by senators increased from 1,749 to 3,554.[64] One result of these developments was to alter the individual senator's role from that of a person who weighs, debates and deliberates public policy to that of a chief executive officer running a small bureaucracy. Susan Webb Hammond, in a study for the Senate, declared: 'the Senate has 100 different bureaucracies at the personal office level. Managing a small bureaucracy thus becomes an important aspect of each senator's job.'[65] To a large extent it is staff who draw up legislation, and discuss that legislation with the staff from other senator's offices.[66] This point was made by Senator David L. Boren (D – Okla) who claimed: 'very often I will call a senator on an issue, and he won't know anything about it. He'll ask me to get someone on my staff to call someone on his staff. It shuts off personal contact between senators.'[67]

Alongside the reforms in the formal rules governing the committee system and the distribution of staff in the Senate, the early 1970s also saw some important changes in the rules that the *parties* used to select committee chairmen. By 1971 the Democratic committee roster, which is drawn up by the Democratic Steering Committee, was made subject to Caucus approval. Majority leader Mike Mansfield (D – Mont) announced that a meeting of the Democratic Caucus would be held at the request of any senator, and that any senator could challenge any Steering Committee nomination of a committee chairman. This procedure was revised in 1975 when the Democrats decided to select committee chairmen by secret ballot whenever twenty per cent of the Caucus requested it because of fears that any senator who was unsuccessful in his challenge to a chairman would be exposed to retribution by that chairman. The Caucus also adopted a 'bill of rights' for committee members which reduced the power of committee chairmen. It gave Democratic members of each committee the right to elect their subcommittee chairmen. Previously the committee chairmen had appointed members to the subcommittees and chosen their chairmen.

Although the changes in the procedures of the Democratic Party were more significant, the Republicans also acted against the seniority system when in 1973 they adopted a proposal sponsored by Senator Howard Baker (R – Tenn) which permitted members of each standing committee to elect the ranking Republican on that committee, subject to approval by a vote of the Republican Conference (caucus). However despite the fact that several ranking members were challenged by their Republican colleagues in 1973, all those with top seniority prevailed. Indeed, there has been no dramatic revolt in the Senate against either incumbent chairmen or ranking members to match that which occurred in the House of Representatives in 1975 when rank-and-file Democrats asserted their power by unseating three chairmen: W. R. Poage (D – Texas) of Agriculture, F. Edward Herbert (D – La) of Armed Services, and Wright Patman (D – Texas) of Banking and Currency.

The extent of the reforms in the Senate during the early 1970s illustrates very clearly the nature of the interaction between the parties and the institution. Dramatic changes in the membership of the Democratic Party in particular generated demands for institutional change which significantly altered both the distribution of power within the Senate and the role of individual senators. In this way membership changes led directly to institutional change. This point is very important because during the late 1970s the Republican Party underwent profound changes in its membership which were linked to new developments in the electoral environment. These membership changes also had an effect on the structure of the Senate, though in a less direct manner than the earlier changes in the Democratic Party, and in order to understand them fully it is necessary to look in some detail at the nature of the electoral environment prevailing at the time.

3 The electoral environment

The electoral environment of the late 1970s may best be characterised as in a state of flux. Demographic changes, the emergence of new issues and the development of new techniques of electioneering combined to undermine the traditional party loyalties of the electorate and transform the role of the political parties in campaigns. These changes, although having an impact at all levels of electioneering, were felt acutely in campaigns for the US Senate where the size and nature of the constituencies involved were ideal for the effective use of campaign techniques such as direct mail and television. The revival in the Republican Party's fortunes in the chamber between 1974 and 1980 was, in fact, a consequence of the increasingly volatile and competitive electoral environment which was generated by these developments in electioneering. Indeed, as so many Republican senators were the *direct* product of this climate it becomes clear that an understanding of its nature is essential to any attempt to comprehend both the changes that occurred in the party during the late 1970s and the breakdown of the existing norms of behaviour in the Senate.

The changing electoral environment

The New Deal coalition of white southerners, ethnic working-class groups, middle-class voters and blacks which produced Democratic majorities at local, state, congressional and presidential levels dominated American politics from 1932 until the election of Dwight Eisenhower as President in 1952. Since then this coalition has gradually unravelled as changes in the voting population and the rise of new issues have led to a general decline in partisanship among the electorate. Reforms such as the 26th Amendment (1971) which lowered the voting age to eighteen, the dramatic post-Second-World-War expansion of higher education, and population migration from the city centres to the suburbs and from the North to the South and Southwest, produced a younger, better-educated electorate which was less attached to traditional party ties than the earlier generation.[1] Party identification was also undermined by the emergence of issues such as racial strife, Vietnam and crime in the 1960s and abortion, unemployment and inflation in the 1970s which cut across the well-settled lines of cleavage between the Democrats and Republicans.[2] The abortion issue, in particular, cut into two of the traditional bases of Democratic support in the Midwest and South; working-class Catholics and fundamentalists.[3] Some indication of the extent of this breakdown in the electorate's allegiance to the parties can be observed in the growth in the number of voters describing themselves as 'independents', and the increase in 'ticket-splitting' during the 1970s. In 1978 38 per cent of the electorate regarded themselves as independents compared with only 22 per cent in 1952.[4] These figures are mirrored in the statistics for ticket-splitting between, for example, Presidential and House candidates. In 1980 32·8 per cent of the congressional districts were carried by a Presidential candidate of one party and a House candidate of another party compared with only 19·3 per cent in 1952.[5]

Perhaps the most important consequence of these developments was that a smaller number of voters taking their main voting cue from the parties meant that a greater proportion of the electorate became 'up for grabs' at each election.[6] However, although the Republicans were able to attract support from disenchanted Democrats and independents at the Presidential level from 1952 onwards, it was not until the late 1970s that they were able to make major gains in the US Senate. Prior to then it was found that as the importance of party as a voting cue in Senate races declined in the 1960s, that of incumbency increased, thereby reinforcing the Democratic advantage in the chamber.[7] Throughout the 1960s and early 1970s the re-election rates for senators remained above 70 per cent, peaking at 87·5 per cent in 1966.[8] Some commentators have even argued that between 1964 and 1974 incumbency served as a more important determinant of the vote than party.[9] It was only after 1974 that new developments in the techniques of electioneering began to nullify the advantages of incumbency, and the re-election rates for senators fell from 85·2 per cent in 1974 to 64·0 per cent in 1976, 60·0 per cent in 1978, and 55·2 per cent in 1980 before rising again to 93·3 per cent in 1982.[10]

A number of studies have shown that the re-election rates for incumbents are related more to the visibility of the challenger than to any advantages accruing to the holding of office.[11] Incumbents generally enjoy visibility, the advantage of staff support and a positive reputation, and when the challenger is unrecognised the incumbent will have an electoral advantage. If, on the other hand, the challenger enjoys high visibility he will be able to pose a far more serious threat to the incumbent. This analysis in important because it helps explain why the New Deal coalition unravelled at varying speeds at the different levels of elected office. Looked at this way it becomes apparent that the New Deal coalition broke up quickest at those levels where challengers were able to gain the visibility they required for electoral success. This meant that the initial inroads into the Democratic majorities were made at the Presidential level where candidates have always been highly visible, and slowly permeated downwards as advances in the techniques of electioneering gradually allowed challengers for lower political office to compete effectively with incumbents. The decline in the re-election rates for senators in the second half of the 1970s may therefore be viewed as being related to changes in the electoral environment which allowed challengers to develop more effective campaigns. With traditional party loyalties and labels declining in significance as determinants of voting behaviour, organisation and the mastery of the new campaign techniques began to assume a far greater importance in deciding the outcome of elections.

The greater visibility of challengers in races for the Senate was the result of a revolution in the nature of campaigning brought about by the increasing use of television as a campaign tool. During the 1970s television became the principal influence acting on the voter, and his chief source of information in the campaign, causing political scientists such as Martin P. Wattenberg to argue that 'the most important factor in reshaping the American electoral scene in recent years has been the tremendous growth of the media'.[12] The rise in television's influence in Senate campaigns can easily be traced. In 1950 GOP candidate John Marshall Butler's spot announcements in Maryland's US Senate campaign assisted his victory over incumbent Democrat Millard Tydings.[13] Since then candidates have evolved strategies that have become increasingly dependent upon television as the centrepiece of their campaign efforts, and have become highly skilled in attracting as much television exposure as possible.[14] Indeed, one important consequence of the new methods of campaigning has been the change it has wrought in the type of candidate likely to be politically successful. Recruiters have become extremely conscious of a candidate's ability to look impressive and perform before the camera.[15]

Television exposure can take either of two forms: the candidate can either attempt to be featured on news broadcasts, or he can buy time for commercial advertising. One recent study has shown that Congress attracted just over 20 per cent of all the newstime on network news, with a substantial amount of this coverage being campaign news.[16] Candidates for the Senate are well aware that television is a visual and entertainment-orientated medium which requires action shots and simple messages. The best way to achieve television exposure, therefore, is not to give a speech on a major foreign policy concern, or to issue position papers, but to do something which is colourful and has human interest potential. During the early 1970s the major campaign gimmick was walking from one end of a state to the other. In this way Lawton Chiles, who was previously unknown, won a Florida seat in 1970, and Dick Clark defeated a Republican incumbent in Iowa in 1972. A similar use of television was made by the veteran Senator Strom Thurmond (R – SC) in 1978 when seeking re-election against a young Democrat who made an issue out of Thurmond's age. The senator fitted out a 'Strom-trek' van and took his family campaigning across the state. During the campaign he held a birthday party for one of his children, and to the delight of the television cameramen repeatedly slid down a firepole to show how fit he was.[17]

The other method of gaining television exposure was to buy time for commercial advertising in the same manner that a company might buy advertising space to market its product. In fact, many analysts regard television advertising as the 'most effective campaign tool in American politics today', and its use in Senate races has been standard practice since the early 1970s.[18] A more recent development has been the buying of television time by independent PACs such as the National Conservative Political Action Committee (NCPAC) to advertise against those incumbent senators whom they did not wish to see re-elected. Although negative advertising *per se* has a long history in American politics—with the Johnson for President Committee running a famous commercial in 1964 which showed a small girl picking petals out of a flower as a nuclear bomb exploded behind her in an attempt to link nuclear war and a Barry Goldwater victory—the campaigns run by NCPAC were a new development because they were carried out by an independent organisation with no connection with any of the candidates. Wes McClure, director of the political consultancy firm

Group Research Inc., even claimed that these campaigns were 'probably the most important development on the right since 1964'.[19]

The increased use of advertising by PACs, particularly those associated with the New Right, during the late 1970s was directly related to what Larry Sabato has described as a 'particular anomaly' of the federal election rules: the independent expenditure loophole.[20] In the 1976 case *Buckley* v. *Valeo* the Supreme Court decided that the spending limit of $1,000 per year which Congress had tried to impose on PACs and individuals who desired to advocate a candidate's election without consultation with his campaign committee interfered with freedom of speech and was therefore unconstitutional under the First Amendment.[21] The Federal Election Commission (FEC), acting after the Court's decision, defined an independent expenditure as one made by a person or committee 'expressly advocating the election or defeat' of a candidate that is not made with the co-operation, or with the prior consent of a candidate or any agent or authorised committee of the candidate.[22] Both these guidelines and the Supreme Court's ruling were very controversial, and were opposed by groups such as the public interest lobby Common Cause. Fred Wertheimer, the executive director of Common Cause, claimed that 'the activities of NCPAC and other independent spenders are undermining the concepts of free competition and accountability that are so basic to our political process'.[23]

Using the independent expenditure loophole in the federal election laws, the groups of the New Right financed a number of infamous negative advertising campaigns against liberal senators in the elections of 1978 and 1980. Senators Dick Clark (D – Iowa), and Floyd K. Haskell (D – Colo) in 1978, and Frank Church (D – Idaho), Alan Cranston (D – Calif), John Culver (D – Iowa), George McGovern (D – SD) and Birch Bayh (D – Ind) in 1980, were targeted for defeat by a number of single-issue and multi-issue groups on issues such as gun control, the Panama Canal and abortion.[24] These New Right campaigns differed from earlier examples of negative advertising in their heavy expenditure on television advertising, and the early message development in the campaigns which on some occasions began up to a year and a half in advance of the election itself. In 1979, for example, NCPAC spent $700,000 on television commercials to attack liberal senators up for re-election the following year.[25] The rationale behind these early campaigns was to focus attention on the legislative record of the senators involved. Stuart Rothenberg, director of the Political

Division of the Free Congress Research and Education Foundation, claimed that: 'they started early and forced the electorate to focus attention on the incumbent-defined context of Senate races . . . The overriding aim of incumbents is to get reelected, they prefer to run as people sending newsletters to constituents. NCPAC forced the electorate to look at their (the incumbent's) voting records.'[26] The NCPAC campaign against Senator George McGovern in 1979–80 provides a perfect illustration of this approach. One television commercial showed a basketball player dribbling a ball while a voice-over stated that: 'Globetrotter is a great name for a basketball team, but it's a terrible name for a senator. While the energy crisis was brewing, George McGovern was touring Cuba with Fidel Castro. He also took a one month junket to Africa. All at the taxpayers' expense. No wonder he lost touch with South Dakota. With so many problems at home we need a senator and not a globetrotter.'[27] Another commercial highlighted McGovern's support for HR.10481 (1975) which provided federal assistance to bankrupt New York City, and claimed that 'George McGovern voted against you when he voted to bail out New York City and its labour unions, bureaucrats, and crooked politicians, and cost South Dakota more inflation'.[28]

In their efforts to defeat targeted incumbents, groups such as NCPAC and the CSFC also developed special interest coalitions with anti-ERA groups, pro-life groups, and the religious right. In late 1978 and early 1979 Paul Weyrich, Richard Viguerie and Howard Phillips of the Conservative Caucus began to approach Christian School lobbyists like Robert Billings of the Christian Action Coalition with the suggestion of a New-Right–Christian alliance. It was felt that the Evangelical Right would prove to be useful allies in lobbying Congress and supporting candidates for electoral office from the local to the Federal level. As Jerry Falwell of the Moral Majority once stated: 'What can you do from the pulpit? You can register people to vote. You can explain the issues to them. And you can endorse candidates, right there in church on Sunday morning.'[29] Furthermore, the churches could also send mail to their members urging them to support or oppose certain candidates.

The links between the New Right and the Christian Right were cemented in the late 1970s when a number of New Right activists helped to found Christian organisations such as Moral Majority and Religious Roundtable. Late in 1978 Viguerie started providing his direct-mail expertise to the evangelical groups. In 1979 Robert Billings joined Falwell to set up the Moral Majority,

Gary Jarmin, previously with the American Conservative Union, moved to Christian Voice, and Conservative Caucus field organiser Edward McAteer created the Religious Roundtable.[30] However, despite claiming credit for the election of Senators Jeremiah Denton in Alabama, Don Nickles in Oklahoma, and John East in North Carolina, there is little to suggest that the Christian Right added much more than a few new votes to the conservaitve totals.[31] Where the Christian Right was important was in engaging evangelists in politics, and in helping shape the electoral environment of the late 1970s.

A similar conclusion can be drawn regarding the impact of the pro-life groups who were active in the campaigns against Senators Clark, Bayh, Culver and McGovern. The pro-life campaign against these senators followed a similar pattern: early commercials which highlighted each senator's views on abortion, and then the distribution of leaflets at church meetings in each state. In South Dakota, for example, George McGovern faced early negative advertising by the Life Amendment PAC of South Dakota. In the spring primary McGovern faced the first challenge of his career from a pro-life Democrat, and on the Sunday before the primary the Life Amendment PAC distributed a brochure at South Dakota's churches. The brochure, titled 'Stop the Baby Killers', carried a photograph of a foetus in a womb, followed by the charge that McGovern 'continuously votes your tax dollars to kill preborn children' and a brief comparison with his opponent's views on abortion.[32] McGovern won the primary, but with a smaller margin than he had hoped, winning only 62 per cent of the vote against a relative unknown. The pro-lifers felt rewarded by their efforts, and repeated their operations in the general election.

Financial returns submitted to the Federal Election Commission revealed that $222,044 was spent on negative advertising against George McGovern in 1979–80.[33] This in itself was more than the total of $168,125 spent on independent expenditures in 1977–78.[34] McGovern, moreover, was only one of five Democrats targeted for defeat by NCPAC and the other groups of the New Right. A further $339,068 was spent on commercials against Senator Frank Church, $192,059 was targeted against Senator Alan Cranston, $186,613 against Senator John Culver and $180,723 against Senator Birch Bayh. The scale of this negative advertising campaign against the five senators becomes apparent when the fact that only $245,611 was spent in independent expenditures against President Carter during this period is taken into account.

The effectiveness of independent expenditure on negative advertising has been the subject of a great deal of debate. Philip Williams and Graham Wilson have, for example, questioned the New Right's role in the defeat of Senator Dick Clark in 1978. They have suggested that 'the main surprise about Iowa's rejection of Senator Clark was that it chose him in the first place'.[35] Early in 1979 National GOP strategists were concerned that negative advertising might actually backfire on the Republican challengers. 'It's like a loose cannon on the deck, although I know they mean well' commented Norm Turnette, director of political operations of the Republican National Committee (RNC).[36] In mid-1979 Don Parrish, the chairman of the South Dakota Republican Party, had attempted to distance GOP candidate James Abdnor's campaign from the activities of NCPAC when he stated: 'I don't think you can defeat George McGovern by standing up cussing him.'[37] In mid 1980 Abdnor even filed a complaint with the Federal Election Commission charging NCPAC with using his name without authorisation.[38] Similar criticisms were made by Bill Fay, an aide to Steven Symms, who claimed that: 'I think if anything such groups as NCPAC probably hindered Steve Symms. I think people got tired of trash.'[39] A prime example of the type of advertising that Fay was complaining about was an early NCPAC television commercial that showed a Republican state legislator standing in front of an empty missile silo to underscore the complaint that 'Senator Church has always opposed a strong national defence'. Church struck back at the advertisement by claiming that it was misleading and fabricated, and noted that it was empty because it was designed for a now mothballed Minuteman, which Church had supported.

The fears that NCPAC's campaigns might harm the prospects of the Republican challengers eventually proved to be unfounded, and four of the five Democratic senators targeted by NCPAC in 1980 were defeated. In terms of votes, however, McGovern, Church, Culver and Bayh did no worse than the other northern Democrats up for re-election whose average percentage drop in support since 1974 was identical with theirs.[40] All four defeated senators were in conservative states where the Republican Party had made major efforts, and in changing hands these seats were merely reverting back to the patterns of the 1950s. Where groups such as NCPAC may have been more important was in setting the tone of the elections. This point was made by New York opinion researcher Arthur J. Finkelstein who remarked: 'I think the most important thing that NCPAC did was set the agenda. From the beginning they put McGovern on the defensive. Even more so Church.'[41] It was NCPAC's ability to focus attention on the voting records of incumbent senators, rather than its success in determining the outcome of elections either in 1980 or in 1982 when it spent $4,046,756 to little avail, that proved the most significant feature of its advertising campaigns because they forced senators to be constantly aware of their constituencies.[42] In other words the activities of the ideological PACs served to emphasise the importance of constituency politics in election campaigns. The difference this made to the behaviour of senators was described by Senator John Danforth (R – Mo) who declared: 'The Senate is on a hair-trigger. There's an absence of a long view. People are running for reelection the day they arrive. It's unbelievable.'[43]

The NCPAC campaigns provide an interesting illustration of the extent to which the role of the political parties as conveyors of campaign information was undermined by television. Increasingly candidates tended to base their campaigns around television, and were advised by media and public relations experts rather than by the political parties. The provision of campaign information was, however, only one area where the political parties appeared to have been squeezed out of the electoral process. During the late 1970s both the cost of campaigning and the nature of fundraising changed dramatically. Television is a very expensive medium, and its increased use in Senate races was reflected in the growth in Senate campaign expenditures between 1974 and 1982. In 1982 sixty-four candidates for the Senate spent a total of $114 million in their campaigns compared with the $28·5 million that sixty-five candidates had spent in 1974.[44] At the same time that the cost of campaigning was increasing, the enactment of the Federal Election Campaign Act (1971), and its major amendments of 1974, 1976, and 1979, placed severe limitations on the size of contributions that could made to a candidate. An individual was limited to a maximum of $1,000 per candidate per election, up to a ceiling of $25,000 to all candidates annually. PACs were limited to $5,000 per candidate per election with no overall spending limit. A PAC could also give up to $5,000 a year to other political committees. An individual could donate up to $20,000 to a national political party and up to $5,000 to PACs and other political committees, but such gifts were to be subtracted from the overall $25,000 ceiling. Candidates for the Senate could also accept direct contributions totalling $17,500 from the Republican National Committee, the National Republican Senatorial Committee, and the National Republican Congressional Committee.

One unforeseen consequence of FECA was to increase the importance of PACs at the expense of the parties. Between 1974 and 1982 the number of PACs grew from 608 to 3,371 as they began to play a more prominent role in campaigns.[45] FECA's $1,000 contribution limit on individual gifts to candidates obviously benefited the PACs, which with their $5,000 contribution limit offered a greater reward for a more efficient expenditure of a candidate's time and effort as individual donations were usually solicited at high overhead dinners while PACs were organised and centralised. FECA placed a heavy premium on an ability to generate very large numbers of small contributions, and the best technique for this purpose was direct-mail solicitation of many thousands of names on computerised lists of persons who had previously made contributions to causes and candidates.[46] In this way FECA largely rendered obsolete the traditional money-raising techniques of the parties, and enhanced the techniques most suitable for PACs. Two companies, PAC Associates and PAC Information Services, even began to offer candidates in the late 1970s computerised lists of PACs broken down by area of interest and past donations.[47] Consequently PAC contributions increased both absolutely and as a proportion of total campaign funds throughout the late 1970s. In 1974 non-party PACs accounted for 11 per cent of all Senate funds, and by 1980 for 19 per cent.[48] The most dramatic changes of all occurred within the Republican Party. In 1974 non-party PACs accounted for 7 per cent of the funds raised by Republican candidates, and for 21 per cent by 1980 when for the first time they replaced the Democrats as the main recipients of PAC money.[49]

The increased share of PAC money going to the Republicans in the 1980 elections was due, in part, to the fact that corporate PACs began to support Republican challengers rather than merely giving money to incumbents. When the Federal Election Commission had ruled in 1975 that the Sun Oil Company's Political Action Committee (SUNPAC) could use company funds to solicit political contributions from salaried employees, Republicans had hoped, and Democrats feared, that this new source of funds would benefit the GOP.[50] Mark A. Siegel, the executive director of the Democratic National Committee, had predicted in 1976 that 'most of the money will be heavily Republican, although some will go to Democratic incumbents. It's clear that the proliferation of corporate PACs will be a boon to the Republicans.'[51] Until the later stages of the 1978 elections, however, corporate PACs tended to support incumbents regardless of party. It was not until late October 1978 that corporate PACs started to give more to Republican challengers than incumbents as they began to identify Republicans with good chances of unseating Democrats.[52] In 1980 corporate PACs contributed $7·7 million to Senate candidates of which 42 per cent went to Republican challengers, and only 28 per cent to Democratic incumbents.[53] This compares with the $3·6 million they donated to Senate campaigns in 1978, of which only 20 per cent went to Republican challengers while 37 per cent went to Republican incumbents, and 15 per cent to Democratic incumbents.

The other new source of funds for Republican candidates came from the non-connected or ideological PACs which contributed $1·9 million to Senate candidates in 1980, of which 52 per cent went to Republican challengers.[54] These groups, especially those associated with conservative causes, proved able to raise large amounts of money through the use of direct-mail solicitation. In the period 1979–80, for example, conservative groups were able to raise $27·3 million comapred with the $2 million which the liberal groups were able to raise.[55] The right's advantage in fundraising can be attributed to two factors. First, the modern use of direct mail originated on the right when Richard Viguerie formed a direct-mail corporation in 1965 to raise money for the Young Americans for Freedom. This initial investment gave the conservative groups a technological advantage which the liberal groups were unable to eliminate. Second, the key to successful fundraising letters is fear. PACs stirring strong sentiments among small but intense parts of the population were able to raise large sums while moderates generally fared badly because of their inability to arouse their constituency.[56] Terry Dolan, director of the NCPAC, stated that his organisation's fund-raising letters tried to 'make them angry' and 'stir up hostilities'. The 'shriller you are', he said, 'the easier it is to raise funds. That's the nature of the beast.'[57] An example of such an approach can be seen in a letter which NCPAC sent out in the autumn of 1977 asking recipients to 'send $5 or $10 contributions today to help defeat liberal senators who want to give our Panama Canal away'.[58] The letter then proceeded to present a scenario where the Canal was blocked to American warships but wide open to the Russian navy.

In addition to raising funds such letters were often used to involve people in an issue. After reciting a list of horrors about to be perpetrated the signatory, usually a prominent right-wing activist or politician, would ask for help from the recipient. For example, as well as a request for a donation the letter might also ask the recipient to send a letter to his congressmen. NCPAC claimed that it had stimulated a million letters to Congress in 1977 during consideration of a proposal by the Carter administration to allow unregistered voters to enrol at the polls.[59] In this way direct mail was used to raise funds and mobilise grass-roots opinion. Not only did it undermine the funding role of the parties but it also enhanced the importance of constituency politics.

During the late 1970s ideological PACs, of both the left and right, also began to supply campaign services to candidates. Fashioning itself after the National Committee for an Effective Congress (NCEC), a liberal organisation which had been founded in 1948, the NCPAC started providing campaign consultants, media advice, polls, voter targeting services and precinct organisers. Commenting on these activities Richard Viguerie disclaimed any originality: 'all we are, are very good Japanese. We make copies. We didn't invent single interest groups. The liberals did.'[60] The NCPAC also ran training seminars for candidates and prospective campaign organisers as ways to set up a campaign structure, to use telephone banks and mail contacts, to follow up on prospective voters, and to take polls. The successful campaign of Senator Gordon Humphrey of New Hampshire in 1978 was built around trainees from these seminars.

To a certain extent reforms such as FECA and the increasing sophistication in the techniques of electioneering weakened the traditional function of the parties in campaigns, facilitated the emergence of a corps of professional campaigners who offered their services to candidates on a profit-making basis, and threatened to reinforce the fragmentation of American political life. The use of political consultants was not a new phenomenon in American politics. As early as 1958 professional campaign management firms were organising traditional precinct activities on an *ad-hoc* basis.[61] By 1970 a *National Journal* study of US Senate candidates indicated that of the sixty-seven candidates with opposition that year, sixty-two employed advertising firms, thirty hired professional media consultants, twenty-four used national polling firms, and twenty acquired the servives of a campaign management and public relations firm.[62] The use of political consultants, however, had reached such a level by the end of the 1970s that candidates for the Senate were able to develop what amounted to their own political parties. They were candidate-centred organisations established to serve the immediate end of an individual's election, and used a wide variety of professional consultants. As

Gary C. Jacobson has written, the most striking feature of congressional elections during the late 1970s was the 'ascendant importance of individual candidates and campaigns'.[63] This view was echoed by Nelson Polsby who argued that by the late 1970s candidate-based organisations had replaced the candidate's dependence on 'party regulars and state party organisations'.[64] The acquisition of campaign resources, the campaign organisation, strategy formulation, and media selection became, for the most part, the province of the candidate rather than the party organisation.[65]

The most impressive of these candidate organisations was the Congressional Club, a direct-mail group created by Tom Ellis, a friend of Senator Jesse Helms (R – NC), in 1972 to further Helms's and other like-minded congressional candidates' chances of electoral success.[66] Tom Ellis described the Club as 'an effort to counterbalance the political activities of the union bosses, the ERA crowd, and other far left political campaigns'.[67] As such the Congressional Club was the recipient of large campaign contributions from traditional conservative groups across the United States. H. E. Alexander has shown, for example, that Helms's successful re-election campaign in 1978 received funds from groups like the National Rifle Association and the American Conservative Union and from the PACs of major oil companies and large corporations such as Ashland, Conoco, Texaco, Gulf, Getty, Amoco, Shell, Sun, Alcoa, Sears, J. P. Stevens, Republic Steel and Kemper Insurance.[68] Donations from these groups, however, amounted to less than 10 per cent of Helms's total funding. The rest was raised in a direct-mail campaign organised by Richard Viguerie which concentrated on small contributors, more than half of whom lived outside North Carolina. These operations were extremely successful. In 1978 the Congressional Club raised $7·4 million to support Helms's re-election bid, and in 1980 was able to spend $4·6 million on independent expenditures.[69]

The main beneficiary of the Congressional Club's activities in 1980 was John East, a professor at East Carolina University with no previous political experience, who was selected by Helms to run against incumbent Senator Robert Morgan (D – NC). Campaigning hard on East's behalf the Congressional Club ran a number of commercials which attempted to portray Morgan as a Washington-orientated, liberal-minded Democrat. More than $600,000 was spent on television commercials in the last six weeks of the campaign which stated that Morgan had supported the 'giveaway of the Panama Canal', had voted 'to send hard-earned American dollars to help communists in Nicaragua', had opposed efforts 'to strengthen our defense by voting against the B-1 bomber', and finally, had voted in favour 'of giving away our tax dollars to aid New York City'.[70] Morgan was unable to match this barrage, and lost the state, winning 49 per cent of the vote to East's 50 per cent. It was the closest race in the nation in 1980, and the activities of the Congressional Club undoubtedly influenced the outcome. As Tom Ellis stated:

> When John East started running for the Senate, less than 5 percent of the people in the state knew who he was. We turned that around and gave people a chance to know John. That's why he was able to win and that's what it's going to take to elect more people like him to government. The Congressional Club can be the most effective organisation in the country when it comes down to doing the hard work it takes to win an election.[71]

The important point here is that the Congressional Club allowed East to gain the visibility which enabled him to challenge Morgan.

Some observers have suggested that candidate-centred organisations like the Congressional Club, which raised most of their money from out of state sources, threatened the very nature of the federal system.[72] This point was made by Fred Wertheimer of Common Cause when he stated that 'When most of their funds come not from constituents, but from out of state contributors, citizens have a right to ask "Whom do these people represent?" '[73] On the whole, however, such concern was misplaced. An examination of the voting records of senators shows that they still tended to put their constituency interests above ideological purity. Of far more importance is the impact that the development of candidate-centred organisations had on the parties.

The political parties in campaigns

Although the political parties may never quite have performed the roles often attributed to them retrospectively, it is clear that during the 1970s their role in campaigns changed considerably, and that by the 1978 elections this role was basically that of a support agency for the candidate's campaign organisation. As Edie N. Goldenberg and Michael W. Traugott have written: 'The parties have shifted from providing voter-centered to candidate-centered services.'[74] In particular, the Republican Party began to acquire the techniques of the political consultants to further the chances of its own candidates. With fewer voters identifying with the parties, and with much less loyalty among those who did, the GOP recognised the voting had become increasingly candidate-centred.[75] Winning elections, therefore required good candidates and vigorous campaigns. The Republicans were fortunate in being better placed to take advantage of the new campaign technology than the Democrats. First, the party had begun businesslike, broad-based financial solicitation in the 1930s, some twenty years ahead of the Democrats.[76] Second, the disadvantages that the party suffered in having been so long in the minority acted as an important incentive in trying to capture exposure in competition with officeholding Democrats.

When Bill Brock became chairman of the Republican National Committee in 1977, following the failure of his 1976 re-election bid, he concentrated on rebuilding the party's state and local base in the belief that these were the prime recruiting grounds for future congressmen, senators and governors.[77] In this respect, Brock's reforms had a precedent in Ray Bliss's programme of party rebuilding following the disaster of the 1964 elections. Bliss had also attempted to strengthen the GOP's local base, arguing that 'We are building from the basement up, not from the roof down', but Brock's actions went far beyond anything that had previously been achieved.[78] Early in 1977, for example, the RNC took the unprecedented step of backing one Republican among two or more competitors in party primaries, and Senator Bob Packwood (R – Ore), the chairman of the National Republican Senatorial Committee, embarked on an unusual recruiting drive for Senate candidates.[79] He wrote to all Republican state and county chairmen in states with 1978 Senate races, asking each of them to name the ten best potential candidates. Where one individual ranked uniformly high with party leaders, Packwood called to persuade him to run and enlisted other Republican leaders to do the same.

In addition to good candidates, the ability to wage vigorous campaigns requires technical expertise, a set of issues which resonate with the voters, and money. In an attempt to provide its campaign managers with technical expertise the Republican National Committee ran a Campaign Management College to train managers for House and Senate campaigns in which they were given sophisticated training in campaign techniques.[80] The RNC also provided candidates with studies of voters, non-voters, campaign managers and polls conducted by national polling firms. In order to help them solicit PACs and political consultants the

RNC provided candidates with a list of PACs that had donated to Republicans in the past, and an evaluative list of political consultants.[81] The RNC even paid more than $800,000 in 1978 to Wright-McNeill and Associates, a Georgia-based group of black political consultants, in an effort to attract black votes for white Republican candidates.[82]

A similar attempt to provide Republican senators with help with their campaigns was initiated by Senator James McClure (R – Idaho) following his election as chairman of the Republican Conference in 1981. McClure hired Carter L. Clews, the former director of public relations for the National Right to Work Committee, as the director of the Conference's communications division, and greatly expanded the media facilities available to senators. The communications division had a staff of ten and was divided into three subdivisions. A print division became responsible for mailing reports on Republican senators to news editors across the United States. Telephone and television requirements were met by an electronics division which set up a recording studio in the Capitol to provide a rapid video recording service and installed an audio system which allowed senators to transmit recorded statements over several long-distance telephone lines. Finally, the graphic arts division assisted Senate offices in preparing newsletters and press releases.[83]

In an era of candidate-centred campaigns the GOP tried to ensure that Republican candidates were in a better position to exploit the new campaign technology than their Democratic opponents. This not only involved providing services and money to the candidates but also led to an attempt to improve the image of the Republican Party generally by developing a set of issues which appealed to the electorate, and in particular, those describing themselves as 'independents'. To do this the Republican Party switched to 'genre' advertising rather than running commercials for individual candidates.[84] As early as January 1975 Mary Louise Smith, who was the chairman of the Republican National Committee at that time, announced a television campaign to restore Republican fortunes following the 'Watergate' election of 1974.[85] This idea was developed by Bill Brock, and in a series of television commercials called 'America Today' shown in late 1977, the GOP sought to re-establish its credibility by concentrating on a human issue topic. After the 'America Today' spots had run their course, a new series of commercials called 'Issues of the 80s' was shown which stated standard Republican policy on a number of issues. For the 1982 elections a series of commercials titled 'Stay the Course' was shown.

One problem faced by the Republicans when attempting to unseat incumbent Democrats was that during the late 1960s and early 1970s the electorate had tended to evaluate individual members of Congress highly despite feeling that the institution was performing poorly.[86] During the late 1970s, however, the anti-establishment sentiment which had been prevalent in American society since the late 1960s became increasingly personalised.[87] A poll taken by the RNC in January 1980 indicated that voters not only blamed the Democratic Party for what they regarded as an inadequate performance by Congress but also felt that their own senators and representatives, identified by name, shared the blame for that performance.[88] The poll also showed that the Republicans were favoured 39 per cent to 22 per cent as the party most likely to control government spending, 33 per cent to 25 per cent as the party most likely to control inflation, and 32 per cent to 25 per cent as the party most likely to hold down taxes.

As a result of the poll Bill Brock announced that the Republicans would make the economy and the need for change 'the centerpiece of our campaign'.[89] Under the overall theme of 'Vote Republican—for a Change', a slogan which was reminiscent of the 'Had Enough? Vote Republican' under which the Republicans had captured both houses of Congress in 1946, the GOP launched a $9·4 million advertising campaign designed to blame the country's problems on the twenty-five years of Democratic control of Congress.[90] The first commercial, shown on 29 January 1980, featured a Tip O'Neill look-alike driving a Lincoln Continental until it ran out of petrol while a voice-over declared: 'The Democrats actually passed laws that cut back energy exploration here at home, and made us dependent on foreign oil.' Other commercials showed a dollar bill shrinking in the hand of a worker to the size of a postage stamp to illustrate inflation, and another showed a pair of hands counting out money at what was described as the congressional spending rate of 'a million dollars a minute'. One effect of these commercials was to increase the electorate's perception of the differences between the two parties. In a survey taken in 1980 58 per cent of the electorate perceived important differences in what the two parties stood for, compared with figures of 49·9 per cent in 1952 and 46·1 per cent in 1972, years when, as most observers would argue, the differences were in reality even stronger.[91]

The $9·5 million spent by the Republican National Committee on the 1980 advertising campaign was a record for a party, and was an indirect result of FECA's limitations on contributions to candidates. By taking advantage of what were known as the 'coordinated expenditure' provisions of FECA, however, the Republican Party was also able to offer direct assistance to selected candidates in Senate races. Co-ordinated expenditures can be made for almost any campaign activity as long as the party retains some control over how the money is spent. Direct party contributions to individual candidates are limited by FECA to a total of $17,500 per candidate from all national committees, but the ceilings on co-ordinated expenditures are much higher. The limit for co-ordinated expenditures in Senate races is two cents multiplied by the state's voting-age population, adjusted for inflation since 1974. This formula meant that in 1980, for example, states like Alaska, Idaho and Rhode Island had ceilings of approximately $30,000, and California, the most populous state, had a co-ordinated spending limit of $485,024. By 1982 population growth and inflation had raised the limit in California to $665,874.[92] These ceilings were effectively doubled by the Republican Party when it adopted an interpretation of the law which permitted the party's national committee to act as the agent of the state parties which are allowed to spend on co-ordinated expenditures an amount identical to the national committees. The Republican Party's strategy meant that if a state party proved unable to meet its expenditure limits the national party was able to make up the difference.

Relying heavily upon the co-ordinated expenditure provisions of FECA, the Republican Party made a modest revival as a source of funds for candidates during the late 1970s. In 1976 the party had contributed a mere 6 per cent of the money used by Republicans in their campaigns for the Senate, but by 1982 this figure had risen to 17 per cent.[93] The importance of co-ordinated expenditures to this revival in party funding is revealed in the pattern of contributions made by the National Republican Senatorial Committee between 1976 and 1982. In 1976 the NRSC gave $445,902 in direct contributions to Senate candidates and spent only $113,976 on co-ordinated expenditures. By 1982 these figures stood at $558,327 and $8·7 million respectively.[94] Comparable figures for the Democrats in 1982 were $530,000 and $1·9 million.

Generally speaking it was challengers rather than incumbents who received most financial aid from the National Republican Senatorial Committee. All of the nine Senate candidates who received more than $200,000 from the Republican national committees in 1980 were challengers, with the biggest recipient of party funds being Alphonse D'Amato who received $754,497. This sum was surpassed by the $1·3 million which the party spent on Pete Wilson's campaign in California in 1982. Twelve of the sixteen Republicans who received more than $200,000 from party funds in 1982 were challengers.[95] There can be little doubt that such expenditure by the national party committees was extremely important in enabling Republican challengers to mount effective campaigns against Democratic incumbents. As Gary Jacobson has pointed out: 'campaign spending is more useful to nonincumbents because of its greater effect on how frequently they are remembered by voters'.[96] A study of Senate expenditures by election outcomes shows that when incumbents won with 60 per cent or more of the vote they had outspent their challengers by considerable amounts.[97] To mount an effective campaign the challenger's expenditure had to exceed a certain threshold which varied from state to state, and from election to election, depending on a number of factors including incumbent popularity and the prior visibility of the challenger.

The ability of the Republican national committees to give financial aid, and offer services to its candidates was, of course, dependent upon their ability to raise funds. By the late 1970s both the Republican National Committee and the National Republican Senatorial Committee were running successful direct-mail operations. Between 1977 and 1980 the RNC expanded its donor base from about 350,000 contributors to 1·2 million, and for the 1980 elections was able to raise approximately $50 million.[98] The NRSC began building an independent financial base in 1977 using the services of two direct mail organisations: Stephen Winchell and Associates, and Lewis and Associates.[99] By the end of 1979 the NRSC was raising about 80 per cent of its funds from direct mail, and had approximately 332,000 donors.[100] For the 1980 election the NRSC raised $23·3 million, more than twice the amount raised in 1978, and vastly more than the $1 million raised in 1976.[101]

There was no Democratic equivalent of the advanced Republican direct-mail programme, and in almost every respect the Democratic Party's operations were inadequate compared with the GOP's. There can be little doubt that during the late 1970s the Republican Party was 'light years' ahead of the Democratic Party in its use of sophisticated electioneering techniques, and as a consequence was able to give considerable campaign assistance to its candidates, both directly and indirectly. It is crucial, however, that the nature and implications of this assistance are fully understood. Although the Republican electoral gains at the senatorial level during the late 1970s were impressive they should not be interpreted as a triumph for the Republican *Party*.[102] The Republicans fought a nationwide campaign and were rewarded for their efforts, but given the nature of the electoral environment, the only credit that the party could be given for the Republican success was for providing valuable support to Republican candidates. A close examination of electioneering in the late 1970s and early 1980s underlines the crucial role of individual candidates and campaigns, and gives little ground for thinking that strong direct links between national political forces and individual voting decisions had been reforged.[103] This point is important given the link between the way power is distributed in the Senate and the party's role in elections. An enhanced role for the national party in the electoral process would have been reflected in factors such as party loyalty and the authority of the party leadership in the Senate.[104]

The electoral resurgence by the Republicans during the late 1970s was, in fact, very shallow. In 1980 many individual races were extremely close, and if a mere 50,000 votes could have been moved back into the Democratic column then the Republican victories in Alabama, Alaska, Georgia, Arizona, Idaho, New Hampshire and North Carolina would not have occurred.[105] Such an observation merely emphasises the competitiveness of the electoral environment, and provides an explanation for both the increased importance of constituency politics and the generational changes within the Republican Party during this period. Not only did the Republican's electoral success alter the regional and ideological composition of the party in the Senate but it also led to important generational changes. The latter were the direct result of the new skills required for success in what was an extremely volatile electoral environment. These skills included above all else an ability to take advantage of the new campaign techniques. Quite simply, the Republican Party in the Senate during the late 1970s and early 1980s was the product of its electoral environment.

4   The New Party

An examination of the composition of the Republican Party in the Senate is vital to any understanding of that party's reaction to specific policy proposals, and to its interaction with the institution. Not only may a change in party strength transform the policy agenda of an institution, as occurred following the elections of 1936, 1958 and 1980, but the geographical, ideological and generational composition of the parties will also affect the manner in which the institution's rules are applied, or even generate a demand for those rules to be changed.[1] Any examination of either the Senate or the party, therefore, must necessarily take account of the membership of the party.

The highly volatile and competitive electoral environment of the late 1970s had an important impact on the composition of the Republican Party in the Senate. As the New Deal coalition of white southerners, blacks, blue-collar workers and the ethnic groups gradually unravelled in the face of complex social change the Republicans proved able to speak to the newly ascendant concerns and constituencies, and were able to fashion a majority. As a consequence of opening itself up to these new social forces, however, the composition of the Republican Party in the Senate underwent significant change. In addition to the fact that the traditional relationship between the various geographical regions were transformed as the GOP in the Senate experienced changes in its geographical distribution, the party also experienced considerable changes in its ideological and generational make-up. By 1980 these changes had combined to make it a different party from that found in the early 1970s.

The changing geographical distribution

In the late 1960s and early 1970s a number of political analysts predicted the break-up of the New Deal coalition forged by Franklin D. Roosevelt in the 1930s.[2] They foresaw the emergence of a new Republican majority based in the 'sunbelt' states of the

South and Southwest and the traditionally Republican states of the Midwest.[3] Initially, however, such forecasts seemed to be premature since Republican fortunes suffered such setbacks in the post-Watergate elections of 1974 and 1976 that one commentator could title a chapter of his book 'The Unmaking of the Republican Party'.[4] Another could suggest that 'from the presidency, to Congress, to the governorships, to the state legislatures, the Republical Party in 1976 was worse than decimated . . . it hardly looked like a governing party at all, let alone the "normal governing party" of the country'.[5] Yet those who had predicted a GOP revival finally seemed to be vindicated by the results of the 1980 elections. Not only did Ronald Reagan, a Californian, carry all the Midwest and 'sunbelt' states with the sole exception of Jimmy Carter's home state of Georgia but the GOP won an unprecedented number of US Senate seats in these areas. The victories of four right-wing Republicans in the South—former Public Service Commissioner Paula Hawkins in Florida, state Republican chairman Mack Mattingly in Georgia, Professor John East in North Carolina, and former Admiral and prisoner-of-war Jeremiah Denton in Alabama—left the Democrats holding a bare majority of the twenty-two Senate seats in that region.[6] In the Great Plains states the victories of Dan Quayle in Indiana, Charles Grassley in Iowa, Mark Andrews in North Dakota, James Abdnor in South Dakota and Robert Kasten in Wisconsin meant that the Democrats' share of the seats in this region had fallen to a mere 25 per cent.[7]

The 1980 elections, in fact, accelerated certain general trends which had been evident for some time as the New Deal coalition gradually began to break up: most notably, the decline of the Northeast, and its replacement by the South and West as the main regions of GOP support.

TABLE 4.1 *The regional distribution of Republican Senators, 1974–84*

Congress	94th	95th	96th	97th	98th
South (11 states)	6	5	6	10	11
Border (5 states)	4	4	3	3	3
New England (6 states)	3	4	5	6	6
Mid-Atlantic (4 states)	6	5	4	4	4
Midwest (5 states)	3	3	2	4	4
Plains (6 states)	5	4	7	9	9
Rocky Mountain (8 states)	7	9	10	11	11
Pacific Coast (5 states)	4	4	4	6	7
Total	38	38	41	53	55

The extent of the change in the geographical distribution of Republican senators becomes even clearer if the number of seats that the Republican held in each region is stated as a percentage of the total party strength.

TABLE 4.2 *The geographical composition of the Republican Party in the US Senate, 1974–84 (%)*

Congress	94th	95th	96th	97th	98th
South	15·8	13·2	14·6	18·9	20·0
Border	10·5	10·5	7·3	5·7	5·5
New England	7·9	10·5	12·2	11·3	10·9
Mid-Atlantic	15·8	13·2	9·8	7·5	7·3
Midwest	7·8	7·9	4·9	7·5	7·3
Plains	13·2	10·5	17·1	17·0	16·3
Rocky Mountain	18·4	23·7	24·4	20·8	20·0
Pacific Coast	10·5	10·5	9·8	11·3	12·7

Although the changes in the regional composition of the Republican Party in the Senate in the years between 1974 and 1984 were dramatic, a comparison with earlier Congresses is useful in providing a historical perspective. In the 68th Congress (1923–4) the New England and Mid-Atlantic regions accounted for approximately 30 per cent of Republican strength in the Senate, and in the 86th Congress (1959–60) for 37 per cent of the seats held by the GOP.[8] Even allowing for the fact that Republican strength in the 86th Congress had fallen to thirty-five seats, leading to a distortion when comparing percentages, this figure still represents a source of considerable Republican strength in the Northeast.[9] Moreover, this was a strength which was mirrored in the House of Representatives, where the Northeast accounted for 38 per cent of Republican strength in the 68th Congress, and 34 per cent of the 86th Congress.[10] By the 94th Congress (1975–6), however, the New England and Mid-Atlantic regions accounted for only 23·7 per cent of Republican strength. By the 98th Congress (1983–4) this figure had been reduced to 18·2 per cent.

There are several explanations for this decline in Republican strength in the Northeast. First, Republican strength in what might be termed the 'urban' states of both the Northeast and Midwest declined significantly. Indeed, by the 97th Congress (1981–2) the sole Republican senator representing a Midwest urban state—the homeland of 'Mr Republican' Robert Taft—was Charles Percy of Illinois.[11] This decline in numbers was the consequence of a fall in the support given to Republican candidates by middle- and lower-status white northern protestants. During the early 1950s this group had provided approximately one-third of the support for the Republicans but by the 1970s this percentage had fallen to nearer 20 per cent.[12] In part this fall in support was due to the extent of the population shift from the industrial East to the sunbelt. The 1980 census showed that California, Florida and Texas had gained 9·6 million people in a decade. This was more than 40 per cent of the total population increase of the United States. By contrast, rates of population growth in the Northeast tended to be negative.[13] To a certain extent, therefore, the reduced role that middle- and lower-status white northern protestants played in the Republican Party was the result of a decline in their numbers rather than a shift in their political allegiances. This explanation might also help explain why the Republican Party made gains in the rural New England states of Vermont, New Hampshire and Maine, where the population increase was more in line with the South and West than the Northeast. New Hampshire experienced a 25 per cent increase in population between 1970 and 1980 while Vermont enjoyed a 15 per cent increase, and Maine a 13 per cent increase.

An over-reliance on demographic factors to explain the decline in support given to the Republican Party by middle- and lower-status white protestants in the North, however, obscures the shift in allegiance that occurred among this group. Traditionally protestants had dominated both the Republican Party and American society as a whole. Most Republicans were of Anglo-Saxon, German or Scandinavian backgrounds, and their adherence to protestantism led to the party's hostility to what they saw as the social evils of drinking, prostitution and gambling.[14] The influence of protestantism on the Republican Party and American society declined during the twentieth century, and the election of John F. Kennedy to the presidency effectively ended protestant dominance in national politics. Moreover from 1960 onwards protestants began to identify with the Democratic Party. Between 1948 and 1960 northern protestants constituted about 15 per cent of the total Democratic support, but by 1976 this figure had risen to 21 per cent.[15] These figures suggest that at least some protestants switched allegiance from the Republican Party to the Democratic Party. Indeed, it may be that the liberal Republican senators, who tend to represent states in New England and the Mid-Atlantic, managed to survive only because of their ability to attract support from liberal Democrats and 'independents'.[16]

However, as liberal Democrats found that they had more attractive candidates in their own party, and as liberal Republicans began to face determined primary opposition from conservatives, so their ability to attract support from Democrats declined. The defeat in 1978 of Senator Edward Brooke, a black liberal Republican from Massachusetts, may be viewed as an example of the former, while the defeats of Senator Clifford Case (R – NJ) in 1978 and Senator Jacob Javits (R – NY) in 1980 were certainly examples of the latter.

Senators Brooke and Case had faced determined primary opposition from challengers supported by the groups of the New Right. Brooke, in particular, the Senate's only black, came in for much criticism. A fundraising letter sent to Republicans in Massachusetts in 1978 charged that Brooke had 'done a great deal to oppose conservatives' and had voted much of the time with Senator Edward Kennedy (D – Mass), the Senate's 'Mr Liberal'.[17] So disturbed were some Republican senators over the right-wing challenge to Brooke and Case that eight of them wrote a letter to Bill Brock, the RNC Chairman, on 7 November 1977 appealing to him to stop what they called the 'cannibalisation of the Republican Party by fellow Republicans':

> We have become increasingly disturbed by the talk of 'hit lists'— undisguised efforts to purge members of Congress who vote contrary to the wishes of dedicated, emotionally committed interest groups . . . Funds are being accumulated by committees operating on a nationwide scale, and available for a blitz in any local race that attracts its ire or attention.[18]

Brooke survived the primary challenge but went down in defeat to Paul Tsongas, a liberal Democrat, in the general election. Clifford Case, however, lost in a low-turnout primary election to Jeffrey Bell, who failed to defeat the popular basketball player Bill Bradley in the general election. In 1980 Senator Javits, aged 76 and suffering from a degenerative disease, was defeated in the primary election by the conservative Alfonse D'Amato.

If the Republican Party lost ground in one region where historically it had once been strong, then the late 1970s were also a period when it regained its dominance in the Great Plains states, and improved its competitiveness in the South and West. In the space of four years from 1976 to 1980 the GOP improved its position in the Plains states from that of a rump consisting of Senators Carl T. Curtis (R – Neb), Milton Young (R – ND), Bob Dole (R – Kansas) and James Pearson (R – Kansas) to that of the dominant party holding 75 per cent of the region's Senate seats.

Interestingly, this revival in Republican fortunes was mirrored at the gubernatorial level but not at the congressional level. Of the eight states defined as Plains states only Kansas had a Democratic governor after 1980, but Republicans from this region constituted a mere 9 per cent of the party in the House of Representatives.[19] The high re-election rates enjoyed by representatives served to limit a Republican resurgence in the House of Representatives. Throughout the 1970s the re-election rates for representatives remained about 90 per cent.

The Republican revival at the senatorial level in the Plains states was spectacular but it was a success which was matched, and in some respects exceeded, by the GOP gains in the South where the party almost doubled its strength in the eight years from 1974 to 1982. Whereas Republican Party organisation in most of the Plains states had traditionally been strong, until the mid-1960s the party in the South had been almost non-existent.[20] The weakness of the GOP in the South was a consequence of the post-Civil-War settlement and, in particular, the 1896 election when it became evident that the region was unnecessary to the new national Republican majority.[21] By 1932 when the GOP realised that it once again needed the South, Democratic dominance in the region had become entrenched. In 1952 Alexander Heard wrote in his book *A Two-Party South* that 'to many citizens of the South, a Republican is a curiosity. They have heard about the Negro undertaker who goes to Republican conventions . . . but a genuine breathing Republican is a rarity in most of the counties of the South.'[22]

One of the most important obstacles to the growth of two-party competition in the South was the importance of the Democratic primary in state and local politics. As long as the Democratic primary remained the only important area of competition, potential candidates, political activists and voters had little incentive to transfer their attention and allegiance to the state Republican party.[23] Until the mid-1960s most of the Republicans who sought statewide office were either nominated in state conventions or were chosen in primary elections without opposition. Typically, Republican parties in the South either failed to challenge Democratic candidates or waged only token campaigns.[24] For example, John Tower, who won the GOP's first Senate seat in the South since Reconstruction in a special election in 1961 caused by Lyndon Johnson's elevation to the vice-presidency, had a year earlier when challenging Johnson in the general election commented: 'I'll tell you honestly, there wasn't much of a struggle to get that nomination. The party felt a moral obligation to run a candidate against the Democratic majority leader, and after others had refused to run they came to me and said "You can articulate the party philosophy: you do it." '[25]

John Tower's victory in 1961 represented the most important Republican breakthrough at the sub-presidential level since 1877. It showed that forces such as population migration, economic change, and the small isolated areas of traditional Republican support could be harnessed by Republican candidates at all levels.[26] Although these forces had been in evidence since the Second World War it was not until 1957 that the chairman of the Republican National Committee, H. Meade Alcorn, had decided to try to accelerate the growth of Southern Republicanism by creating a Southern Division in the National Committee staff under the control of a Virginian, I. Lee Potter. Potter spent the next seven years concentrating on publicity, recruitment and the consolidation of existing Republican support.[27]

The impression that the South had always voted for the Democratic Party at all levels is not entirely accurate. There had always been permanent flaws in the Democratic fabric, especially in the Ozurks, southwestern Virginia, western North Carolina, and Eastern Tennessee.[28] Farmers in these areas had generally not been in agreement with the lowland planters on the issues of slavery and secession, had often fought for the Union, and had tended to vote Republican ever since. The mountain Republicans of eastern Tennessee had continuously elected Republicans to the House of Representatives, and together with their brethren in Virginia and North Carolina provided a basis for future GOP development.[29]

The development of Republicanism as a state-wide force in these states, and the South in general, however, owed as much to divisions within the Democratic Party as it did to Lee Potter's activities. Without the increasing alienation which many southerners felt towards the post-Second-World-War Democratic Party, it would have proved much more difficult for the Republican Party to have broken out of its mountain redoubts into the lowlands, and become a competitive force at the senatorial level. As Numan V. Bartley has pointed out: 'Strong and persistent conflicts between southern and nonsouthern Democrats became a cardinal feature of the New Deal system.'[30] When the Democratic Party ceased to be the party of white supremacy it ceased to command the undisputed loyalty of white southerners. This point was made in an editorial of a newspaper published in Birmingham, Alabama when it proclaimed that 'When the Democratic Party ceases to be the party of white supremacy, the deepest basis of Democratic loyalty has been destroyed'.[31] Faced with the Democratic Party's commitment to civil rights many southerners initially transferred their allegiances to Strom Thurmond's States Rights Party, and then to George Wallace. Others, no longer in bondage to the party of white supremacy, felt free to vote in accordance with their economic convictions.

During this period southerners were subject to cross-pressures from various aspects of social change: industrialisation, mass migration from the farms and small towns to the cities, rapid economic development that expanded middle-class values and the in-migration of managers and professionals and their families from outside the South.[32] After World War Two the developing middle- and upper-class suburbs reacted against the neglect of one-party, rural-orientated local governments which failed to respond to the need and demand for new services. Throughout the South during the 1950s and 1960s the emerging upwardly mobile middle class identified with Republican policy on economic issues and became centres of GOP support. For example, John Tower had his most substantial majorities in the suburbs of Houston, Dallas, San Antonio, Fort Worth and El Paso.[33] Economic change, in effect, brought the South into line with the sunbelt states of the South-west where the GOP had enjoyed electoral success since the early 1950s when the first period of sunbelt growth had spawned a new generation of Republicans: Howard Pyle, Barry Goldwater and Paul Fanin in Arizona, Edwin Meecham in New Mexico and Henry Bellmon in Oklahoma.[34] Republican strategists believed that a similar movement into the South would be possible once the race issue had been confronted.

The Republican decision to take advantage of the race issue manifested itself in a speech made by Senator Barry Goldwater in Atlanta in 1961 when he told a gathering of southern Republicans that 'We're not going to get the Negro vote as a block in 1964 and 1968, so we ought to go hunting where the ducks are'.[35] In an attempt to draw support away from the independent candidacy of George Wallace, Goldwater confirmed his belief that school integration was 'the responsibility of the states. I would not like my party assume it is the role of the Federal Government to enforce integration in the schools.'[36]

This strategy proved successful, and when Goldwater was nominated by the Republicans on 15 July 1964 George Wallace's support began to crumble almost immediately.[37] Barry Goldwater went on to win the five Deep South states of Mississippi, Alabama, Georgia, Louisiana and South Carolina, and appeared to have shown George Wallace's electorate that there was a home for them in the Republican Party. Nowhere was this conversion more visible than in Senator Strom Thurmond's decision to become a Republican and campaign for Goldwater. Speaking to a statewide television audience Thurmond declared: 'The Democratic Party has turned its back on the spiritual values and political principles which have brought us the blessing of freedom under God and a bountiful prosperity . . . It is leading the evolution of our nation to a socialistic dictatorship.'[38] In the long run this capture of the Wallace electorate was to have important consequences for the Republican Party for it introduced a style of southern politics into the party that was to be exemplified by the likes of Senators Jesse Helms and John East of North Carolina, and to a lesser extent by Paula Hawkins of Florida, Thad Cochran of Mississippi and Jeremiah Denton of Alabama. Not only were all these senators very conservative but they also brought a 'populist' style of politics into the party. To this extent the Goldwater strategy ended the possibility of the Republican Party assuming the role of reform in the South, and meant that the GOP increasingly attracted the most reactionary elements in the region.

In the short run, however, Republican strategists such as Kevin Phillips and John Mitchell, echoing a strategy which had been suggested by William Rusher in 1963, saw the South as forming the basis of a Nixon presidential victory in 1968. Rusher had argued that the Republicans should forget about carrying New York and California, and instead should strike a conservative pose for a victory in the South which, together with the traditionally Republican states of the Midwest and Mountain regions, could produce a national Republican plurality.[39] The Phillips–Mitchell 'southern strategy' basically involved ensuring that the Wallace electorate remained in the Republican Party.[40] With this in mind Nixon actively courted the South. In a private session with southern Republican National Convention delegates he advocated policies more tolerant of segregation.[41] He also made Strom Thurmond a special adviser, and vice-presidential candidate Spiro Agnew toured the region making colourful anti-Eastern Establishment speeches. Howard Calloway, Nixon's southern co-ordinator, summed up the strategy when he commented: 'I think the ideas expressed by George Wallace are the ideas that a great many Republicans espouse.'[42] By combining the Wallace electorate with the growing support for the Republican Party found in the urban South, Nixon hoped to turn the region into a Republican heartland.

Nixon won 38 per cent of the vote in the South in 1968, and once in office continued to campaign for the 32 per cent of the vote which Wallace had gained.[43] Former Thurmond aide Harry Dent became Deputy Counsel to the President to keep a 'Southern eye' on administration policies.[44] The president also ordered chief of staff H. R. Haldeman to 'establish and enforce a policy on this administration that no statements are to be made by any officials who might alienate the South'.[45] The 'southern strategy', however, failed to help any of Nixon's senatorial running mates. In 1970 William Brock of Tennessee was elected to the Senate, but in terms of senatorial elections the 'southern strategy'—the explicit appeal to the Wallace electorate—failed to produce any substantial results. Early Republican success at the senatorial level was confined to those 'Southern Rim' states where there had been either a tradition of Republican support or the growth of urban centres had produced a sizeable Republican electorate. Of the six Republican senators from the South in the 94th Congress (1975–6) only one, Senator Strom Thurmond (R – SC) represented a Deep South state. The others, Senators Howard Baker (R – Tenn), William Brock (R – Tenn), Jesse Helms (R – NC), William Scott (R – Va), and John Tower (R – Texas) represented 'Southern Rim' states.

William Brock was defeated in the 1976 elections, and it was not until 1978 that the Republicans made further gains in the South. The 1978 elections saw former Navy Secretary John Warner replace William Scott as Senator for Virginia after the latter had decided not to stand for re-election. Scott had been elected in 1972 but had not proved a success in the chamber. Of far more importance was the fact that Thad Cochran of Mississippi became the first Republican to be elected to the Senate from a Deep South state. This Republican breakthrough, however, must be kept in perspective. Cochran's triumph in Mississippi owed as much to divisions within the Democratic Party where the vote was split between the official candidate Maurice Danton and a black independent, Charles Evans, as it did to any Republican breakthrough in that state. Divisions within the Democratic Party also aided the election of Jeremiah Denton in Alabama in 1980. Indeed, by the 98th Congress there were still only four Republican senators from Deep South states while the number coming from the Rim states had increased to seven.

There was thus a slow diffusion of Republican support throughout the South at the senatorial level which lagged a decade behind that at the presidential level.[46] The initial success came in the Rim states of Texas, Florida, Tennessee and Virginia which had been carried by Eisenhower in 1952, and this was followed by success in the Deep South states when Barry Goldwater carried them in 1964. This improvement in Republican competitiveness was generally brought about by the economic and demographic changes which drew the South into the mainstream of American life,[47] a process which altered the balance of power between the major regions of the United States.[48]

Linked to this changing balance between the regions was the GOP's consolidation of its position in the West. As the sunbelt states of the southwest increased in economic power so the Republican Party tightened its grip on these states. By the 98th Congress the GOP held five of the eight Senate seats in this region. When added to the traditionally Republican states of the Rocky Mountains where the Republicans held seven of the ten Senate seats these two areas formed a considerable conservative bloc within the party. Together, the sunbelt, South and Rocky Mountain states provided twenty-three Republican senators in the 98th Congress. This was a sizeable proprotion of the senatorial party which threatened to eclipse, both numerically and ideologically, the previously dominant New England and Mid-Atlantic sections of the party. Not only was there a transfer of power from one region to another but this process led to the Republican Party adopting new policies, reordering existing priorities, and evolving new electoral strategies. The change in the geographical distribution of Republican senators thus led to changes in its ideological composition: increasing the influence of conservatives while decreasing that of liberals.

A new ideological make-up

The changing geographical distribution of the Republican Party in the Senate had an important impact on the party's political agenda. Neither the parties nor their factions have ever been bastions of ideology but, rather, have tended to represent different regions and interest groups. Indeed, the importance of regionalism in the Senate was shown by the development of bipartisan regional caucuses during the late 1970s. Although their development was hindered by a Senate rule which prohibited the joint hiring of staff by senators, and by the traditional independence of senators, three such bipartisan caucuses were in evidence in the 98th Congress: the Northeast–Midwest Senate Coalition, the Senate Western Coalition, and the Senate Border Caucus.[49] Of these, the Northeast–Midwest Senate Coalition, with a membership drawn from nineteen states and led by Senators Arlen Specter (R – Penn) and Alan Dixon (D – Ill), was by far the best organised and worked closely with its counterpart in the House of Representatives.[50] The Senate Western Coalition had been founded in 1977 by Senators Paul Laxalt (R – Nev) and Dennis DeConcini (D – Ariz), and with a membership drawn from fifteen western states met every two or three months to discuss issues common to the western states: energy, water and federalism. Due to its diverse membership, however, the coalition found it difficult to agree on specific issues. The Senate Border Caucus had been founded by Senators Dennis DeConcini and Peter Domenici (R – NM) and was concerned primarily with law enforcement along the border between the United States and Mexico.

The emergence of regional caucuses in the Senate reflects the fact that the actions of most senators are often more related to constituency concerns and the need to build a successful electoral coalition than to any desire to act in accordance with some theoretical construct. This concern for a constituency was clearly expressed by Senator Jesse Helms when attacking plans to provide New York City with a federal subsidy in 1975: 'the taxpayers of my state, and I believe the other states, are repeatedly asking why they should be taxed to bail out the city of New York'.[51] As a result of such constituency concerns the divisions within the political parties are very complex, and any broad categories must give on specific issues. One study, for example, has found that the relationship between federal spending on agriculture, education and space and roll call patterns in the Senate corresponds closely with constituency concerns.[52] Senators coming from states receiving high benefits in those areas would only rarely vote against bills containing such benefits. Even Senator Jesse Helms, who built his career around an uncompromising conservative image, and through the use of direct mail managed to capitalise on that image, supported the tobacco subsidy to North Carolina producers, and voted for federal protection of the North Carolina textile industry.[53]

Despite claims by Senator John Tower (R – Texas) that 'there are no serious ideological differences in the party', three groupings broadly categorised as moderate, mainstream and right wing can be identified within the senatorial party.[54] These groupings have no formal structure, overlap considerably around their edges depending on the issue involved, and have fluctuated through time in size and influence depending on the geographical distribution of Republican seats in the Senate. During the late 1970s the large number of Republican senators coming from the South and West was reflected in an increased number of right-wing Republicans in the Senate, while the relative decline of the North as an area of GOP support was matched by a corresponding decline in the relative size and influence of moderate Republicans.

TABLE 4.3   *Ideological divisions within the Republican Party in the Senate, 1974–84*

Congress	94th	95th	96th	97th	98th
Moderates	13	13	12	12	13
Mainstream	10	9	11	12	14
Right Wing	15	16	18	29	28
Total	38	38	41	53	55

Source: Compiled from the voting records, interest group ratings, and policy statements of the senators concerned.

The moderate wing of the party was descended from two quite different movements within the GOP that date from the New Deal. The 'Western Progressives' or 'Sons of the Wild Jackass' such as Senators William E. Borah of Idaho, George W. Norris of Nebraska and Charles L. McNary of Oregon supported the domestic social policy of the New Deal but opposed intervention in the Second World War.[55] The 'Eastern Wing' under the leadership of Wendell Willkie, Thomas E. Dewey and Fionella La Guardia, initially opposed the New Deal but then adjusted to the new order and actively endorsed the 'internationalist' foreign policies of Presidents Roosevelt and Truman.[56]

Progressivism, which had been in decline since the First World War, all but disappeared from the Western Wing of the party following the Second World War as its philosophy proved to be outmoded and insufficient to meet the problems of an industrialised, urbanised world power. Gradually the Democratic Party supplanted the GOP as the party of advanced liberal reform. Only in Oregon in the persons of Senators Mark Hatfield and Bob Packwood, and in Washington State in the persons of Senators Slade Gorton and Daniel Evans, did Western Progressivism survive in the 1980s. Senator Hatfield, for example, was one of the major proponents of a nuclear freeze in the early 1980s, and co-authored a book on the subject with Senator Edward Kennedy (D – Mass).[57]

The 'Eastern Wing', however, managed to adapt to the new circumstances and proved willing to accommodate the social change which they regarded as inevitable in a developing society. In 1940 a committee headed by Dr Glenn Frank accepted most of the New Deal when it published its report, *A Program for a Dynamic America*.[58] This willingness of moderate Republicans to go along with the New Deal quickly led to them being labelled 'me-too' Republicans by their conservative colleagues. Later they would be accused by Senator Barry Goldwater's supporters of having 'no ideology of their own. No loyalties of their own. No character of their own.'[59]

Rejecting such charges, the moderates regarded themselves as pragmatists. Senator Jacob Javits (R – NY) argued in his book *Order of Battle* that: 'our political system has shunned the doctrinaire and ideological approach to public affairs . . . the main function of politics is to serve the practical needs of life as those needs present themselves in different forms and in different settings'.[60] This pragmatic approach to politics meant that moderate Republicans were often willing to employ government to deal with social and economic problems which they believed could not adequately be met through private means. They also often acted as spokesmen for corporate business, particularly for the business communities of New York, Boston, Philadelphia and Baltimore. They regarded a relatively close association between business and government as not only inevitable but in many respects beneficial to society.

Under the leadership of Thomas Dewey and Nelson Rockefeller the moderates exerted considerable influence over the party from the end of the Second World War to the 1960s. During the 1970s, however, moderate Republicans became an isolated and demoralised force. By the 97th Congress (1981–2) the number of senators identified with the 'Eastern Wing' of the party had been reduced to eight: Lowell Weicker (R – Conn), Charles Matthias (R – Md), John Heinz (R – Penn), Arlen Specter (R – Penn), Charles Percy (R – Ill), John Chafee (R – RI), Robert Stafford (R – Vt) and William Cohen (R – Me). This group, together with Senators Bob Packwood, Mark Hatfield, Slade Gorton and Nancy Kassebaum (R – Kansas), constituted a broad moderate Republican faction within the Senate associated with the Wednesday Group. The Wednesday Group had been formed in 1968 by Senator Marlow Cooke, a newly-elected Republican from Kentucky, to further the interests of moderate Republican senators.[61] It developed into a lunch group which met every week to discuss forthcoming issues but did not attempt to provide comprehensive information or voting cues.

Although the total number of senators identified as moderates in the 97th Congress was only two less than in the 94th Congress (1975–6), two of the new members were not as clear cut liberals as Senators Edward Brooke (R – Mass) and Clifford Case (R – NJ) who had lost their seats in 1978, or Senators Jacob Javits who lost his seat, and Richard Schweiker (R – Penn) who retired in 1980.[62] The *National Journal and Barone Report* for the year 1981, for example, showed that Senator Cohen had a perfect conservative record on foreign policy votes, a distinction he shared only with the more conservative Senators Gordon Humphrey (R – NH) and Warren Rudman (R – NH) among Eastern Republicans.[63] Moreover, Senator Kassebaum, the daughter of the 1936 Republican presidential nominee Alf Landon, voted for S.951 (1981) which aimed to prevent the Justice Department from bringing legal action that could lead to court-ordered busing. Indeed, the absence of Senators Brooke, Case and Javits from the ranks of Republican moderates left the group seriously weakened, and bereft of the leadership that Javits had shown in the early 1970s as co-author of the War Powers Resolution of 1973.[64] It was this leadership which had helped make the Republican Party in the Senate much more moderate than its counterpart in the House of Representatives or the country as a whole.[65]

By the late 1970s young GOP conservatives from the South and West had established themselves as the virtual leaders of the Republican opposition in the Senate and the moderate wing had all but been eclipsed. Rather than leading the party as they had done a generation earlier, Eastern moderates acted, at best, as a brake against a more rapid rightward push by conservative activists. In particular they consistently opposed the 'social issues' legislation propounded by more right-wing Republicans. For example, Senators Weicker and Packwood were instrumental in blocking attempts by Senator Jesse Helms to gain the passage of anti-abortion legislation through the Senate. In 1982 they filibustered anti-abortion and school prayer amendments which Helms had attached to H.J. Res 520 (1982), and in 1983 Weicker successfully opposed S.J. Res 73 (1983) which proposed a constitutional amendment to permit organised, recited prayer in public schools. Speaking after the defeat of S.J. Res 73 (1983) Weicker declared: 'I knew I couldn't lose. Because if I had lost, everything in the Constitution would have been up for grabs.

If people were willing to allow the First Amendment to go, if this concept of religious freedom fell, anything could have happened.'[66]

The distance between the moderates and the rest of the party in the Senate was clearly shown by the lack of support among Eastern Republicans for the positions taken by the majority of their Republican colleagues. In 1980 Senator Mathias supported the party position only 23 per cent of the time, Javits supported it 29 per cent, Weicker 34 per cent, Stafford 39 per cent, and Chafee 40 per cent.[67] In 1981, owing to the skilful manipulation of the Senate's agenda by majority leader Senator Howard Baker (R – Tenn), the divisions within the Republican Party were largely obscured, and the support given to the party position by the Eastern moderates rose slightly. Mathias and Weicker supported the party position 56 per cent of the time, Heinz 63 per cent, Specter 65 per cent, and Chafee 70 per cent.[68] Events, however, proved that this high degree of party unity was temporary, and based mainly on support for President Reagan's economic policy. The president's initial popularity enabled him to push through his economic measures—the bill cutting taxes was opposed only by Senator Mathias among Republicans—but as Reagan's popularity waned, so the Eastern moderates increasingly went their own way, mindful of their own electoral vulnerability and the fact that many of their states were in economic decline and thus heavily dependent upon federal subsidies. In doing so they showed an increased willingness to pursue their own policy and political interests: a pattern typical of the Senate under Democratic rule.

While the moderate wing of the party found itself at odds with the rest of the GOP, and declining in influence in the Senate, the faction once led by Senator Robert Taft, and generally based in the Midwest, experienced a minor resurgence. This revival in the size and influence of the mainstream Republicans was due almost entirely to the increased number of Republican senators coming from the Plains states. Although mainstream Republicans traditionally derived their greatest strength in the 'rock-ribbed' constituencies dominated by small and middle-sized towns and their rural hinterlands in the Midwest they also drew support from some sections of the Border states and the South.[69] In general they regarded themselves as speaking primarily for small business rather than for the giant corporations and New York banks. Like the Eastern Republicans with whom they were often in conflict, their approach to the economy was pragmatic, in the sense of being responsive to political interests, rather than doctrinaire. The

TABLE 4.4 The geographical breakdown of ideological divisions within the Republican Party in the Senate during the 94th and 97th Congresses

	94th			97th		
	Mod	Main	RW	Mod	Main	RW
South	–	2	4	–	2	8
Border	1	2	1	1	1	1
New England	3	–	–	4	–	2
Mid-Atlantic	3	2	1	2	1	1
Midwest	2	1	–	1	1	2
Plains	1	2	2	1	5	3
Rocky Mountains	–	–	7	–	–	11
Pacific Coast	3	1	–	3	2	1
Total	13	10	15	12	12	29

major differences between mainstream Republicans and their Eastern counterparts may thus be regarded as due to the special conditions in the states which they represented.[70] As Nelson Polsby has pointed out: 'There is a sizeable jump from the cultural milieu of the Normal Rockwell painting represented by the (Main St.) strand of the Republican Party's heritage, to the Museum of Modern Art and the sophisticated moneyhandlers and entrepreneurs who adopted the Republican Party as their own because of its permissive—indeed, encouraging view of economic development.'[71]

Mainstream Republicans may be viewed as conservative in the sense that they sought to preserve the social system in its existing form, but they have not opposed all change. Senator Robert Taft, perhaps the most important mainstream Republican of the post-New-Deal era, once wrote to a disapproving friend: 'We cannot blindly oppose every measure looking towards the improvement of conditions in the field of social welfare.'[72] In fact, Taft was relatively liberal on welfare measures, uncommitted in the area of fiscal and economic policy, conservative on questions of power and resource development, and only moderately nationalist in his approach to foreign policy matters.[73] Indeed, one of his more conservative colleagues Senator Ralph Flanders (R – Vt) described Taft as 'one of the great liberals of [his] generation'.[74] Although opposing each step in the growth of the welfare state, the mainstream Republicans of Taft's generation tended to move their line of defence to a new position rather than seriously try to restore the former *status quo* once a particular welfare measure had been enacted.[75]

Following Senator Taft's death in 1953, mainstream Republicans suffered a loss of strength in the Senate which mirrored the general decline in Republican fortunes. During the years of the Carter presidency, however, a number of factors combined to improve the electoral viability of mainstream Republicans. First, the economic depression tended to support the argument that the growth of the Federal Government had led to a curtailment of individual freedom and enterprise, and reinforced the mainstream Republican belief, as expressed by Taft, that 'the whole history of America reveals a system based on individual opportunity, individual initiative, and individual freedom to earn one's living in one's own way'.[76] To this extent Midwestern Republicanism was a reflection of the protestant work ethic prevalent among the German and Scandinavian populations of the region. Secondly, the foreign policy failings of the Carter administration reinforced the isolationism that tended to lie just below the surface in the Midwest, especially in the Plains states, and worked to the advantage of the mainstream Republicans.[77] This factor would later bring many Midwestern Republicans into conflict with the more aggressive interventionalism of other Republicans. In the debate over the 1982 Budget, for example, Nancy Kassebaum and other Midwestern Republicans attempted to reduce outlays for defence spending. Kassebaum introduced an amendment to the Budget Bill, S. Con Res 92 (1982), which would have reduced defence spending by $13·9 billion over three years. The amendment was tabled on a 53 to 44 vote.

The number of mainstream Republicans in the Senate increased from ten in the 94th Congress to twelve in the 97th Congress. Although numerically they were no stronger than the moderate Republicans, those belonging to the mainstream of the party were able to exert more influence in the Senate owing to their control of the party leadership. Both Senator Howard Baker, the majority leader, and Senator Ted Stevens (R – Alaska), the majority whip, were mainstream Republicans.[78] Moreover, by the mid-1970s traditional mainstream policies such as fiscal discipline, tax cuts and anti-communism had been taken over by the right wing of the party. This offered mainstream Republicans numerous allies on many issues, and led one committee aide to argue that there were '30–35 centralists ranging from John Danforth of Missouri to Jake Garn of Utah' on the Republican side of the Senate.[79]

The rapid growth of the right wing of the party from 1974

onwards altered the traditional relationships between the party factions in the Senate. Traditionally the struggle for control of the party had been between a moderate wing centred on the New England and Mid-Atlantic regions, and a bloc centred in the Midwest and identified with Senators Robert Taft and Everett Dirksen. Taft had on one occasion even stated that 'the discomfiture of the Eastern intelligentsia gives me as much pleasure as that of the radical farm leaders'.[80] By the late 1970s, however, the contest was between the inheritors of the Taft–Dirksen conservative tradition and the right wing of the party. Indeed, after the Republicans captured the Senate in November 1980, Senator Baker was only assured of his unanimous election as majority leader after President Reagan backed, and Senator Paul Laxalt (R – Nev) nominated, him in the interests of party unity.

Right-wing conservatism developed in the United States after the Second World War in response to a number of economic, social and moral concerns which were felt most deeply in the South and West. The rapid economic development in the region following the Second World War tended to reinforce a belief in economic individualism, and heightened a deep mistrust of the Federal Government. In this respect right-wing Republicanism differed little from the tradition exemplified by Robert Taft. Taft's brand of conservatism was, however, modified by several concessions to the demands of expediency and responsibility. He accepted, for example, that the Federal Government should concern itself with 'seeing that every family should have a minimum standard of decent shelter', should 'assist those states desiring to put a floor under essential services in relief, in medical care, in housing, and in education', and should 'underwrite the states in providing a basic minimum education to every child'.[81] In contrast, right-wing Republicans believed that economic individualism could still be ruthlessly applied to American life. Senator Charles Percy (R – Ill), who belonged to the moderate wing of the party, emphasised the difference between the new conservatism and the traditional conservatism of the Republican Party when he claimed that 'the philosophy of these men does not even reflect conservatism as it has been practiced in the GOP by such men as Senator Robert Taft, Senator Arthur Vandenberg, and President Hoover'.[82] In his book *Conscience of a Conservative*, for example, Senator Barry Goldwater not only ruled out any more federal welfare programmes but also advocated a staged withdrawal from all existing domestic programmes except those he deemed to be part of the Federal Government's constitutional mandate.[83] He argued 'government must begin to withdraw from a whole series of programs that are "outside its constitutional mandate" including social welfare programs, education, public power, agriculture, public housing, urban renewal . . .'[84] In other words, right-wing Republicans, unlike the mainstream of the party, were no longer content with moderating the rate of change. They believed that change had gone too far and demanded a return to an earlier condition of society where racial tensions, permissiveness, drug abuse and increases in crime were believed to be unknown. Patrick Buchanan, a speechwriter for Richard Nixon, summed up this sentiment when he called for a 'counter-reformation'.[85]

Until the mid-1960s right-wing Republicans were rare in the Senate, and numbered only five: Barry Goldwater, Peter Dominick of Colorado, Strom Thurmond, John Tower, and Carl Curtis of Nebraska. As the party reached out beyond its previous power bases, however, and sought to take advantage of the new social forces in the South and West, so the number of right-wing Republicans gradually increased as the GOP managed to attract some support from groups like white southerners and Roman Catholics who had previously not been attracted to the party. The fact that the Republican Party was becoming more acceptable to some Catholics was shown by the increased number of Roman Catholics in the Republican senatorial party.

TABLE 4.5 The religious affiliations of Republican Senators, 1974–84

Congress	94th	95th	96th	97th	98th
Catholic	4	3	4	8	8
Jewish	1	1	2	3	4
Baptist	3	3	5	6	6
Episcopal	9	11	12	15	16
Methodist	5	7	6	9	8
Presbyterian	7	5	2	2	2
All other	9	8	10	10	11

Source: Ornstein, Mann, Malbin, Bibby, op. cit. p. 252; and Congressional Quarterly 1984 Almanac, p. 223.

Although not all of the Roman Catholic senators belonged to the right wing of the party they generally gave their support to the social issues agenda: the campaign against abortion, busing and the restrictions on school prayer.

By the 94th Congress there were fifteen right-wing

Republicans in the Senate, of whom seven came from the Rocky Mountain states of the West, four from the South, two from the Plains and one from Oklahoma. It is perhaps one of the greatest ironies of American politics that the Rocky Mountain states, which to a large degree may be viewed as wards of the Federal Government, should produce so many rugged, independent frontiersmen who are ready to denounce the Federal Government for its every transgression.[86] In 1979, for example, Nevada became the leader among Western states in the 'Sagebruch Rebellion' which showed that the old ownership–largesse relationship with Washington had broken down. The Nevada legislature passed, and the Republican Governor Robert List signed, a measure declaring state sovereignty over 49 million acres of Nevada territory owned by the Federal Bureau of Land Management. The issue eventually ground to a halt in the courts, but the bill struck a chord in thirteen other states with heavy federal land owner-ship. By the 97th Congress the number of right-wing Republicans representing Rocky Mountain states had increased to eleven but it was in the South where they made the greatest gains. In the 97th Congress there were eight right-wing Republicans from the South. Gains were also made in New England with the election of Senators Gordon Humphrey (R – NH) and Warren Rudman (R – NH) in 1978 and 1980 respectively.

The years 1974 to 1980 might thus be characterised as a period when right-wing Republicanism made major gains across the United States. In the Rocky Mountain states and in New Hampshire these gains were built upon the strong sense of individualism which existed in those states, combined with a general discontent with the liberal policies of the previous fifteen years.[87] New Hampshire, although a Northeastern state, displayed many of the characteristics of a 'sunbelt' state. The dominant newspaper, the Manchester *Union-Leader* was pro-development, anti-planning and anti-tax in a state with low social services, and the unique status in modern America of not having a single land-based tax. Instead the state tried to subsist off so-called 'sin' taxes on liquor, tobacco, racing and sweepstakes which were designed to draw in out-of-state money to pay New Hampshire's bills.[88] In the Southern states, the extraordinary gains made by right-wing Republicans were largely the result of the economic changes which were occurring in the region, and the racial tensions generated by court-ordered integration. Walter Dean Burnham, in fact, has suggested that right-wing Republicanism had many of the characteristics of a general protest movement created by

Republican strategists to take advantage of the white lower-middle- and working-class backlash against the Great Society programmes of the 1960s and their non-white beneficiaries.[89] It would be a mistake, however, to treat right-wing Republicanism as a unified movement. Not only were there divisions between what became known as the 'old right' and the 'new right', but there were also considerable differences of opinion even between those senators usually identified as belonging to the 'new right'.

The first reported use of the term 'new right' was in 1975 when the right-wing political analyst Kevin Phillips used it in a newspaper article which examined the links between Joseph Coors, a member of the Coloradan brewing family, Paul Weyrich, director of the Committee for the Survival of a Free Congress, and Richard Viguerie, the direct-mail fundraiser.[90] In his article Phillips suggested that the Coors/Weyrich/Viguerie network differed from more traditional conservative groups such as the Americans for Constitutional Action by its concentration on social or moral issues. This view was supported by Weyrich who stated that 'the very essence of the new right is a morally based conservatism . . . our view is not based in economics but in a religious view'.[91] This description of the new right was generally accepted by Senator Barry Goldwater who, in a speech on 15 September 1981, declared: 'In the past couple years I have seen many news items that referred to the Moral Majority, pro-life and other religious groups as the "New Right" and the "New Conservatism". Well I have spent quite a number of years carrying the flag of "old conservatism" and I can say with conviction that the religious issues of these groups have little or nothing to do with conservative or liberal politics.'[92]

One of the distinguishing features of those senators associated with the new right, therefore, was their emphasis on social issues. In the Senate during the period 1974 to 1984 these social conservatives considerably outnumbered old right senators who generally opposed government intervention of any sort into family life. Of the twenty-nine right-wing senators in the 97th Congress, for example, only Senators Barry Goldwater, Sam Hayakawa (R – Calif), Warren Rudman, John Tower, Malcolm Wallop (R – Wyo) and Alan Simpson consistently voted against banning abortions. Senators Wallop and Simpson, in particular, found themselves isolated from their Rocky Mountain colleagues on this issue. Moreover not all of the twenty-three senators who might be termed social conservatives supported the new right's social agenda. Rather, support tended to vary from issue to issue. Of the twenty-three social conservatives, only a small minority consisting of Senators William Armstrong (R - Colo), Jake Garn (R - Utah), Orrin Hatch (R - Utah), Roger Jepsen (R - Iowa), Jesse Helms and John East gave whole-hearted support to the new right agenda.

An overriding concern for the social agenda, however, was only one feature linking those senators described as belonging to the new right. Equally important was their determination to succeed, and dislike for the institutions of government. In many respects they regarded themselves as replacing an old conservative generation demoralised by defeat, reluctant to organise, and unwilling to promote their ideas among the electorate. 'They've laid the groundwork for what we do, but they've been banging their heads against a wall. Some of them are tired' stated Senator Hatch in 1978.[93] This sentiment was echoed by Senator Garn who described the old right as lacking a will to win: 'As long as they were able to express their philosophical viewpoint, the outcome didn't matter. They went home and said they tried.'[94] The conservatism of Senators Garn, McClure, Hatch and Helms represented an *aggressive* call for a return to traditional values packaged in the most contemporary style.

An illustration of this new mood among conservatives can be seen in the formation of the Senate Steering Committee in 1974 by Senators Curtis and McClure.[95] In explaining his reasons for forming the Steering Committee Curtis stated: 'I got tired of being defeated on the floor. I was disappointed that one of my colleagues would have a good amendment that was defeated because nobody knew anything about it. I decided what we needed was a little organisation.'[96] The key word here is organisation. The formation of the Steering Committee may be viewed as an attempt by like-minded conservative senators to organise themselves effectively, and thus play a more active part in the Senate's proceedings: better able to defend conservative proposals, and defeat those with which they disagreed. Margo Carlisle, who became executive director of the Steering Committee in 1979, described the Committee's members as 'more activist now. People used to consider conservatives as protecting the status quo, but there is nothing conservative about the status quo. We are in favour of change.'[97]

The Senate Steering Committee began operating in May 1974 when Senators Curtis and McClure hired Tom Cantrell from Senator Dewey Bartlett's (R - Okla) staff as its first executive director, and immediately became active in the legislative battles over the Consumer Protection Agency. From that date the Steering Committee met regularly over lunch each Wednesday while its staff members co-ordinated legislative activities, planned strategies, assembled coalitions, wrote speeches, drafted legislation and assisted their members' personal and committee staffs. Members were often assigned to take the lead on specific issues. For example, Senator Garn was told to take responsibility for the Strategic Arms Limitation Talks, Senator Hayakawa for education and Senator Helms for school prayer and abortion.

Between 1974 and 1981 the number of senators associated with the committee rose from nine to seventeen. A close examination, however, of the type of senator associated wih the Steering Committee during this period reveals a gradual broadening of the Committee's base. Among those senators contributing money to the Steering Committee in 1981 were senators as ideologically diverse as Jesse Helms, Barry Goldwater and Larry Pressler (R – SD). Pressler, in particular, was not noted for his radical conservatism, and his inclusion suggests that in trying to broaden its base the Steering Committee reduced its ideological coherence, thereby making it more difficult to agree on joint action.

Prior to 1980 the Senate Steering Committee had some success in co-ordinating the efforts of its members to defeat or obstruct legislation with which they disagreed. It has been argued that its activities helped to kill a Carter Labor Law Reform Bill, HR.8410 (1978), and almost prevented ratification of the Panama Canal Treaties. In its opposition to these and other measures, the Steering Committee, and the new right in general, demonstrated all of the obstructionist techniques that had become commonplace in the Senate during the late 1970s. The Labor Law Reform Bill was killed by a filibuster organised by Senators Helms and Richard Lugar that held up the Senate from 16 May to 22 June 1978. Senator Strom Thurmond and Senator Orrin Hatch also killed a Fair Housing Bill, S.506 (1980), by maintaining a filibuster throughout December 1980 until the Bill was withdrawn through lack of time. With Senate leaders unwilling to bring bills to the floor without an agreed time limit on debate, members of the Steering Committee were usually able to extract compromises from sponsors anxious to see their bills brought to the floor. Time constraints caused by an overburdened schedule gave inordinate power to a handful of members.

One important new feature of Senate obstruction during the late 1970s was the development of the post-cloture filibuster by Senator James Allen (D –Ala).[98] Facilitated by the passage of S.Res 268 in April 1976 which changed the Senate's rules to allow amendments to a bill to be introduced right up until the result of a cloture vote was announced, in June 1976 Senator Allen broke the unwritten rule that a filibuster ended when cloture had been invoked.[99] He charged that the leadership had cut him off before he had actually begun to filibuster, thereby violating his minority rights, and in retaliation he called up dozens of amendments, demanding roll call votes and quorum calls until offered a compromise. To a certain extent such tactics were reminiscent of the methods of obstruction employed in the House of Representatives during the Speakership of Thomas B. Reed (1889–91) and were used by new right senators, either to defeat legislation or to exact compromises.[100] As one Senate staff director stated: 'We are always up against some deadline, and some one senator can always exercise monopoly control. I can't count the number of times there have been that senator X, usually Hatch or Armstrong, has 100 amendments in his pocket. So we start out by watering the bill down.'[101] In an effort to limit the post-cloture filibuster a change in Rule 22 was made in 1979. After cloture had been invoked a final vote had to occur after one hundred hours of debate. All quorum calls and votes were included in the one hundred hours, but provision was made to extend the time for debate if approved by a two-thirds vote.

In their efforts to defeat 'liberal' legislation, new right senators benefited from their contacts with certain ideological Political Action Committees. Almost every new right senator seemed to have his own links with new right organisations such as the Committee for the Survival of a Free Congress and the National Conservative Political Action Committee. These links were generated and sustained by the close personal association of various senators with the new right groups. Paul Weyrich, director of the CSFC, had been instrumental in setting up the Senate Steering Committee and knew Senators McClure and Helms well. Charles Black, a former aide to Helms, was largely responsible for creating the NCPAC. Senator Humphrey was once a state director for the Conservative Caucus. Two more aides of Helms—John E. Corbaugh and James P. Luiser—ran the Institute of American Relations, a right-wing foreign policy think tank financed by the Texas billionaire Nelson Bunker Hunt. Senators Hatch, McClure, Jepsen and Humphrey also served on the advisory board of Christian Voice, an organisation of the Christian Right.

The various elements of the new right network were also brought together in a series of more formal meetings. Perhaps the most important of these was the Kingston Group: a weekly meeting of Senate and House staff members, Senate Steering

Committee members, administration staff members and leaders of the conservative organisations. At these meetings, which dealt mainly with economic issues, 'information was exchanged, resources combined, and new ideas aired' in an attempt to mobilise grass-roots support behind legislature initiatives and to co-ordinate strategies to defeat 'literal' initiatives.[102] There were two other less well-known groups operating in much the same way as the Kingston Group and having close links with it. The first of these was the Stanton Group which met at the headquarters of the CSFC and dealt with national security issues. It had a membership which ranged fromt he new right Committee for a Free Afghanistan to such pillars of the Washington establishment as the Veterans of Foreign Wars and the American Legion. The second group was the Library Court Group. This group met less frequently than the others and dealt primarily with social issues.

A disregard for the Senate's rules, and an unwillingness to compromise in pursuit of their aims, was one of the major distinguishing marks of the new right from 1974 to 1984. Older conservatives such as Senator Goldwater placed an ultimate value on what might be termed 'institutional maintenance' and were generally unwilling to see the Senate's rules abused. Referring to a filibuster by Senator Hatch in 1984 against a Civil Rights measure Goldwater made his views plain when he exclaimed: 'I think the Senate is beginning to look like a bunch of Jackasses.'[103] It was for this reason as much as for any deep-rooted ideological opposition which led Senators Goldwater and Hayakawa to kill Senator Helms's attempt to pass an anti-abortion measure, H.J. Res 520 (1982), when they moved to table the bill after Helms had proved incapable of breaking a filibuster by Senators Max Baucus (D – Mont), Lowell Weicker and Bob Packwood.

The distinction between the 'old' and 'new' right was largely generational: the new right senators tended to be younger than their more traditional colleagues and had less political experience. To this extent the new right senators were typical of many senators of all political persuasion elected during the 1970s, and may be viewed as symptomatic of the deep changes which were occurring in American electoral behaviour during this period.

Generational changes

While the changing geographical distribution of the Republican Party in the Senate had an important impact on the party's ideological make-up—strengthening the conservative element of the party at the expense of the moderate element—many of the changes in the way that the GOP operated in the chamber can be traced to certain generational changes which occurred in the 1970s. These changes were related to changes in the electoral environment: the increased turnover in Senate seats, changing patterns of recruitment, and the general dealignment of American politics of the late 1960s and 1970s.

Beginning in 1976 an increase in the turnover rate, and the spectacular success of the Republicans in the 1978 and 1980 elections, altered the relationship between senior and junior senators. By the 97th Congress there were thirty-five Republican senators in their first term compared with only fourteen freshmen Republicans in the 94th Congress. This change generated considerable tensions within the Republican Party. Of the thirteen Republican senators in the 97th Congress who had served two terms or more, six belonged to the moderate wing of the party, and were called 'country club Republicans' by the new breed of aggressive GOP conservatives who called for a more activist agenda.[104] These aggressive conservatives constituted the vast majority of the Republican freshman class, and were frequently in conflict with the more senior members of the party who held most of the major committee chairmanships.

Although the high turnover rates of the late 1970s frustrated efforts to centralise power once more within the party or committees, equally important to the operation of the chamber was the type of person gaining election. The changes in the electoral environment during the 1970s meant that most senatorial candidates tended to be self-starters who put together their own political organisations with help and finance from the ideological PACs, and succeeded with relatively little help from the party. In fact, the Senate Steering Committee and the new right network in general were indicative of the reduced role of the parties, both in elections and in the legislative process. First, many of the friendships between the leaders of the PACs and senators had been forged during election campaigns, with the former providing both help and finance for candidate-centred campaign organisations. Second, the fact that senators could turn to the PACs for assistance with legislation undermined the Senate leadership's ability to control the legislative process. Such assistance allowed individual senators to assert their independence as they were no longer forced to rely on party or committee staff for aid.

To a certain extent it was the new breed of senator with his aggressive individualism and emphasis on 'issues' that made the

GOP in the Senate during the late 1970s appear much more ideologically-motivated than had previously been the case. It was no coincidence that the increase in the number of Republican senators coming from states in the South and Southwest where the party organisation was generally weaker than in the Northeast and Midwest, corresponded with the development of aggressive conservatism in the Senate. Indeed to all intents and purposes, 'organisation' is a misnomer for the collection of personalities and factions which compose the Democratic and Republican Parties in California, the West and Southwest and, as a result, many senators from states in these regions owed very little to the party for their election.[105] Furthermore, having taken advantage of the anti-establishment feeling found in these regions, senators were in no mood to compromise with that establishment upon reaching Washington DC.

This unwillingness to compromise was exacerbated by the fact that a large number of this new breed of senators had little or no previous political experience and, consequently, little understanding of the institution in which they served. In the 97th Congress there were fifteen Republican senators with no previous experience of elected political office compared with only two in the 94th Congress. The effects of this increase in the number of Republican senators without previous experience of elected office were accentuated by changes in the age structure of the party.

TABLE 4.6   *The age structure of the Republican Party in the US Senate in the 94th and 97th Congresses (ages calculated at the beginning of each Congress).*

Age	30-35	36-45	46-55	56-65	66-75	75
94th	0	5	15	9	8	1
97th	2	10	22	14	3	1

In the 94th Congress only five senators, or 13·25 per cent of the party, were under the age of 46 years. By the 97th Congress a total of twelve senators, or 22·8 per cent of the party, were in this category. These changes in the age structure were reflected in the decline in the average age of Republican senators from 57·2 years in the 94th Congress to 52·1 years in the 97th Congress. In many respects it was this relative youth and lack of political experience, as much as any ideological differences, which distinguished the new generation of conservatives from the generation of Senators Barry Goldwater and John Tower.

The Republican Party in the Senate during the 97th and

98th Congresses was younger, more aggressive and more conservative than that found in the 94th Congress. In managing to broaden its appeal to sections of the electorate where previously it had had little support, the GOP managed to fashion itself a majority, but in opening itself up to the new social forces of the South and West, and by taking advantage of the new electoral climate, the nature and style of the party were transformed. The new Republican senators were less willing to compromise, were more independent of the party and more ideologically motivated. To this extent they were the product of the electoral environment which existed at the end of the 1970s.

5 The party leadership

Although the Constitution does not mention the role of the political parties in the legislative process, party leadership has become one of the most important factors influencing the manner in which the US Senate operates. Since the late nineteenth century when the two-party system became firmly established on Capitol Hill, congressional leaders have tried to develop methods which advance their party's legislative effectiveness.[1] To that end they have attempted, with varying degrees of success, to strengthen party unity, utilise and shape the institution's rules to facilitate enactment of the party's legislative goals, and in the process, enhance the party's national image and electoral future. During the early 1980s this last function assumed an ever increasing importance, with the leadership attempting to schedule Senate floor action to suit senators seeking re-election: a development which was not welcomed by all senators. Senator Barry Goldwater (R – Ariz), for example, complained in May 1980 that 'I personally am getting a little tired of having to jam the work of the Senate into three days to take care of the senators who are running for re-election, and I happen to be one of them.'[2]

The reason for the mixed success that Senate party leaders have experienced in pursuit of their goals lies in a variety of circumstances which impinge upon their ability to respond to a complex and changing environment. On occasions, leaders such as Senator Lyndon B. Johnson have been able to use their authority to shape the setting and the institution in which they serve, but traditionally the authority of the leader has been limited by the degree of independence afforded to individual senators. As David B. Truman pointed out: 'the acknowledged independence of senators . . . both delimits and defines the roles of party leaders.'[3] Woodrow Wilson recognised this fact when in his book *Congressional Government* he wrote: 'The public now and again picks out here and there a senator who seems to act and speak with true instincts of statemanship . . . But such a man, however eminent, is never more than *a* senator. No one is *the* senator.'[4]

During the 1970s and early 1980s the power of the party leadership was further weakened by the development of a more decentralised committee and subcommittee structure, the emergence of new election laws, and the reform of congressional rules and practices, all of which tended to reinforce the independence of individual senators. Increasingly, senators owed little to the party leadership, and electoral necessity meant that they were more and more eager to make a quick name for themselves by sponsoring their own legislation. As one congressional aide stated: 'Congress gives the impression of a football team which goes to the line of scrimmage not having had a huddle. When the ball is snapped, every player runs the play he would have called if there had been a huddle.'[5] Nowhere were these developments more pronounced that in the Republican Party of the late 1970s where geographical, ideological and generational change had transformed the nature of the party. Few observers believed that when the 97th Congress (1981–2) convened on 5 January 1981 the new majority leader, Senator Howard Baker (R – Tenn), would be able to hold the various elements of the majority party together.[6]

Leadership in the Senate

The task faced by Senator Baker, like that confronting all majority leaders, was to attempt to bring some coherence and efficiency to what was a 'decentralised and individualistic legislative body'.[7] In other words the Senate's leadership had to endeavour to bring the chamber's 'fragmented activity . . . into some sort of harmony'.[8] This function involved a dual and at first sight conflicting responsibility. On the one hand the leadership had to ensure that the business of the Senate ran smoothly, that legislation was scheduled, that work was done, and that disruptive conflicts were avoided. On the other hand they led one of two opposing parties in the Senate and were responsible for their party's programmes and responsibilites.[9] These dual responsibilities may, in part, be viewed as a consequence of the very nature of the chamber. Unlike most other legislatures, which have tended to relinquish power and authority to the executive, the Senate has remained an extremely powerful institution. Not only does it possess considerable legislative powers but it also has certain judicial and executive functions which include the right to try all impeachments, ratify treaties and confirm presidential appointments. The very existence of these powers means that the chamber has a national responsibility, and it thus needs to be seen acting in a manner which transcends mere *party* interests. The Senate's leadership, therefore, must ensure that the chamber is seen to be taking account of its national responsibilities, and yet at the same time be aware that they are also party leaders. These two roles are not easy to reconcile although, as Roger Davidson and Walter Oleszek have pointed out: 'Both kinds of function point towards the parties' objective of influencing policy-making in uniformity with their political leanings.'[10] If the floor leader failed to perform his 'institutional' function it would prove almost impossible for him to guide his party's programme through the Senate.

In performing this difficult function, however, the majority leader has few institutional powers. Unlike the Speaker of the House of Representatives whose powers include the right to preside over the House, decide points of order, refer bills and resolutions to the appropriate committees, schedule legislation for floor debate and appoint members to select, joint and House–Senate conference committees, the majority leader in the Senate has few formal powers.[11] The only power that the majority leader possesses is derived from the fact that he is at the centre of communications within the Senate, and has the parliamentary right to be recognised first on the floor. The latter was used in 1975 by majority leader Senator Mike Mansfield (D – Mont) to defeat opposition by Senators Jesse Helms and James Allen to bill HR.6219 extending the provisions of the Voting Rights Act. On 18 July 1975 Helms and Allen had attempted to block consideration of HR.6219 by calling up another controversial bill but Mansfield managed to forestall this manoeuvre by demanding recognition on the floor to call up the Voting Rights Bill. The right to prior recognition was also used with impressive results in 1978 when majority leader Senator Robert Byrd (D – WVa) and minority leader Senator Howard Baker employed it to cut off a post-cloture filibuster being conducted by two maverick Democrats who were determined to kill legislation designed to end controls on the price of natural gas. After a vote of cloture had ended their standard filibuster, Senators James Abourezk (D – SD) and Howard Metzenbaum (D – Ohio) had attempted to amend the bill to death by calling up for consideration, and demanding quorum calls on, the 508 amendments which they had filed just before cloture. Senators Byrd and Baker decided to break the filibuster by having the amendments ruled out of order. With Vice-President Mondale in the chair, Byrd and Baker, using their parliamentary right to be recognised first on the floor, called up one amendment after another to have them ruled out or order. With Mondale refusing to recognise any other senator, and agreeing with the two leaders' argument that an amendment which had been ruled out of order was no longer pending business before the Senate with the consequence that a quorum call was not in order either, the leadership managed to defeat the filibuster.[12]

The breaking of the Metzenbaum–Abourezk filibuster was accompanied by a large number of complaints concerning the violation of minority rights which the leadership's tactics were deemed to have involved, and serves to emphasise the difficult environment in which the party leaders in the Senate must operate. Senator Byrd once told the Senate that being minority leader was a more onerous task than being president because: 'It is extremely difficult to deal with the wishes and needs of ninety-nine other senators . . . and I cannot fire any of them'.[13] In general, party leadership in the Senate has tended to be collegial in nature, with the majority leader needing to co-operate with committee chairmen and individual senators.[14] This has meant that the evolution of Senate leadership patterns has tended to reflect changes in the chamber's membership, committee structure, norms and rules.[15] Changes in the style of leadership from the 1950s to the early 1980s, for example, reflected more general changes in the Senate: from the largely Southern-dominated, senior-controlled, committee-centred institution of the 1950s to the relatively decentralised, much more egalitarian institution of the late 1970s and 1980s. Senator Mike Mansfield, who succeeded Lyndon Johnson as majority leader in 1961, viewed his position as one among equals. 'I can see a Senate of real egalitarianism, the decline of seniority as a major factor, and the new senators being seen and heard and not being wallflowers', he commented.[16] Mansfield and Senator Hugh Scott (R – Penn), the Republican floor leader, chose to abandon Johnson's domineering style of leadership, and preferred to lead by 'gentle persuasion' and compromise. Mansfield explained: 'I never twisted arms. My predecessor did and gathered chits. I didn't know how. But even if I did, I might have lost down the road because people who have their arms twisted are less cooperative later.'[17] The problem faced by all majority leaders has been to organise the Senate within the limitations imposed by the Senate's structure. With few formal powers it is a problem which each leader has attempted to solve in his own particular manner depending upon the incumbent's personal style, interests, and circumstances in which he operated.

Republican leadership

The circumstances faced by Republican floor leaders are slightly different from those confronting their Democratic counterparts. Having been in the minority for most of the period when the party's leadership posts in the Senate were evolving, the leadership of the Republican Party developed in a different way to that of the Democratic Party. Bereft of standing committee chairmanships to dispense, for example, the GOP was forced to create rewards within the party by providing a large number of leadership posts.[18] Thus unlike the Democratic floor leader who also chaired his party's three most important instruments—the Caucus, the Steering Committee and the Policy Committee—the Republican floor leader chaired no other party committee. Rather, with the exception of the Chairman of the Committee-on-Committees who was appointed by the Chairman of the Conference (caucus), the Republican leadership was elected by Conference at the beginning of each Congress.

Research by Donald A. Gross has shown that the corporate structure of the Republican leadership has generally meant that there are fewer differences between the leadership and Republican senators than there are between the Democratic leadership and Democratic senators.[19] Indeed an examination of the Republican Party's leadership between 1974 and 1984 shows that the geographical and ideological changes which occurred within the party were reflected in the holding of party office.

Table 5.1 *Republican Party leadership in the US Senate, 1974–84*

Congress	94th	95th	96th	97th	98th
Floor leader:	H. Scott	H. Baker	H. Baker	H. Baker	H. Baker
Whip:	R. Griffin	T. Stevens	T. Stevens	T. Stevens	T. Stevens
Conf. Ch.:	C. Curtis	C. Curtis	B. Packwood	J. McClure	J. McClure
Conf. Sec.:	R. Stafford	C. Hansen	J. Garn	J. Garn	J. Garn
Ch. Pol. Comm.:	J. Tower	J. Tower	J. Tower	J. Tower	J. Tower
Ch. NRSC:	T. Stevens	B. Packwood	J. Heinz	B. Packwood	R. Lugar

The leaders of the Republican Party in the 94th Congress (1975–6) were drawn from most of the regions of the United States, and the two main officers, Senator Hugh Scott (R – Penn) and Senator Robert Griffin (R – Mich), may be viewed as representatives of the old northern base of the party. By the early 1980s, however, the leadership was concentrated in the hands of senators from southern and western states. These changes were reflected in the more conservative bias of the leadership during the 97th and 98th Congresses. Although Senators Baker and Stevens may be regarded as belonging in the mainstream of the party, by the 98th Congress all the other posts were in the hands of conservatives. Senator Bob Packwood (R – Ore), the last moderate in the leadership, was replaced by Senator Richard Lugar (R – Ind) at the beginning of the 98th Congress, largely because of the former's criticisms of President Reagan for ignoring the needs of women and minorities.[20]

As well as affecting the structure of the Republican leadership in the Senate, the years as a minority also influenced the way in which the party committees operated. Whereas the Democrats could depend upon standing committee staff for legislative support, Republicans, despite the provisions of the Legislative Reorganisation Act (1970) which required that one third of each committee's staffing funds should be used for minority staff, were generally denied adequate aid from the 1950s to the late 1970s.[21] It was only with the adoption of S.Res 4 (1977) that the Senate finally instituted a policy of two-thirds/one-third minority staffing.[22] Denied adequate staff aid for so many years, the Republicans came to rely on their party committees and in particular the Republican Conference and Policy Committee as sources of staff assistance.

Although the Republican Conference traditionally provided legislative research facilities for Republican senators, under the leadership of Senator James McClure (R – Idaho), and in line with the increased emphasis placed upon elections by the leadership in the 1980s, it began dedicating most of its resources to providing the mass media and public with a steady flow of publicity about the views and accomplishments of Republican senators. This meant that the task of providing legislative research for Republican senators tended to be left to the staff of the Policy Committee. The Senate provided for the creation of Republican and Democratic Policy Committees in the Legislative Reorganisation Act of 1946 following recommendations by the Joint Committee on the Organisation of Congress in 1946 concerning the need for a body to express formally the main policy lines of the majority and minority parties. Despite this, the House of Representatives deleted the provisions from the Bill, and the Senate had to wait until 1947 before establishing the committees by attaching them as riders to a Legislative Money Bill.

Hugh Bone has argued that: 'right from the outset the conclusion is inescapable that the policy committees were misnamed. They have been "policy" bodies in the sense of considering and investigating alternatives of public policy on few occasions, but they have never put forward an overall congressional party program'.[23] In fact the influence of the Policy Committee has varied over the years. Each tends to assume greater importance when its party does not control the White House. Senator John Tower (R – Texas) stated in 1976, for example, that: 'After the election, I felt that with the Republicans out of the White House, I wanted to do more to arrive at Republican positions here in Congress. During the Republican Administration, of course, we were generally taking the initiative from the White House.'[24] Using his position as Chairman of the Policy Committee and ranking member of the Armed Services Committee, Tower managed to forge an alternative Republican national security policy which offered a clear contrast to that of the Carter administration. In May 1978 the Senate Republicans issued a *Declaration on National Security and Foreign Policy*, a thirty-page critique of the Carter administration's policies, together with some alternative policy recommendations. It accused the administration of 'failing to understand adequately, and communicate to the American people the nature of the Soviet threat', warning that 'Carter's defence decisions, unless reversed, could be disastrous to the U.S. within a few years'.[25]

The *Declaration* was issued unanimously, though a mild disclaimer which was appended noted that 'individual Republican senators reserve the right to disagree with some of the specifics'.[26] Generally speaking, the decentralisation and fragmentation of power in the Senate was so well established that few senators were willing to place power in the hands of a Policy Committee, and the unity achieved in the *Declaration* must be viewed as a triumph for Senator Tower's energy and perseverance. He personally negotiated with all of his Republican colleagues, and the result should be interpreted as a personal victory rather than as heralding a new role for the Policy Committee. During most of the Carter administration the Republican Policy Committee served principally to provide additional staff aid to Republican senators and for discussing the problems associated with legislative scheduling.[27]

The problems of legislative scheduling in the Senate can best be illustrated by comparison with the House of Representatives. In the House the route to floor action usually lies through the Rules Committee. This Committee is empowered to report 'rules' setting the guidelines for floor debate on legislation. The chairman of the committee that favourably reported the bill, supported by the bill's sponsors and other committee members, appears before the Rules Committee to request a rule: technically a resolution specifying a special 'order of business'. This rule, which specifies such procedures as the time limit on general debate and the amending process, is then submitted to the floor for approval.[28] Normally rules are approved routinely, though on occasions the strategy of the bill's opponents has been directed towards defeating the rule as a means of killing the bill. In the past the Rules Committee has not always been amenable to the wishes of the leadership in granting rules for bills. During the 1960s, when Rep. Howard W. Smith (D – Va) was Chairman of the committee, it regularly blocked or delayed civil rights and consumer-orientated legislation. At other times the committee has forced substantive changes in bills as the price for granting a rule allowing floor action. Since the era of Rep. Smith, however, the committee has usually done the leadership's bidding.[29]

Unlike the House, the Senate has few elaborate rules or procedures for bringing bills to the floor, and it has no counterpart to the House Rules Committee.[30] Theoretically, under the Senate's rules any senator at almost any time may offer a motion to call up a bill. A simple majority is sufficient to adopt the motion. During the so-called 'morning hour'—the period before 2 p.m. at the beginning of the legislative day—such a motion is not debatable.[31] At other times it is subject to debate, and thus to a filibuster. Occasionally, controversial bills meet defeat at this stage.

The lack of a formal body which deals with legislative scheduling in the Senate means that some other method of co-ordinating action and ensuring the smooth functioning of the institution is required. In practice the role of the House Rules Committee has tended to be undertaken by the majority leader with the aid of his party's Policy Committee. The majority leader will consult with the minority leader and other interested senators in an effort to work out, and gain agreement for, a unanimous consent agreement. This places controls on further debate, and will sometimes include a specific time for conducting roll calls. In effect, it may be viewed as an equivalent of the rule granted by the House Rules Committee in that it places conditions on the floor debate of legislation. The fact that a unanimous consent agreement may be blocked by a single objection means that the role of the Policy Committee is to ensure that the feelings of interested senators are taken into account when drawing up such agreements. This role is performed mainly by the Policy Committee of the majority party, and while the Republicans were the minority the real value of the Republican Policy Committee was its staff, which, unlike those of the Democratic Policy Committee, were available to individual Republicans as well as the leadership.[32] When the Republicans gained the staff resources of a majority party in 1981 this need for staff declined and the Policy Committee took over the role of a scheduling body.

Overall the Republican floor leader has fewer means of acquiring power than his Democratic counterpart, who with the greater staff resources and authority which result from his chairmanship of the Democratic Caucus, the Policy Committee and the Steering Committee, has acces to considerable *potential* power. These resources were used to the full when Lyndon Johnson was majority leader. As Chairman of the Policy Committee Johnson had considerable control over legislative scheduling, which not only gave him the power to 'help or hinder' but also presented him with an unequalled knowledge of legislation on the calendar, and who supported what and why. Furthermore, as Chairman of the Democratic Caucus, Johnson was quite happy to allow the body to lie dormant. In his heyday the Caucus 'would be convened just once or twice during the session, usually to hear the majority leader's State-of-the-Union message or some similar Johnsonian pronouncement'.[33] The main virtue of the Republican form of corporate leadership is that it allows greater participation in the affairs of the party. This provides a strong leader with the opportunity to draw the various elements of the party together.

Howard Baker

The leadership style of Senator Howard Baker, both as minority and majority leader, was the product of a number of factors: his own nature and background, the institutional developments of the 1960s and 1970s which had dispersed power within the Senate, and the particular circumstances which the Republican Party found itself in during his period of leadership. The size and composition of the party in the Senate, its inexperience, and the lack of alternative power centres within the party, were all important factors in determining the effectiveness of Baker's leadership. Probably the two most important influences on his leadership style, however, were his father Howard H. Baker Sr who represented Tennessee's Second District in the House of Representatives from 1951 to his death in 1964, and his father-in-law Senator Everett Dirksen, minority leader from 1959 to his death in 1969.

Baker had entered the Senate in 1966 after running and losing in 1964, and during his early years he spent a great deal of time with Dirksen learning the art of leadership.[34] In 1969 he sought the Republican leadership but was defeated by Senator Hugh Scott, and lost again in 1971 when he was the candidate of conservative Republicans opposed to the leadership of the Eastern moderate Scott. When Scott retired in 1977 the favourite to succeed him was Senator Robert Griffin (R – Mich), the Republican Whip, but Baker was able to put together a coalition of older moderates and younger conservatives to win by an 18 to 17 margin. Between 1971 and 1977 Baker had become known to the nation as the ranking Republican on the Senate Watergate Committee. Without breaking all of his ties with the Nixon White House he was able to project himself as a fair-minded and intelligent investigator whose intention, he said, was to determine what the president knew and when he knew it. Baker's conversational style was ideally suited to the important medium of television, and his election as floor leader in 1977 was the result of a desire by many of the younger conservative senators to have a leader who could speak for the party and represent it on television.

The political environment faced by Howard Baker was very different from that faced by Dirksen or Scott. By maintaining tight party unity, Dirksen had been able to put a Republican imprint on many measures inspired by the Democrats.[35] He had also benefited greatly from the large percentage of Republicans from the Midwest in the senatorial party who could generally be expected to support him.[36] Baker, however, could depend on no such support. Indeed, the very process that enabled the Republicans to become the majority—their electoral inroads into the South and West—paradoxically created leadership problems for Baker. The Republican state parties in the South and West were traditionally weak: the party in the South because of the century of Democratic dominance, and the party in the West as a result of the progressive tradition in that region. Consequently, most senators from states in these regions owed very little to the party for their election. Furthermore, having taken advantage of the anti-establishment sentiment found in these regions, senators were unwilling to compromise on those issues which they believed had enabled them to gain election. Baker thus had to cope with an influx of ardent conservatives, impatient with the accommodating ways of the party veterans, who as the minority believed their mission was to obstruct Democratic programmes, and as the majority felt their purpose was to undo the 'damage' caused by liberal legislators.

As minority leader from 1977 to 1981 Howard Baker managed to convert this opposition to Democratic programmes into unified party positions on such issues as the economy, taxes and national security. Senator William Armstrong (R – Colo) confirmed the importance of this role when he stated: 'Baker pulls us together to marshal a constituency for Republican ideas.'[37] Baker was especially concerned to present a unified front and look after Republican interests as elections loomed.[38] As one of Baker's aides declared: 'He is responsible for representing Republican interests with regard to floor scheduling. That's a major part of the floor operations.'[39] In addition to looking after Republican interests Baker also provided critical help to the Carter administration in securing a degree of Republican support, and thus ratification of the Panama Canal Treaties, winning approval of arms sales to Saudi Arabia, and an end to the arms embargo against Turkey.[40] The end result of Baker's concern with Republican interests and his support for the Carter administration was a form of muted partisanship in line with his 1977 statement: 'I wish the President well. I hope he succeeds and prospers, but we must ensure our constitutional authority to disagree.'[41]

The basis of Howard Baker's success in marshalling both Republican support for those of Carter's measures he felt to be important, and the impressive display of Republican unity on economic issues, was his ability to bring the disparate elements of the Republican Party together. A relaxed manner and close friendships with many of his Republican colleagues were Baker's principal assets as majority leader, and he relied on these ties to win support for the party's positions, working assiduously to fashion a compromise which could be accepted by all elements of the party. His Democratic collegaue from Tennessee, Senator Jim Sasser, described Baker as 'a genius at finding the compromise point and pushing it through'.[42] Baker also took advantage of the corporate nature of the Republican leadership in the Senate to bring more senators into the leadership process, and spent much of his time with individual senators, listening to their complaints and catering to the particular problems that they or their states might have. In other words Baker's highly personal and collegial style of leadership generally kept senators in line by making them feel important and needed. Senator William Roth (R – Del) described Howard Baker as being like 'a political neutron bomb. He destroys his opponents and leaves their egos standing'.[43]

The first example of Howard Baker's skill as *majority* leader occurred in February 1981 when the Senate considered a bill to raise the federal debt ceiling: the authorisation that allowed the federal government to run a budget deficit. This was a highly emotive issue for many Republicans, especially those on the right of the party who viewed it as a symbol of government run rampant. Many of them had previously refused to vote for a debt ceiling increase even though the alternative would have been the government's default on its obligations. 'It was a tough issue, but the facts of life were we had to do it' said Senator Ted Stevens.[44] By using Senate elders such as Senator Strom Thurmond (R – SC), the Senate's President Pro Tempore, and senior conservatives such as Senator Paul Laxalt (R – Nev), Baker managed to head off a potential revolt among conservative freshmen in a manner which made Thurmond and Laxalt feel needed, the freshmen comfortable, and Reagan grateful. Senator Laxalt proved especially effective in this role because of his close association with President Reagan which had developed when they were the governors of California and Nevada during the late 1960s and early 1970s. As Senator Roger Jepsen (R – Iowa) commented: 'I have found that if I want something magical to happen involving the President personally, the person to talk to is Paul Laxalt. It's like talking to the President himself.'[45] While Laxalt told the freshmen that the President was depending on their vote, Thurmond gathered them together and told them: 'Gentlemen, I understand you are concerned that you always opposed an increase in the debt limit. Some of you served in the House and you never voted to increase it. Well neither have I. But I never had Ronald Reagan for President before, so I'm going to vote for it and I believe you should too.'[46] In this way Baker not only distanced himself from an unpalatable measure but also ensured its success.

In an attempt to improve the efficiency of the Senate, and at the same time re-establish an element of control over an institution which during the late 1970s had seen a growth in individual assertion, Baker tried to institute higher scheduling of floor sessions. Using the Republican Policy Committee as a means of sounding out the likely reactions of senators, both Republican and Democratic, to legislative proposals, Baker tried to use this information to schedule floor activity in advance, and cut down on late night sessions, Saturday sessions, Sunday sessions and roll call votes.

To a certain extend Howard Baker was successful in bringing more regularity to Senate business. As a result of his tighter scheduling of floor sessions the average number of hours per day that the Senate was in session fell from 6·5 hours during the 96th Congress to 5·8 hours in 1981.[47] Such figures, however, obscure certain problems which continued to plague Baker throughout the 97th and 98th Congresses. Although tighter scheduling resulted in a shorter Senate day it generally failed to expedite the chamber's business. For example, the ratio of measures passed to measures introduced in the Senate remained at approximately the same level as during the 1970s.[48] As a consequence Howard Baker decided to propose televising Senate debates in the belief that television would act as a lever for major changes in the way that the Senate conducted its business.[49] Referring to the Founding Fathers' conception of the Senate as a restraining, stabilising counterweight to the House of Representatives, he argued that television coverage of selected debates was 'an opportunity for the Senate to actually become the great deliberative body which it was thought to be when it was created, as it has sometimes been in the past, and that we would all like it to be every day'.[50] Baker planned to 'implement scheduled debates on the great issues of the day, intentionally to lay out for ourselves and for the public the parameters of current or impending public policy issues'.[51] Instituting these 'town-meeting' sessions, Baker argued, would lead logically to other innovations, including greater regularity in Senate floor sessions, streamlined procedures for disposing of routine business, briefer sessions over the calendar year, and finally a thorough rewriting and recodifying of the Senate's rules and procedures.[52]

The procedures of the Senate are much looser and more flexible than those of the House of Representatives, and it is this flexibility which causes problems for the leadership. Routine business such as the receiving of messages from the President, communications from department heads, messages from the House, reports of standing and select committees, and the introduction of bills and resolutions, are meant to be dealt with during the two hours designated as the 'morning hour'. Following morning business the Senate moves on to unfinished business or to the business planned by the majority leader. Unlike the more orderly House the Senate frequently interrupts consideration of a bill to take care of other legislation. The Senate may take up a bill, lay it aside temporarily to consider another, return to debate on the first, then pause for speeches unrelated to the subject technically under consideration. As a result it may take days or weeks to dispose of a single bill. Howard Baker attempted to improve this situation through the implementation of television coverage of Senate proceedings. Television, he believed, would put pressure on senators to dispose of routine business more rapidly, and create a need for more orderly debate. Unfortunately for Baker S.Res 20 encountered stiff opposition from senators who expressed reservations that the regulations for television broadcasts would be set without review by the full Senate.[53] Faced with the threat of a filibuster Baker withdrew the measure and reintroduced it in the 98th Congress as S.Res 66. On 17 September 1984 he once again reaffirmed his belief that television would restore 'vigorous and well-informed debate' in the Senate.[54] S.Res 66, however, faced the same problems as S.Res 20, and, unable to break a filibuster, Baker was forced to withdraw the measure.

With the defeat of his proposals for televising the Senate's proceedings Howard Baker was forced to rely on a 'two-track' system to expedite the Senate's business. The two-track system had been instituted in the early 1970s by majority leader Mansfield, with the agreement of minority leader Hugh Scott, and basically allowed the Senate to have several pieces of legislation pending on the floor simultaneously by designating specific periods during the day when each proposal will be considered.[55] By reserving a certain period of time each day for particularly controversial bills the two-track system tries to ensure that a much-debated bill does not interfere with other business. As Democratic Whip Senator Alan Cranston noted, the two-track system means that the Senate 'can now continue to work on all other legislation on one 'track' while a filibuster . . . is . . . in progress on the other "track" '.[56] The use of the two-track system is implemented by the majority leader after obtaining the unanimous consent of the Senate.

In terms of influencing legislative business and behaviour, however, the two most important functions a floor leader can exercise are control over committee assignments and control over the legislative agenda: two important and interlocking factors which help determine the relationship between the floor leader and the standing committee chairmen.[57] Republican floor leaders have traditionally had little control over committee assignments. The Senate Republican committee assignment process is the simplest in Congress with committee assignments being determined solely by seniority.[58] Each member makes his committee preferences known, and the assignments are handed out routinely. Previous members of the House of Representatives take precedence over other freshmen with the remainder being ranked alphabetically until a rule change in 1983 sponsored by Senator Arlen Specter (R – Penn) led to seniority in these circumstances being determined by lottery rather than name.[59]

When committee chairmen have considerable experience, this inability to shape the composition of the committees severely limits the floor leader's power. In this respect Howard Baker was rather fortunate in that the Republican chairmen, and the new Republican committee staff aides, were comparatively inexperienced, and were slow in developing agendas. 'It took us a while to sort out the agenda' commented Senator Alan Simpson (R – Wyo).[60] Unlike Robert Byrd, his immediate predecessor, Baker was not initially faced with the problem of strong alternative sources of power in the form of powerful committee chairmen such as Senators James Eastland (D – Miss), Warren Magnusson (D – Wash), Henry Jackson (D – Wash) and Russell Long (D – La). His one-time rival for the leadership post, Senator Paul Laxalt, did not have a strong legislative record, and proved unwilling to challenge Baker's authority. In the words of one leadership aide: 'Senator Laxalt has never done anything but let the mantle of leadership fall on the shoulder of Howard Baker.'[61] Even the 'new right' senators, who when in the minority had disrupted much of the Senate's proceedings, found it difficult to adapt to majority status: feeling uneasy with their previous role as obsrructionists but unable to play a constructive role in the formulation of legislation.[62] The new right's lack of political experience was clearly demonstrated by the hearings held by Senator John East (R – NC), Chairman of the Judiciary Committee's subcommittee on the Separation of Powers, on Senator Jesse Helms's anti-abortion bill S.158 in 1981. Senator East, who favoured his colleague's bill, had hoped to dispose of the matter in two days of hearings confined to the biological question of where life begins. This hurried schedule, and an initial witness list that was construed as biased, isolated East. Senator Max Baucus (D – Mont), the subcommittee's ranking Democrat, distributed a three-page letter questioning whether hearings would be scheduled for pro-choice groups after East had barred the Democratic counsel from questioning witnesses. East had also refused to schedule witnesses selected by the Democrats. A parade of seven witnesses opened the hearings by giving support to the bill's central thesis that 'scientific evidence indicates a significant likelihood that actual human life exists from conception'.[63] The eighth witness, Dr Leon E. Rosenberg, pointed out the unbalanced witness list when he stated: 'I hope that you and the rest of the subcommittee would not take the ratio of 7-to-1 to reflect the scientific opinion of the American scholar. If you wish to know more about how American scientists feel on this issue, I would hope that you will continue to seek additional opinion.'[64] To counter the charges of biased hearings East assured everyone that 'we intend to have extensive and exhaustive hearings so that all points of view ultimately and finally will have been heard. I would ask only that every person judge us by the final result, and not by any given day of hearings.'[65] Although the Helms Bill was eventually reported out of the subcommittee, the controversy over the hearings helped delay it and added to the mounting conflict over the issue.

Republican senators had spent the better part of a quarter of a century perfecting their skills as 'guerilla fighters' in innumerable parliamentary ambushes. They had freely indulged their individual egos and ideologies, enjoying what Senator Mark Hatfield (R – Ore) described as 'the luxury of being dissidents', and it took them a while to become accustomed to their new role as the majority party.[66] As Senator Richard Lugar (R – Ind) stated: 'It's a different experience for us so it's been difficult.'[67] The election of Ronald Reagan as President, and the GOP's seizure of the Senate, meant that Republican senators were no longer able to proceed merely by disrupting the chamber's business. 'We had to make this place work' remarked Senator Hatfield.[68] In fact, the only senator able to adapt immediately to the new circumstances was Senator Bob Dole (R – Kan), chairman of the Finance Committee. Not only did Senator Dole play a major role in enacting President Reagan's tax-cut programme in 1981 but he also came to Senator Helms's aid when the latter's farm bill fell apart. Senator Helms, as chairman of the Agriculture Committee, proved unable to cope with the difficulties involved in guiding legislation through its various stages, and was forced to rely on Senator Dole for advice.[69]

Howard Baker was able to take advantage of this leadership vacuum by presenting committee chairmen with a legislative strategy which concentrated on President Reagan's economic policies. In meetings held each Tuesday morning before the weekly lunch of all Republican senators, Baker attempted to co-ordinate the activities of the Senate's scattered committees by forming a 'chairman's committee' composed of himself, all Senate committee chairmen, the Whip Ted Stevens, Conference Chairman James McClure, Paul Laxalt and two representatives of the Senate Republican freshmen who served on a rotating basis. In March 1981 his staff canvassed all the committee chairmen to obtain their plans, and a large chart was prepared detailing the proposed schedule for floor debates.[70] Although this schedule could not be carried out in its entirety, key parts of it—mainly economic issues—were fulfilled. In fact Howard Baker asked his colleagues to give top priority to President Reagan's budget and tax cuts, and to postpone their own legislative goals. 'I want the big controversial social issues to wait for next year. I want this year to be Ronald Reagan's year' he declared.[71] Otherwise, Baker explained, the crush of bills competing for the Senate's time would slow the pace of the Republican economic recovery programme. To reassure conservatives pressing for action on social issues such as abortion and school prayer, Baker promised to set aside time for these matters at a later date. Although conservatives such as Paul Weyrich of the Committee for the Survival of a Free Congress complained that Baker treated the new right's agenda as 'second-class issues', most Republicans wanted Reagan to succeed, and were prepared to back him.[72] Senator Orrin Hatch (R – Utah), for example, agreed to delay consideration of a balanced budget amendment until 'after President Reagan's program is enacted.'[73] To a certain extent, Republican senators regarded themselves as part of the Republican movement, rather than individual Republicans, and believed that President Reagan had received a clear electoral mandate for his policies.

President Reagan went to great lengths during his first year in office to forge close links with the legislative branch, and frequently spoke of his partnership with Congress in a manner which contrasted strongly with President Carter's poor relationship with the Senate. Carter's style often left Senator Byrd and the Democrats operating in a vacuum, whereas Reagan's approach enabled Howard Baker to portray much of his work as carrying out the mandate of an enormously popular president.[74] Thus during consideration of the 1981 Budget Reconciliation Bill, HR.3982, Baker was able to overcome jurisdictional problems which threatened to derail the measure by limiting the power of the Budget Committee, when he convinced Senator Dole, chairman of the Finance Committee, and Senator Hatfield, chairman of the Appropriations Committee, to work together and defer to the Budget Committee. 'He did an exceptional job when he convinced Dole and Hatfield to step aside and leave reconciliation to the Budget Committee' said Senator Laxalt. 'We'd still be floundering around in a Carter-like fashion if not for Howard's leadership on that.'[75]

Howard Baker's effort to convert Republican senators from articulate opponents of Democratic policy to powerful and friendly supporters of the Reagan administration began in December 1980 when he hosted a dinner at his home to discuss the first hundred days of the Reagan administration. Heading the guest list was prospective White House Chief of Staff James A. Baker, Office of Management and Budget director David Stockman, Treasury Secretary Donald T. Regan, President Reagan's principal domestic adviser Martin Anderson, and four senators about to become chairmen of the key committees dealing with economic policy: Bob Dole, Mark Hatfield, Pete Domenici (R – NM), chairman of the Budget Committee, and Jake Garn (R – Utah), chairman of the Banking, Housing and Urban Affairs Committee.[76] At that and subsequent meetings the group reviewed President Reagan's campaign commitments, public needs and expectations in order to advise the White House on how its goals could be achieved. Once Reagan formally submitted the spending and tax cut proposals Howard Baker became his chief advocate to all Senate Republicans. Senator Packwood described Howard Baker's attitude by using a football analogy: 'Howard said we are a team, and the President is the quarterback and we are his blockers, and we can't say now we don't like the plays.'[77] Unlike Robert Byrd, who as majority leader had played a very limited role on behalf of President Carter's economic and energy programmes—merely scheduling action and urging senators to resolve disputes—Baker gave Reagan's economic package his nearly total attention. The key strategy decisions such as putting all of Reagan's spending cuts in one package—ostensibly to reduce the impact of lobbyists, but also to promote Republican unity—were Baker's responsibility. As he once stated: 'I'm the President's man in the Senate, but he is aware that I reserve a high degree of independence.'[78]

In his attempts to build a consensus among Republicans for President Reagan's economic politics, Howard Baker benefited greatly from the large degree of unity that prevailed amongst Republicans on economic issues. To a large extent the consensus was already present, and all Baker had to do was shape it into some form of legislative strategy. There was no such consensus, however, over the administration's plan to sell AWACs (Airborne Warning and Control Systems) to Saudi Arabia. Indeed, preliminary vote counts suggested that there were only twelve senators in favour of the sale, while sixty-five, led by Senator Packwood, opposed it.[79] On 24 June 1981 Packwood sent Reagan a letter expressing deep concern over the sale. The letter stated that: 'It is our strong belief that this sale is not in the best interests of the U.S. and therefore recommend that you refrain from sending this proposal to Congress.'[80] Realising that he faced serious political problems, Howard Baker persuaded the White House to defer formal ratification of the sale until 25 August 1981.

Even by August, however, Howard Baker still faced considerable opposition to the sale, and his ability to push the measure through the Senate was perhaps his greatest achievement as majority leader, providing an illuminating example of his leadership skills. His first step was to attempt to establish a degree of bipartisanship on the issue, and with this in mind he approached Senator Sam Nunn (D – Ga), the leading Democratic spokesman on defence policy, Senator David Boren (D – Okla), the leader of the informal conservative caucus in the Senate, and Senator John Warner (R – Va), a former secretary of the navy, to ask for their help. Senators Nunn and Warner suggested that a letter from the president to the Senate containing assurances that the Saudis had consented to a detailed plan as to just how the AWACs were to be used would be useful in persuading some senators to vote for the sale. Howard Baker and James Baker worked closely together on this suggestion, and eventually persuaded President Reagan to write such a letter. The next problem facing Howard Baker was in the Foreign Relations Committee where the success of the measure depended on the vote of Senator Larry Pressler (R – SD). Howard Baker telephoned Maxwell Rabb, Ambassador to Italy and a close personal friend of Senator Pressler, to find out what would persuade Pressler to vote for the measure. He learned from Rabb that Pressler felt he needed a telephone call from President Reagan asking for his support. Baker immediately telephoned the President, and twelve minutes later Reagan called Pressler who confirmed his support for the sale. Furthermore, between mid-September and late October Reagan saw seventy-five of the one hundred senators, talking alone to forty-four of them, seventeen of them between Monday morning 26 October and 2 p.m. of 28 October when the vote in the Senate was finally taken.[81] This sustained lobbying paid off, and a considerable number of senators who were committed to voting against the sale, including the Republicans Roger Jepsen (R – Utah) and Slade Gorton (R – Wash), changed their mind after talking with the President, and the vote not to block the AWACs deal was won by 52 votes to 48.[82]

Leadership problems

The passage of the 1981 budget proposals and the AWACs deal undoubtedly represented the high point of Howard Baker's leadership. President Reagan himself stated: 'I don't think that we could have had the successes that we've had up there without his leadership.'[83] On closer inspection, however, it becomes apparent that the success of the 1981 budget and the AWACs deal depended a great deal upon President Reagan: his close participation in legislative battles, and the degree of support which he was deemed to enjoy in the country as a whole. As Senator Gorton explained: 'Every president had a honeymoon, but a number of factors caused the aberration in 1981. They included a new president with a big victory and strong views, a large number of new senators and a Republican majority for the first time since 1954.'[84] The result was a degree of support for the president's legislative position in the Senate which had not been bettered since 1955 among Republicans. In 1981 the support for President Reagan's position among Senate Republicans was 84 per cent. This compares with the 85 per cent which President Eisenhower received in 1955, and was ten percentage points higher than the level of support given to President Carter by Senate Democrats in 1977.[85]

Beginning in late 1981, however, the degree of support given to President Reagan began to wane as he started to play a less active role in legislative battles, and the electoral mandate he was perceived to have received faded. The decline in support given to Reagan mean that Howard Baker faced a much more difficult task in securing the passage of measures such as the 1982 budget, and he was unable to repeat the success of the 1981 AWACs deal. In October 1983 the Senate defeated a Reagan proposal to arm and support two brigades of the Jordanian Army as a rapid deployment 'strike force' in the Middle East, and in March 1984 pressure from Senator Packwood caused President Reagan to withdraw a proposal to sell Stinger anti-aircraft missiles to Jordan and Saudi Arabia. Moreover, without the unifying lead provided by the President the various disparate elements of the party began to fall apart. Party-line voting among Senate Republicans declined from 81 per cent in 1981 to 76 per cent in 1982 to 74 per cent in 1983 and rose slightly to 78 per cent in 1984.[86] This was in itself a fairly small decline, but it meant that Howard Baker was unable to guarantee 51 votes on any proposal which Reagan might send to the Senate. The moderate and conservative wings of the party, in particular, began taking stands which were independent of both

Baker and the White House. One study carried out by *Congressional Quarterly* revealed that of the ten senators whose support of Baker's legislative position declined by over ten percentage points between 1981 and 1982, six belonged to the moderate wing of the party, and three belonged to the conservative wing.[87] In December 1982, for example, Senator Helms tried to filibuster a gasoline tax measure which Baker had co-sponsored with Tip O'Neill, the Speaker of the House of Representatives. To Helms the gas levy was a tax and spend heresy, and aided by his North Carolina colleague Senator John East, Senator Gordon Humphrey (R – NH) and Senator Don Nickles (R – Okla) he tried to talk the bill to death. The four senators were able to delay a final roll call until two days before Christmas, hoping that by then enough senators would have gone home to prevent the leadership from mustering enough votes to force cloture. Baker retaliated by using a fleet of eleven military jets to bring back senators for the vote and ensure them a quick flight home when it was all over. 'The sky was dark with Airforce planes bringing back senators, kicking and screaming' complained Helms.[88] Cloture was finally invoked, however, by an 81 to 5 vote, and the gas tax passed by a 54 to 33 vote.

In addition to the reduced role played by President Reagan in legislative battles, another important factor in explaining the decline in Republican Party unity was the increased confidence and competence displayed by standing committee chairmen as they gained in experience. 'There may be increasing independence as chairmen begin to develop their own constituencies' stated Senator Bob Kasten (R – Wisc).[89] With committee chairmen beginning to develop their own agendas the power vacuum which Howard Baker had successfully taken advantage of during his first year as majority leader began to disappear. Moreover, many of the proposals developed by the committee chairmen, most notably the 'social issues' agenda of the new right, were divisive and led to filibusters and other forms of obstruction by moderates such as Senator Lowell Weicker. Senator Weicker, for example, was instrumental in defeating Senator Helms's 1982 anti-abortion measure (H.J. Res 520), and a 1983 proposal (S.J. Res 73) to permit public prayer in schools.

One of the most important factors in allowing committee chairmen to develop their own agendas was the growing competence of Republican staff. When the Republicans became the majority in 1981 the number of staff they were entitled to doubled. They were thus faced with the problem of hiring a full staff complement in the space of a few weeks: a problem compounded by the fact that experienced Republicans were in demand for administration posts as well. Indeed, a number of veteren Hill staffers were themselves recruited by the administration to take key posts in departments or agencies. As a result many of the staff aides hired by the Republicans were relatively inexperienced and unable to provide the support to committee chairmen which would enable the latter to develop their own agendas. Only after a few months' experience were the new staffers able to provide the support required and expected of them.

The transfer from majority to minority status also reduced at a stroke the number of Democratic staff by half, and left the Democrats in considerable disarray. In an attempt to compensate for their staff losses the Democrats were forced to pay more attention to organisation and consensus-building than they had previously done. The Senate Democratic Caucus began to gather weekly for lunch, and the Policy Committee's staff and role were expanded along Republican lines. A series of task forces was appointed by Senator Byrd to highlight issues, and new press aides were hired to bolster the party's image.[90] As a consequence of these reforms the Democrats were able to present alternatives to Republican initiatives in 1982. Spurred by political expediency, for example, they put up a solid front against a tax measure drafted by Senator Dole. Senator Bill Bradley (D – NJ), who chaired the Caucus's economy task force declared: 'As we look at the legislation . . . it is our conclusion . . . that it places a disproportionate burden on middle and lower income people, and that it benefits upper income groups.'[91] The Democratic Caucus's alternative would have deferred President Reagan's plans for a 10 per cent tax cut for high-income groups, deleted the Dole Bill's increases in cigarette and telephone excise taxes, restored some Medicare spending, raised federal unemployment payments and raised minimum deductions for unreimbursed medical and casualty expenses. Among Democrats, only Senator Ed Zorinsky (D – Neb) voted against this alternative.

These displays of partisanship grew more frequent as the 1982 elections loomed closer, and with the Republicans enjoying only a small majority meant that Howard Baker faced increasing difficulties in guiding legislation through the Senate. He also faced increased scheduling problems. To a certain extent these problems were exacerbated by Baker's pattern of good-natured accommodation which created an environment in which nearly every senator expected the Senate to conform to his own personal needs. In

1981 Baker had used these tactics to unite the party behind President Reagan's economic policies, keeping individual senators in line by appealing to the President's name. By 1982, however, with Reagan's influence waning, individual senators expected Howard Baker to accommodate their every whim. 'It's like children lining up in the elementary school classroom asking when they can go to the bathroom. "Howard, I've got to be in Cheyenne tonight" or "I've got a fundraiser in Dubuque. Can you move up the vote?" ' said Senator Alan Simpson (R – Wyo).[92] William F. Hildenbrand, an aide to Howard Baker, confirmed the problems that the majority leader faced in obtaining Republican votes: 'Howard Baker often had to bleed and die to get their votes because they recognised they would have to be individuals and could not depend on Reagan to get themselves re-elected.'[93]

Howard Baker's problems as majority leader were compounded in the 98th Congress following his announcement on 21 January 1983 that he was not going to seek re-election in 1984. This announcement effectively made Baker a 'lame duck', lacking in authority and unable to hold the party together. In fact the Senate during the 98th Congress might be characterised as reverting back to the pattern of the 1970s, compared with the rather abnormal circumstances of 1981. Although Howard Baker's leadership qualities were considerable, much of his earlier success had been due to a certain element of 'luck'. The changeover from a Democratic-controlled chamber to a Republican-controlled chamber temporarily nullified to a certain extent those institutional factors that had made the Senate a difficult chamber in which to pass legislation. Once institutional factors such as the dispersal of power within the Senate began to reassert themselves, and the divisions within the party reappeared, Baker's leadership suffered accordingly.

6 Presidential–senatorial relations

The experience of Senator Howard Baker's leadership clearly reveals the important impact that a president has on the activity of the Senate. Without President Reagan's active involvement in legislative battles in 1981 it is doubtful whether the almost unprecedented level of Republican unity would have been achieved. On a more general level, an examination of presidential–senatorial relations is important because it helps illustrate many of the developments which occurred in American government during the 1970s and 1980s: the post-Watergate reassertion of Congressional power, the 'democratisation' of the Senate's procedures, a new electoral climate, and a changing policy agenda as President and Congress sought to deal with the energy crisis, 'stagflation', and a revival of the 'cold war' following Soviet aggression in Afghanistan. An analysis of presidential–senatorial relations thus offers an opportunity to examine the context, both institutional and political, in which such interaction takes place.

The institutional context

The notion of presidential domination of Congress during most of the twentieth century has been generally accepted by political scientists and members of Congress alike, with some commentators even suggesting that Congress is 'congenitally incapable of formulating and pushing through a coherent legislative program except under the most unusual circumstances'.[1] It would be a mistake, however, to assume that Congress plays only a minor role in national policy-making. Although one senator quoted by Samuel P. Huntington believed that Congress's role in the legislative process had been reduced to 'filtering legislative proposals from the President', such a process still has a major impact on legislation.[2] During the Carter presidency, for example, the Senate significantly altered or rejected a number of the President's proposals, including such major measures as the first energy programme, comprehensive tax reform, comprehensive welfare reform, the Humphrey–Hawkins Full Employment Act, and the legislation altering the United States's relations with Taiwan. Furthermore, expected opposition led to the withdrawal of the SALT II Treaty from the chamber before it could be ratified. Such evidence would suggest that even though Congress may no longer be a major initiator of legislation, and despite the fact that its agenda is largely determined by the President, it should not be regarded as a mere rubber stamp with little legislative impact.

The shared mandate of American government means that the President, either personally or acting through his aides, must negotiate with a variable set of congressional actors at different times and at different legislative stages.[3] Even if matters are simplified by concentrating on presidential–senatorial relations, thereby reducing at a stroke the number of 'actors' involved by 435, the interaction between the President and the Senate remains 'unpredictable, sometimes unfathomable, and always complex'.[4] Many of the decisions that senators make can only be understood with reference to the individual senator's constituency, party and ideological alignment. Of this complex set of institutional and political factors, perhaps the most important in explaining the tensions that exist between the President and the Senate is the limited nature of the senator's constituency. As Ben W. Heineman and Curtis A. Hessles point out: 'with the exception of Watergate, the tension between the President and Congress has not been between different conceptions of their Constitutional roles, but between the nationalism of the President's view, and the pluralism that is the sum of Congress' parts'.[5] Thus while President Ford's liaison team spent most of its time attempting to muster congressional votes in order to sustain presidential vetoes during a period of constitutional conflict between the President and the Senate, the tension between Presidents Carter and Reagan and the Senate was largely the result of constituency pressure.[6] Generally speaking, the President can claim to speak for all Americans while senators, in the words of James Madison: 'will likely attach themselves too much to local objects . . . Measures will too often be decided according to their probable effect, not on the national prosperity and happiness, but on the prejudices, interests and pursuits of the government and people of individual states.'[7] The result is often a conflict of interest between the President and the Senate: between the 'national interest' and parochialism.

The fact that senators speak for different economic, social and geographical interests has had an important impact on the functioning of the Federal Government. It is the particularism of the Senate that makes it almost impossible for the chamber to initiate and pass a coherent legislative programme. President Ford once complained that Congress: 'wasn't answering the nation's challenges domestically because it was too fragmented. It responded too often to single-issue special interest groups and it therefore wound up dealing with minutae instead of attacking serious problems in a coherent way.'[8] This point was echoed by President Carter who in 1978 stated that 'the average member of Congress has a very narrowly focused, parochial interest'.[9] The way in which the national interest emerges in the Senate is through bargaining between members and blocs of members responsible to particular interests. Only the President has the centralised, national perspective necessary to set a national agenda.[10]

The successful passage of a President's agenda through the Senate is dependent upon the President and his advisers' ability to put together a legislative coalition that either overcomes or takes account of the various sectional interests within the chamber. Some commentators have suggested that in the post-Second-World-War period such agreement was more likely to be achieved in the realm of foreign policy than domestic policy: an observation which has led to talk about the existence of 'two presidencies—one domestic, and one foreign'.[11] Viewed from a slightly different perspective such observations tend to suggest that Presidents have traditionally found it easier to claim legitimacy for their foreign policy than their domestic policy.

Presidents have generally been able to claim *de facto* authority in the foreign policy field for two reasons. First, in an era of constant crisis it was commonly accepted that only the President possessed the ability to move swiftly and with secrecy to meet any threat to American security. Thus, although the Constitution shared responsibility for the conduct of foreign policy between the President and the Senate, with the former being designated as Commander-in-Chief and given considerable diplomatic powers, and the latter given a role in war-making, the nominating process and the ratification of treaties, in practice the *nature* of international relations since the Second World War has led to presidential domination of the foreign policy-making process. Prior to the Second World War the Senate was much more assertive, and isolationists such as Senator William Borah (R – Idaho) constantly frustrated attempts by 'internationalist' Presidents to commit the United States to a more active role in international affairs. In 1921, for example, the Senate blocked ratification of the Treaty of Versailles, and in 1935 blocked American entry into the World Court.[12] The second factor mitigating against a more active role for the Senate in the foreign policy-making process was the fact that too great a concern with foreign policy tended to be politically inexpedient for senators. One member of the Foreign Relations Committee was quoted by Richard F. Fenno as stating that a concern for foreign policy was: 'a political liability . . . You have no constituency. In my re-election campaign last fall, the main thing they used against me was that because of my interest in foreign relations, I was more interested in what happened to the people of Abyssinia and Afghanistan than in what happened to the good people of my state.'[13]

There are two important points to be made at this stage. First, the fact that a senator who played an active role in foreign policy was liable to be accused of ignoring his state's interests tended to mitigate against the development of foreign policy initiatives by senators. Second, the general lack of constituency interest in foreign affairs meant that the President was more likely to gain agreement for his policies than would have been the case in the realm of domestic policy where his programme might well conflict with the interests of a senator's state. Indeed, many of the conflicts over foreign policy that have arisen between the President and the Senate have occurred precisely on those occasions when the President's programme affected part of a senator's constituency. For example, senators representing states with large Jewish and Greek voting blocks voted against President Carter's plans to sell military aircraft to Egypt and Saudi Arabia and to repeal the arms embargo on Turkey in 1978. Senator Clifford Case (R – NJ) even went so far as to make an impassioned defence of Israel, well aware that 6 per cent of New Jersey's electorate was Jewish: 'The existence of Israel, its strength to defend itself, is essential to the preservation of the West, to the preservation of NATO, and inevitably, in the end, to the preservation of the United States. More than that, it is essential to the preservation of the moderate Arab regimes.'[14]

Developments in the electoral environment during the late 1970s only served to increase the importance of 'constituency politics'. The emergence of new issues which cut across traditional party ties, changes in the Federal Election Campaign Laws and the growth in the number of Political Action Committees, in particular those associated with the 'new right', created a highly volatile electoral climate. Not only did these developments alter the nature of Senate elections but the PACs were able to make use of internal Senate reforms which opened the chamber's proceedings to achieve greater scrutiny of individual senator's voting records. With more of their decisions open to public scrutiny, the desire of senators not to do anything that might possibly harm their constituency became even more pronounced. The result was that senators who concentrated on foreign affairs, and who cast controversial votes against the wishes of vocal groups in their constituencies, stood an increased chance of suffering electorally for their decisions. In the 1980 elections, four of the five members of the Foreign Relations Committee who were seeking re-election were defeated: Chairman Frank Church (D – Idaho), ranking member Jacob Javits (R – NY), George McGovern (D – SD) and Richard Stone (D – Fla).[15] All lost their seats to conservative Republicans. Senators Church and McGovern, in particular, suffered from their interest in foreign policy with the National Conservative Political Action Committee (NCPAC) running television and radio commercials that suggested that they were neglecting their states for the sake of countries such as Cuba.

In the new electoral climate the way to gain re-election was not so much by pleasing people as by not offending them. Senators during the late 1970s found that foreign policy concerns were politically expensive, and the greater emphasis on the re-election goal served to weaken senatorial initiatives in policy-making. In other words, developments in electioneering worked to increase the reliance of the Senate upon presidential policies in the field of foreign affairs. If a senator took too keen an interest in foreign policy he was liable to find his record exploited by his opponent, not usually on ideological grounds but on the assumption that an interest in the world automatically meant a neglect of his home state. These very developments, however, by emphasising the parochialism of the Senate also made it more difficult for the President to pursue his domestic policy. While senators might regard the President as having a legitimate right to pursue un-hindered most aspects of his foreign policy, this legitimacy did not usually extend unchallenged into the domestic sphere.

The problem for the President in the domestic policy sphere is that although his programme may adversely affect a senator's constituency, on many occasions his own personal mandate from that state will be weaker than that enjoyed by the senators from that state. Thus, not only does a senator have a constituency to consider when responding to presidential policy initiatives but he may enjoy greater support than the President in his state, and thus regard the President's legitimacy to act unchallenged as slight. This point can be illustrated by comparing the percentage of the vote gained by Presidents Carter and Reagan in each state with that achieved by that state's senators. Of the sixty-seven Democratic senators and forty-nine Republican senators who sat in either the 95th Congress (1977–8) or the 96th Congress (1979–80) President Carter outpolled only five Democrats and two Republicans.[16] In contrast, of the forty-seven Democratic senators and the fifty-three Republican senators who sat in the 97th Congress (1981–2), President Reagan outpolled six Democrats and no fewer than eighteen Republicans.

The discrepancy between the degree of support given to President Carter's policies and those of President Reagan may, in part, be explained by the fact that Reagan outpolled far more senators than Carter, and was thus regarded as possessing a far greater legitimacy for his domestic policies.[17] This was especially the case for those senators elected in 1980 who supported President Reagan's position on 82 per cent of the votes on which Reagan made his position known compared with a Republican average of 80 per cent.[18] For a short time Reagan was presumed to possess an electoral mandate for his policies, despite achieving a total percentage of the vote almost identical with that achieved by Carter in 1976. In 1976 Carter had gained 50·1 per cent of the votes cast with a turnout of 54·3 per cent of the electorate, and in 1980 Reagan gained 50·8 per cent with a turnout of 54 per cent.

The psychological impact of a perceived presidential landslide on the successful passage of the president's legislation through the Senate assumed increased importance in the late 1970s and early 1980s as institutional reforms weakened the power of party and committee leaders. The growth of individual assertion in the Senate meant that Presidents and their liaison teams could no longer rely upon a few key committee chairmen to secure the passage of their legislation. As Hamilton Jordan, a close adviser to President Carter, stated in an interview with the *New York Times*:

> we faced the fragmentation of political power on the Hill. Twenty years ago a President would have gone along to Lyndon Johnson and Sam Rayburn and George Meany . . . and together they would write a tax bill and the leadership would get it approved. Now you can have the President, the leadership, the committee chairmen, and the sub-committee chairmen all in favor of something, like hospital cost control, and a group of young Turks in the subcommittees can run over you. It means you have to deal with scores and sometimes hundreds of people

to pass a bill.[19]

This view was reinforced by President Carter who claimed that: 'each legislator had to be wooed and won individually. It was every member for himself and devil take the hindmost.'[20]

Although Hamilton Jordan's description of the power wielded by Lyndon Johnson as majority leader in the Senate may have been slightly exaggerated, there can be little doubt that changes in congressional rules and procedures did raise substantial impediments to Carter's ability to influence Congress. Whereas President Ford's problems with Congress had been largely the result of his lack of legitimacy as an unelected president and a desire by Congress to reassert its authority in the wake of Watergate and Vietnam, there is a very real sense in which President Carter's problems stemmed from the internal reforms carried out in Congress during the early 1970s.[21]

Carter's poor legislative record, however, cannot be blamed totally on Congress. As Nelson Polsby points out, it was also the result of 'mistakes, ineptitude, and presidential neglect of Congress'.[22] It is perhaps no exaggeration to claim that President Carter's liaison efforts during the first eighteen months of his administration were marked by chaos. White House liaison efforts under the leadership of the inexperienced Frank B. Moore were unco-ordinated, and repeatedly offended key members of Congress.[23] As one observer wrote: Moore 'had barely laid eyes upon the Capitol before election day'.[24] His early problems ranged from a failure to return senators' telephone calls to complete communications breakdowns.[25] For example, in his lobbying effort to secure passage of the Fiscal 1978 Budget Moore decided that it was not necessary to give members of Congress advance notice of budget deletions which affected their constituencies.[26]

The Carter administration's relations with the Senate reflected the general problems which plagued Carter's liaison efforts: inexperience, incompetence and an almost complete failure to understand the complexities of the institution. In an early remark Carter stated that he would handle Congress just as he had handled the Georgia legislature when Governor of that state in the early 1970s.[27] A year later he was forced to concede that 'it didn't work. They treated me like the governor of Georgia'.[28] Despite an effort to improve relations in the second year of his administration, Carter's liaison never really recovered from the mistakes he made during his first year in office, and his relations with the

Senate remained strained.

The main complaint that senators of both parties levelled against Carter concerned his inability to settle upon legislative priorities, and his reluctance to consult them on measures before they reached the Senate. In the first six months of his administration, Carter sent more proposals to Congress than any other president since Franklin D. Roosevelt in 1933.[29] By failing to indicate which measures he regarded as pirority bills, however, Carter's programme almost ground to a halt in the decentralised structure of the Senate. This caused Carter to complain about senatorial obstructiveness, yet quite clearly senators were not being deliberately obstructive. Rather the extent of Carter's programme had overloaded the Senate's capacity to deal with such a large volume of legislation. The dispersal of power in the Senate during the 1960s and 1970s had resulted in a slowing down of the legislative process. As Senator Byrd stated: 'the fact that Congress doesn't follow through and act as a rubber stamp and give the administration what it wants in every jot and title doesn't mean we aren't cooperating'.[30] Vice-President Mondale also conceded that some of Carter's proposals had suffered from 'fractricide—the concept in missilry [sic] where you fire too many missiles too close together, and they kill each other off'.[31]

Upon closer analysis it becomes clear that President Carter's failure to understand the complexities of the legislative process in the Senate, and his unwillingness to assign priorities to his legislation, were symptomatic of his general failure to consult with senators, both Democratic and Republican. Although Carter claimed in his memoirs that 'during the transition months, I made several trips to Washington, meeting with the Democratic and Republican leaders of both Houses', this consultation did not really go beyond soliciting nominations for his cabinet.[32] Even in the early days of the administration there existed a sizeable communications gap between the White House and the Senate.[33] As early as January 1977 Senator Byrd was complaining that the President 'has never called me for any advice . . . not many presidents have done that. Ford called on his appointment for the vice-presidency, and Johnson would call occasionally.'[34] Byrd went on to suggest that his failure to be briefed by James R. Schlesinger, director of the President's energy programme, had necessitated a second briefing for those senators involved in energy legislation who had not been invited to the initial session. He concluded that Carter 'has to learn that there have to be a number of senators brought into a discussion on any subject, and he better let the leadership know about these meetings so that we can suggest the Senators involved'.[35]

An early example of the result of Carter's failure to consult with those senators who had interests in a specific piece of legislation can be seen in Carter's failure to eliminate nineteen water projects from the Fiscal 1978 Budget. Despite the fact that cutting back on the water projects went to the core of what most senators regarded as their public duty, the decision to cut the projects was made without any prior consultation with the senators who represented states where the water projects were to be cut. Senator Byrd gave Carter an indication of the mood in the Senate by writing to the President and informing him 'that there's a great sense of frustration, the feeling here on the part of members that they haven't been consulted', but such advice was ignored.[36] As a result, on 10 March 1977 the Senate adopted a measure (S.427), proposed by Senator Johnston (D – La), to prevent the Administration from holding back money from the projects by a 65 to 24 vote. Carter responded by inviting eighteen senators from 'water states' to the White House and scolded them for their parochial stands on the water projects.[37]

The inexperience of the Carter liaison team was also shown by their initial decision to structure their liaison effort along issues rather than having specialists for the Senate and the various voting blocs within the chamber.[38] This system meant that different liaison people dealt with the same senator on different issues, thereby hindering the establishment of the personal relationships that are so important on Capitol Hill. Even when the system was changed after six months, and two specialised White House lobbyists, Danny C. Tate and Robert Thomson, assigned to the Senate, there were still no close relationships between the liaison staff and senators.[39] Hamilton Jordan was later to identify the inability of Carter's aides to establish close relationships with individual senators as one of the major failings of the Carter administration: 'It was a mistake, especially in the early months, for me and the others not to have paid more attention to the Hill. If I had to do it over again, I would have gone up there and met people and cemented our relationship.'[40]

The failure of the Carter administration to set up a liaison team capable of dealing with the subunits of the Senate was one of the main factors responsible for shaping the role which the Republican Party was to play as the minority party. If the relations between Carter and the majority Democratic Party were strained, they were largely nonexistant for the minority Republican Party.

Generally speaking, Republican senators were largely ignored by Carter unless their votes were needed on major issues like the Panama Canal Treaties. The result was that the White House, operating under the belief that the Democratic majority in the Senate would be sufficient to ensure the passage of Carter's legislation, forced the Republican Party to abandon its traditional bipartisan support for the President. In the 89th Congress (1965–6), for example, President Johnson had consulted frequently with Senator Everett Dirksen before legislation reached the Senate, with the result that Republican feelings were taken into account at a very early stage. In the 95th and 96th Congresses, Republican participation was limited to a few discussions after the legislation had been introduced. One member of Howard Baker's staff claimed that the White House kept in touch with Baker 'once every three weeks'.[41] Denied of an early opportunity to play a prominent role in the devising of policy the Republicans had little choice but to play a more active role in committee and on the floor of the Senate. This departure from bipartisanship was particularly notable in the area of foreign policy, and the party's publication of its *Declaration on National Security and Foreign Policy* ultimately formed the groundwork for the Republican opposition to SALT II.

Although it was to some extent forced upon them by the inexperience of Carter's liaison effort there is little doubt that the more aggressive Republican opposition to Democratic policies was also due to more general changes in the political environment which generated changes within the Republican party itself. First, developments in the techniques of electioneering left senators of both parties conscious of the need to court their constituencies. For the Republicans this meant presenting an alternative programme and displaying a unified opposition to President Carter's more controversial legislation. Only measures such as the Civil Service Reform Act, and the phased deregulation of the airline industry, attracted strong support from the Republicans.[42] Second, changes in the geographical composition of the Republican Party in the Senate strengthened the influence of the GOP's Western and Southern wings, whose members were ideologically opposed to Carter's brand of middle-of-the-road politics. Although these changes would later prove to be of benefit to President Reagan, they worked to the detriment of President Carter's legislative effort.

President Carter's relations with the Republican Party in the Senate were thus marred by a number of factors. The institutional problems caused by changes in the electoral climate and the reforms of the 1960s and 1970s were accentuated by Carter's inexperience. That these problems could be surmounted was shown by the successful passage of President Reagan's programme in 1981, and by the fact that Carter achieved considerable Republican support for his early foreign policy initiatives. In 1978, for example, on issues such as the ratification of the Panama Canal Treaties, the selling of $4·8 billion worth of military aircraft to Saudi Arabia, Israel and Egypt, and the maintaining of a moderate policy stance towards Rhodesia, Carter received important support from moderate Republicans. The Panama Canal Treaties were ratified by a vote of 68 to 32. In this context the votes of the sixteen Republican senators who supported the Treaties were vital. The sale of military aircraft to the Middle East approved by a 59 to 39 vote with twenty-six Republicans voting for the measure. On Rhodesia the Senate adopted an amendment to the 1978 Foreign Military Aid Bill (S.3075) that had been proposed by Senator Clifford Case (R – NJ), and which stated that US sanctions against Rhodesia could not be lifted until the Rhodesian Government of Ian Smith had committed itself to a conference of all the groups contending for power in the country, and free elections for a new government, supervised by international observers had been held.[43]

To a certain extent Carter's early foreign policy successes were the result of hard lobbying on issues he cared seriously about.[44] He also benefited, however, from the support of an 'internationalist' element within the GOP which habitually backed a bipartisan foreign policy. In most other areas Carter suffered from the new 'sunbelt' complexion of the Republican Party. Not only were many of the new Republican senators very conservative but they were also highly independent and conscious of the fact that Carter was not very popular in their home states. In this respect President Reagan was fortunate in sharing the ideological view of the Southern and Western wings of his party. During the first year of his presidency, however, he did not take the support of these senators for granted. As someone who was as much a political outsider as Carter had been, Reagan took pains to court rather than ignore Congress. From the outset he regularly consulted with the Senate leadership, both Republican and Democratic, with the aim of paying 'very close attention . . . to requests and communications from Congress'.[45] As such he differed considerably from both President Carter and President Ford. Apart from Senators Robert Griffin and Charles Mathias, Ford did not have

close relations with any Republican senators, and only infrequent-
ly consulted minority leader Hugh Scott about legislation.[46]

Early in the transition period Reagan set the tone of his
Administration by attending a breakfast meeting with the
Republican congressional leadership to discuss his economic programme, claiming: 'I think the very evidence of our meeting here
this morning, in the eyes of the public . . . is an indication that we
are prepared to work together, and I'm looking forward to it . . .
So I'll come up to the Hill as often as necessary.'[47] In a television
interview in July 1982 Reagan further claimed that he had 'had
eleven formal meetings with the leadership of the House and
Senate . . . I've gone up to the Hill nine times myself, and I understand that for eighteen months that's kind of a record.'[48] Although
this willingness to meet with congressional leaders declined in
subsequent years of his presidency as Reagan withdrew from most
legislative battles, it was important to the success of his first year
in office because it enabled him to establish close relations with
Senator Howard Baker. This gave Baker the authority to sub-
ordinate the policy preferences of many Republican senators to
those of the President. The co-operation of Howard Baker was
vital to the strategy of initiating legislation in the Republican-
controlled Senate, and Reagan acknowledged his debt to Baker
on many occasions.[49]

Reagan strengthened and consolidated his personal efforts at
liaison by appointing Max L. Friedersdorf, a former congressional
lobbyist for Presidents Ford and Nixon, to be his chief
congressional liaison officer. Under Friedersdorf's direction the
White House liaison effort became highly centralised, and in fact,
mirrored the congressional liaison system set up by Larry O'Brien,
President Johnson's chief liaison officer. Under O'Brien, for
example, the Office of Congressional Relations had a wide-ranging
authority over Departmental liaison offices. This was also the case
during the initial years of the Reagan administration. The Department of Labor's chief lobbyist claimed that: 'One of the first
things Max Friedersdorf said to me is "There's no such thing as a
departmental position. There is an administration position".'[50]
The ability of the White House liaison office to maintain close
control over the lobbying efforts of the government agencies was
made possible by using the Office of Management and Budget's
clearance function to ensure that agency personnel did not free-
lance in support of agency proposals which did not meet with
White House approval.[51]

One effect of the use of central clearance was to sharpen

legislative priorities down to a very fine point, and thus avoid many of the pitfalls that had weakened President Carter's initial legislative effort. Under the guidance of David Stockman, director of the OMB, the Reagan administration prepared a package of domestic and economic policy proposals, and a strategy for enacting them, with a degree of skill that was to make Reagan's first year in office 'seem like a deliberate inversion of the standard catalogue of explanations of stalemated presidential leadership'.[52] Perhaps Stockman's greatest contribution to the White House liaison effort was to meet with Senator Pete Domenici, Chairman of the Senate Budget Committee, and decide that the only way of pushing expenditure cuts through the Senate was by employing the reconciliation provisions of the congressional budgetary process, thus permitting a single vote on an omnibus bill. This meant that the administration was able to reduce or eliminate programmes which would almost certainly have survived had senators been forced to vote on them singly.[53] Indeed, Reagan's limited initiatives to attack specific programmes piecemeal did not get very far as senatorial support, for the programmes remained strong enough to prevent major changes.[54]

The initial success of President Reagan's legislation was thus partly the result of a highly skilled congressional liaison effort. Many of the problems which occurred in the realm of presidential-senatorial relations, for example, as with the sale of AWACs to Saudi Arabia, in 1981, were caused by uncharacteristic lapses in the presidential liaison effort. However, although Reagan did all in his capacity to avoid mistakes on the presidential side of the liaison equation, he also benefited from a number of developments within the Republican Party which ensured a favourable reception for his ideas, and contrariwise, made bipartisan support for Carter almost impossible to achieve.

Party factors

Although the initial level of influence achieved by President Reagan over the GOP in the Senate was due in part to factors such as his strong electoral showing compared with many Republican senators, the experience and competence of his liaison effort and the leadership skills of Senator Howard Baker, he was also aided by changes in the geographical composition of the party in the Senate which shifted its power base from the New England and Mid-Atlantic to the South and Rocky Mountains. The importance of these changes in the geographical composition of the Republican

Party becomes clear if the support given to Reagan by individual senators is broken down on a regional basis, and compared with the support given to Carter and Ford.

TABLE 6.1   *Republican support for presidential legislation in the US Senate 1974–85*[55]

Congress	94th (Ford)	95th (Carter)	96th	97th (Reagan)	98th
South	71·4	36·1	39·1	82·2	79·6
Border	64·7	51·0	61·0	71·8	71·0
New England	50·1	65·5	56·8	68·8	65·2
Mid-Atlantic	49·6	61·1	52·3	70·7	68·6
Mid-West	68·0	51·0	56·7	82·6	80·0
Plains	73·4	44·1	45·2	77·3	73·9
Rocky Mountains	74·4	31·0	34·3	78·9	76·7
Pacific Coast	59·5	51·8	51·7	77·5	75·0

Source: Compiled from data given in the *Congressional Quarterly Almanac* 1975–84.

The most striking feature which emerges from the geographical breakdown for presidential initiatives is the discrepancy between those senators representing New England and Mid-Atlantic states and the rest of the party. While the support given to President Reagan's policies by the majority of Republican senators was much greater than that given to President Carter, the support given to both Presidents by senators from New England in particular remained fairly constant. Senator Jacob Javits (R – NY), for example, supported President Carter on 86 per cent of the votes where the President made his position known in 1978. This degree of support was bettered only by four Democrats: Senators Alan Cranston (D – Calif), Paul Sarbanes (D – Md), John Glenn (D – Ohio), and Patrick Leahy (D – Vt).

The relatively high level of support that Republican senators from the Northeast were willing to give to Carter's programme underlines the failings of the presidential liaison effort during his administration. The group of Northeastern Republicans represented a potential strong source of support for Carter, which when added to the votes of other Republican moderates could have improved the success rate of his programme in the Senate. With the rest of the Republican Party moving to the right, there is little doubt that this group would have responded positively to active leadership from Carter. Instead they found themselves increasingly at odds with the policy positions of their Republican colleagues, and ignored by Carter.

If an analysis of the roll-calls of a number of measures on

which Carter suffered reversals in the Senate is made, the existence of this potential source of support for Carter among Republican senators becomes apparent. For example, on the vote on Senator Johnston's Amendment to the Fiscal 1978 Budget which prevented the administration from holding back funds for water projects, three of the four Republicans who voted against this motion were from the Northeast: Senators Edward Brooke, John Chafee and John Heinz. These three, however, represented only a small fraction of the support that Carter could have expected if he had run an effective liaison effort, and not treated the Senate with disdain. Republicans from the Northeast shared many of his aims and faced no constituency pressure from water-hungry states. A similar failure by Carter to utilise fully all the potential support available to him in the Senate occurred in 1977 when the chamber voted in favour of an amendment to a Bill authorising US contributions to the World Bank (HR.5262) which had been introduced by Senator Dole. The Dole Amendment, which introduced language to HR.5262 that instructed US officials at the World Bank and other international financial institutions to vote against loans to Vietnam, Laos and Cambodia, was passed by a 58 to 32 vote despite being condemned by Carter as 'irresponsible'.[56] The vote represented another failure for the Carter liaison team. Once again Carter failed to exploit the latent support for his position which existed among Northeastern Republicans: Senator Javits opposed the motion claiming 'we have achieved a moral self-righteousness at the cost of complete ineffectiveness'.[57] Only eight Republicans voted against the amendment: Senators Charles Percy, Charles Mathias, Edward Brooke, Clifford Case, Jacob Javits, Henry Bellmon, Mark Hatfield and Bob Packwood.

The inability of President Carter to gain the support of the Northeastern Republicans may be viewed as symptomatic of the failure of his entire liaison effort. Even Senator Javits, one of Carter's most consistent supporters, was finally forced to express his exacerbation over the President's failure to consult with members of the Senate. In 1979, during a debate on the continuation of US sanctions against Rhodesia he exclaimed: 'If the President had come here and said I need x weeks, please give me an extension, I would enthusiastically support it. But the President didn't do that. The President said you are finished Mr Congress, unless you reverse me.'[58] Only on the question of the Panama Canal Treaties did Carter make an active effort to enlist the support of both the Republican leadership and the Republican moderates: an effort which was rewarded by the successful ratification of the Treaties.

The distance between the senators from the Northeast and the rest of their colleagues in the GOP was confirmed by their less than enthusiastic support for President Reagan. Although their initial opposition to Reagan's domestic policies was muted by a feeling that the President had received a mandate for change—the only Republican to vote against the 1981 Tax Bill (H.J. Res 266) was Senator Charles Mathias, and only Senator Lowell Weicker voted against the 1981 Budget Reconciliation Bill (HR.3982)—they maintained a constant opposition to specific measures.

The most important challenge to Reagan's budget cuts came in the form of an amendment to the Senate's Reconciliation Savings Resolution (S.Con Res 9) introduced by Senator John Chafee which aimed to restore $973 million to a variety of urban-orientated programmes. The proposal worried the White House and the Senate leadership enough to cause Vice-President Bush to travel to the Capitol to be on hand to cast a possible tie-breaking vote. Bush used his visit to lobby against the measure, causing Senator Alan Cranston to talk about 'Republican leaders whipping their troops into lock-step conformity'.[59] Once solid opposition to Senator Chafee's amendment was assured Southern and Western Democrats joined their Republican counterparts to defeat it 40 to 59 in a vote which split along regional lines. The Republican Senators voting for the measure were: Lowell Weicker, Charles Percy, William Cohen, Charles Mathias, David Durenberger, John Danforth, Mark Andrews, John Heinz, Arlen Specter, John Chafee and Robert Stafford.

The belief that Reagan had received an electoral mandate for his policies became increasingly open to doubt as his administration progressed, and as a result, opposition to his domestic policies by Republican senators from the New England and Mid-Atlantic states increased in 1982, 1983 and 1984.

This growing opposition may be construed as not only being ideologically based, but also arising from the type of constituency that these Republicans represented: urban, in economic decline, and heavily dependent upon the type of federal spending which the Reagan administration was trying to reduce. Indeed, given the fact that all the Northeastern Republicans, with the exception of Senator Alfonse D'Amato (R – NY), and all moderate Republicans without exception, easily outpolled Reagan in their states, the real question is not why their level of support for Reagan fell in 1982 and subsequent years but, rather, why it was so high in 1981.

TABLE 6.2 *Republican Senators' support for President Reagan in the 97th and 98th Congresses*

	1981	1982	1983	1984
South	84·9	79·5	97·7	84·5
Border	76·0	67·6	68·6	73·3
New England	74·5	63·1	68·0	62·5
Mid-Atlantic	77·0	64·5	69·5	67·7
Mid-West	85·2	80·0	82·7	77·2
Plains	78·5	76·1	67·7	74·1
Rocky Mountains	81·4	76·4	71·7	81·8
Pacific Coast	83·5	73·3	75·4	74·4

Source: Compiled from data given in the *Congressional Quarterly Almanacs* 1981–84.

The answer to this question lies in a combination of factors which have already been examined individually. First, most Republicans regarded Reagan has having received an electoral mandate for his domestic policies, despite the evidence of the polls. Second, Reagan's liaison effort was highly effective, and stood in stark contrast to that of the Carter administration. Third, Senator Howard Baker displayed a degree of skill as majority leader, and was highly successful in his role as the 'president's man in the Senate'. Fourth, the independence of many Republican senators was muted by the Republican takeover of the Senate, and their inexperience as the majority party. As Senator Bob Kasten (R – Wisc) stated: 'The President was fresh. The Republican Senate Majority was fresh. We were all finally committee chairmen or subcommittee chairmen. We knew we had to stick together.'[60] Senator Grassley (R – Iowa), noting the difficulty of being the majority party, commented: 'It's doggone easy being a member of the minority of the House of Representatives.'[61] Unlike their Democratic predecessors, they had not yet built up independent power bases in their committees from where they could challenge presidential policies and develop their own agendas. These factors tended to subdue the impact of constituency-based politics: but as they became less effective in the second year of the Reagan administration, for example, as the committee chairmen began to develop their own agendas, so the importance of constituency politics reasserted itself. As Senator Boschwitz stated: 'The glue is becoming diluted because we're getting close to the next election.'[62] For moderate Republicans this meant assuming an increasingly independent stance from the Reagan administration, and more specifically, attacking the spending cuts proposed in the 1982 Budget. Acceding to pressure from moderate Republicans and partisan sniping from Democrats, for example, GOP leaders decided to remove from the Budget Committee's Resolution (S.Con Res 92) provisions which would have reduced the cost of social security benefits by $40 billion over three years. In 1983 moderate Republican senators also defied GOP leaders when they passed a measure calling for increased taxes and higher domestic spending.

The fact that the moderate Republican senators were unable to do more damage to President Reagan's programme, however, is testimony to their decline in size and influence within the Senate. Indeed, from the point of view of securing passage of their legislative programmes, Reagan benefited, and Carter suffered, from the power shift in the Republican Party which increased the size and importance of its Southern and Western wings. Western and Southern Republicans opposed many of Carter's domestic and foreign policies, including the Panama Canal Treaties, and the Energy Bills, but they were generally unable to influence the content of legislation as they were denied access to the policy-initiating process. Initiatives thus had to be introduced either in committee or on the floor, where the chances of success were limited by the Democratic majority. For example, both Senator Jesse Helms and Senator Harrison Schmitt failed in their efforts to add amendments to the Panama Canal Neutrality Treaty which would have strengthened US rights in the Canal Zone after the Panamanian takeover.[63] Despite these difficulties, however, Western and Southern Republicans did have some success in adding damaging amendments to several of Carter's bills, including the Humphrey–Hawkins Full Employment Bill (S.50) in 1978, and the Taiwan Relations Bill (S.245) in 1979.

In its consideration of the Humphrey–Hawkins Full Employment Bill the Senate's Banking, Housing and Urban Affairs Committee voted 8 to 7 to adopt a zero-inflation goal amendment proposed by Senator Harrison Schmitt. This amendment committed the Federal Government to achieving a zero rate of inflation by 1983, and thus undermined the effectiveness of its full employment provisions which called for increased federal spending. Its acceptance by the Banking Committee was largely due to the high percentage of Republicans from Western and Southern states serving on the committee, but was also in part, a response to a growing belief among Republicans that inflation was the major economic evil. For example, even moderate Republicans like Senator John Heinz began to speak about inflation and its causes: 'inflationary factors—unfair and unnecessarily high taxes for working people, wasteful government spending, overregulation, massive budget deficits, huge trade deficits, and virtually non-existent productivity increases—have plagued us since 1977'.[64] By mid-1978 the annual inflation rate had risen to 10·8 per cent, a symbolic rate which allowed the Republicans to talk about 'double-digit' inflation.[65] Despite opposition from the Democrats the inflation goal in S.50 was retained during floor consideration of the measure, largely because of a threat by Senator Orrin Hatch that he would filibuster the bill if the amendment was removed.

Southern and Western Republicans also led the opposition to President Carter's decision in December 1978 to estalish diplomatic relations with the People's Republic of China (PRC), and terminate the 1955 Mutual Defense Treaty with Taiwan. While Senator Barry Goldwater challenged Carter's constitutional authority to terminate a treaty without the Senate's consent in the Federal Courts, his colleagues attempted to strengthen American guarantees for Taiwan. Senator Goldwater's suit was eventually dismissed by the Supreme Court on 13 December 1979 on technical grounds, however, in the Senate the Republicans managed to add modest amendments to the Taiwan Relations Legislation (S.245) which increased the American presence in, and guarantees for Taiwan. An amendment introduced by Senator James McClure specified that Taiwan would still be eligible for nuclear fuels from the United States; Senator Orrin Hatch introduced an amendment stating that 'boycotts and embargoes' against Taiwan would be considered a threat to the peace in the Western Pacific, and of grave concern to the United States; and Senator Jesse Helms introduced an amendment to ensure that the American Institute in Taiwan would be able to perform the same services for US citizens and businesses in Taiwan as performed by the former embassy. Although all these amendments were accepted, conservative Republicans failed in their efforts to restore the full government-to-government relationship which had existed before the recognition of the PRC.

The effectiveness of the Western and Southern Republican challenge to Carter was limited by the Republican Party's minority status. With both the Humphrey–Hawkins Full Employment Bill and the Taiwan Relations Bill their success was due to general support for their position among all Republicans: support which would have made a vote of cloture almost impossible to achieve. Following the 1980 elections, the power and influence of the Southern and Western Republicans were significantly increased. Not only were their numbers swelled with the elections of Paula Hawkins (R – Fla), Mack Mattingly (R – Ga), Steve Symms (R – Idaho) and John East (R – NC), but they became part of the majority, and had an ideologically-compatible president to deal with. In this respect the power of the Republican senators from the South and West was enhanced by the fact that Ronald Reagan had been elected President. Under a more moderate President it is likely that they would have remained on the fringes of the political process. Reagan's election effectively brought them into the mainstream of American political life.

Unlike President Carter, whose relations with this grouping of Republican senators suffered from the combined factors of ideological incompatibility and his own poor electoral showing in the West, Reagan suffered from neither of these problems. He shared many of the same policy objectives as the senators, and also outpolled ten of them. As a result many of the freshmen from the South and West regarded themselves as being part of a more general conservative movement in American politics, and were willing to act in accordance with the wishes of the leaders of that movement. As Senator John East stated: 'I look upon myself as being a part of the change in government that was brought about in 1980. I'm not here to see bill X, Y, or Z passed. You are part of the whole. One has to understand that, and be modest about one's assessment. You're going to lose your perspective in my judgement if you focus on a specific proposal.'[66] Senator East's statement may be compared with a comment made by Max Friedersdorf when the latter was chief congressional liaison officer for President Ford: 'Appealing to party loyalty was not a very effective argument. On one occasion, I literally got down on my knees in the Republican cloakroom to Senator Mathias asking him for his vote on an issue which would not have hurt Mathias. But he would not give it . . . just to show independence from the White House.'[67] The party support for Reagan's position was enhanced by the changes in the regional balance of power within the Republican Party in the Senate. The election successes of Republicans in the Rocky Mountain states of the West, the South and the Plains states of the Midwest during the late 1970s meant that by the 97th Congress senators from these three regions constituted over half of the party's strength in the Senate. The result was a party dominated by supporters of Reagan's policies.

The importance of a Republican-controlled Senate, and a Reagan-controlled Republican Party in that Senate, to the success of the President's economic programme in 1981 can be clearly seen. By adopting the strategy of using the reconciliation procedure to achieve their budgetary goals, not only did the Republican leaders manage to avoid the piecemeal process that typically characterises congressional decision-making but by acting with uncommon speed, the Senate brought political pressure upon the House of Representatives, and provided House Republicans with an alternative budget to that being proposed by the Democratic leadership.[68] As one commentator noted: 'Early Senate action on reconciliation . . . provided the Republican minority with a set of internally consistent budget numbers when it came to draft Gramm–Latta (The House-passed reconciliation bill was named after Rep. Phil Gramm (D – Texas) and Rep. Delbert Latta (R – Ohio)).'[69]

In a similar move the Senate responded quickly to Reagan's tax programme. Although Reagan's initial tax proposals were unenthusiastically received by Congress, the Senate dealt rapidly with the revised tax plan when it was announced on 4 June 1981. The Senate Finance Committee began marking up the tax bill on 9 June, and approved it a week later. By contrast, the House Ways and Means Committee began its marking up on 10 June, and reported the package on 23 July, with the Democrats trying to slow the process down. In an effort to force the Democrats to comply with Reagan's legislative timetable, the Senate began floor consideration of the tax package while the Ways and Means panel was still marking up its version of the tax bill: an action that was of dubious legality as it infringed upon the House's revenue-raising powers. Article I, Section 7 of the Constitution stated: 'All Bills for raising Revenue shall originate in the House of Representatives'.

Although the Senate ultimately had to wait until the House had passed its tax bill before completing action on its own measure in order to comply formally with the provisions of the Constitution, the early action of the Senate nevertheless helped prod the House to meet the Reagan timetable for enactment of his tax proposals. Furthermore, as with the budget proposals, the Senate's tax bill provided an alternative for House Republicans. This alternative could have been invoked if the so-called bipartisan tax plan, the Conable–Hance Bill, had failed to win on the floor over the Democratic version supported by Ways and Means Chairman Dan Rostenkowski (D – Ill). In the event though, the Senate measure was not needed as heavy lobbying by Reagan secured the passage of the Conable–Hance measure.

The Administration's 1981 economic victories can thus be

attributed largely to the Republican takeover of the Senate. First, it gave the President the leverage to control a significant portion of Congress's agenda. Second, it is highly unlikely that a Democratic-controlled Senate would have responded as positively, cohesively or quickly in dealing with Reagan's spending cuts. Finally, Republican control of the Senate allowed Reagan to concentrate his liaison efforts on winning votes in the Democratic House.

The unprecedented levels of support in the Senate for the President's programme began to fall in 1982 as disillusionment with Reagan's failure to act on social issues affected Western, Southern and Midwestern Republicans, and a reassertion of constituency-based politics further alienated senators from the Northeast. This decline in support however, did not prevent Reagan from using the Senate as the major motive force for his economic policy. Indeed, it was the Senate that rescued his economic package from oblivion in 1982. In a striking reversal from 1981, House Democrats wanted Senate Republicans to originate, take credit for and suffer the electoral consequences of raising voters' taxes in an effort to reduce the deficit. Not only did the House leave the Senate to originate the 1982 Tax Bill but in an extraordinary procedure voted to go straight to conference with the Senate without writing or considering a tax bill of its own. Rep. Bill Alexander (D – Ark), chief deputy Democratic Whip, summed up Democratic feelings about the tax proposals when he declared: 'I don't want my tracks on this.'[70] Reagan also used the Senate in 1984 to fashion a budget compromise after his original proposals had been rejected. By agreeing a deficit-reduction plan with the Senate Republicans which would have reduced the deficit by $150 billion, President Reagan was able to reach an agreement with House Democrats.

The Republican Senate was thus extremely important to the successful enactment of President Reagan's economic programme. The level of support that Reagan could depend upon was in marked contrast to that achieved by Presidents Carter and Ford, and was achieved mainly because of the close relationship which Reagan enjoyed with the dominant faction of the GOP in the Senate. This close relationship was also responsible for changes in the structure of the US foreign policy-making process during the first Reagan administration. Not only did the Republican gains in the Senate following the 1980 elections provide President Reagan with numerous potential allies on foreign policy issues but they also pushed into prominence senators with different perceptions of their proper role in the foreign policy-making process.

Rather than wishing to confront the executive as their Democratic predecessors had done, the new Republican leaders of the Senate went on record to express their feeling that the President should be given more freedom of action to conduct foreign policy. Writing in *Foreign Policy*, Senator Charles Percy, the new Chairman of the Foreign Relations Committee, argued that: 'the pendulum that has swung toward the legislative branch since 1970 ought now to swing back toward a middle ground that could contribute to greater efficiency in U.S. foreign policy making'.[71] Senator John Tower, Chairman of the Armed Services Committee, echoed this sentiment when he wrote in *Foreign Affairs* that: 'By . . . [the mid-1970s] . . . the two branches were locked in a struggle for control of American foreign policy. To a certain extent Congress won, and the balance between Congress and the President has swung dangerously to the legislative side with unfavourable consequences for American foreign policy.'[72] In a manner which reflected these concerns Senator Percy declared that his highest priority as Chairman of the Foreign Relations Committee was 'to determine not only how we can have a bipartisan foreign policy, but one that meshes with the administration'.[73] During the first few months of the Reagan administration the Senate relaxed some of the restrictions which had been placed on the President's freedom to give direct aid to countries which violated human rights, and in September 1981 voted to repeal the Clark Amendment which prohibited aid to Angola when it adopted an amendment sponsored by Senator Nancy Kassebaum to the Fiscal 1982 Foreign Aid Authorisation Bill (S.1196). 'If we're a world power, we need muscle in the President's office to act like a world power' stated Senator Barry Goldwater, Chairman of the Senate's Select Committee on Intelligence.[74]

Explicit in the statements of Senators Percy, Tower and Goldwater was a belief that the effectiveness of US foreign policy had been undermined by a decade of congressional assertion. Not only were the procedures of Congress too open and cumbersome to allow it to move swiftly and with secrecy to meet any threat to American security but its intervention in foreign affairs during the 1970s had derived US policy of much of its coherence. As Senator Tower wrote: 'Five hundred and thirty five Congressmen with different regional interests and objectives in mind cannot forge a unified foreign policy that reflects the interests of the United States as a whole.'[75] Recognition of this point had, in fact, been gaining ground during the late 1970s and had led Senators

Jesse Helms, Paul Tsongas and Jacob Javits to introduce an amendment seeking the repeal of the Clark Amendment in June 1980.[76] That such a measure had the support of Senators as ideologically diverse as Helms, Tsongas and Javits is indicative of the extent of the feeling in the Senate that the executive had been reined in too much by the curbs of the early 1970s.

Throughout the first Reagan administration the Republican Senate generally supported the President's foreign policy initiatives.[77] Indeed, the fact that President Reagan suffered no *major* foreign policy reverse in the Senate between 1981 and 1984 reveals the extent of presidential ascendancy in this area during the early 1980s, and stands in stark contrast to the experience of his immediate predecessors. Unlike Presidents Ford and Carter, Reagan was fortunate in being able to deal with a Senate where the majority were generally in agreement with his foreign policy aims, and equally important, were willing to allow him some leeway in achieving those aims.

In effect changes within the Republican Party in the Senate altered the relationship between the chamber and the executive. Whereas the Ford and Carter administrations had had to confront a hostile Senate, President Reagan faced a much more accommodating chamber. The consequences of this change were twofold. First, the Senate, by failing to challenge seriously Reagan's conduct of foreign policy lost some of its pre-eminence in this area. Second, the fact that President Reagan used the Senate as a vehicle for promoting his economic policies gave the chamber an importance in budgetary politics which it had hitherto not enjoyed.

7 The new individualism

Between 1974 and 1984 the Republican Party in the US Senate was transformed by changes in the electoral environment. Not only did the increased use of political consultants, and the more active involvement of Political Action Committees in campaigns, weaken the ties between candidates and the party but the internal distribution of power within the GOP was altered by the large influx of Republican senators from previously Democratic states. At the most basic level this influx of Republicans from Southern and Western states changed the factional balance of power within the party. Most of the new senators were conservative, and as a result the ideological complexion of the party was transformed. By the 97th Congress the Republican Party in the Senate was dominated by its Southern and Western wings, and had a more right-wing appearance. The once dominant Eastern, moderate section of the party had been reduced to a small, though not insignificant, minority: diminished to a position where its main role was to frustrate the initiatives of the more right-wing members of the party.

These changes had a profound impact on the Republican Party's policy agenda, and its reaction to presidential initiatives. The majority of Republican senators abandoned the bipartisanship that had, with the exception of Vietnam, generally characterised American foreign policy in the post-Second-World-War period, and also assumed a far more conservative stance with regard to economic and social issues. In effect, the Republican Party abandoned the consensual bias which had characteristically marked most of its activities in the Senate, and increasingly took a more partisan stance in its reaction to presidential initiatives.

In addition to altering the ideological make-up of the Republican Party in the Senate, the large influx of new senators also had a more subtle, and perhaps more important impact on the structure of the party. Not only did these changes alter the ratio between junior and senior senators, but they also introduced a new type of senator into the party. The result was an increase in individual assertiveness in the Senate, and the development of a new political style for the Republican Party. The fact that many of the new senators came from traditionally Democratic states like Alabama, Georgia and Mississippi, where the Republican organisation was weak, meant that the demands and goals of these senators differed from those of their colleagues coming from states with strong Republican ties. The weakness of the Republican Party organisation in these states meant that the senators owed very little to the party for their election: their electoral success being largely the result of their own efforts. Moreover, as 'self-starters' with limited party ties, many of the new senators were politically inexperienced, and thus initially lacking in the parliamentary skills necessary for legislative success in the Senate. They owed their electoral success to an ability to take advantage of the new campaign techniques, and gain the support of the ascendant interests in their states: a competence which did not require, and perhaps even discouraged, an understanding of such traditional political skills as the art of compromise.

The impact of these senators on the Senate was considerable, and may be compared with the effect that the new class of Democratic senators had on the chamber following the Democratic landslide of 1958. As one Senate aide stated: 'We've gone from older people to younger people, from more experienced legislative types to less experienced types, from guys who know you don't always get your way to those who are bound and determined to get their way, no matter what. There's a lack of responsibility in governing. They don't think they have to be a part of compromise.'[1] Lacking a deep understanding of the institution in which they served, but at the same time committed to an aggressive conservatism, many of the new Republicans tended to use the Senate's norms and rules to further their aims in a manner which subverted the traditional purpose of those procedures. In particular, the use of obstruction was extended beyond previous practice. Not only did senators such as Jesse Helms develop the technique of the post-cloture filibuster, but they also increased the scope of legislative candidates for obstruction. Whereas in the past the filibuster had been used almost exclusively in debates on the great issues of the day, during the late 1970s right-wing Republicans began to obstruct almost every issue with which they disagreed. In this respect the 1979 revision of Rule 22 was a failure. Senators continued to conduct effective post-cloture filibusters, and in 1982 Senator Howard Baker expressed his feeling that 'I think now we have made Rule XXII a nullity'.[2]

The relative lack of political experience among the new senators was highlighted by Senator Dan Quayle as one of the major causes of the Senate's problems in the 1980s: 'So many of us were new. We didn't think that much about the institution of the Senate.'[3] Part of the problem faced by freshmen such as Senator Quayle was that the high turnover rates of the late 1970s, in effect, reduced the number of senior senators from whom the junior senators could learn about the norms and procedures of the chamber. The high turnover rates meant that by the 97th Congress there were an unprecedented fifty-five senators in their first term. Thus, not only were the freshmen lacking in the political experience that many of their predecessors had possessed as a consequence of working their way up through the party system but there were fewer experienced senators available to educate them once they arrived in the Senate. This point was made by one Senate aide when asked to explain the breakdown of the Senate's traditional norms of behaviour. He explained: 'We usually changed three or four members at a time. The newcomers were absorbed by the comity, the tradition, the club. But now they set the rules of the body. It's no longer the club it used to be.'[4] Another aide expressed similar sentiments when he declared: 'The giants of the Senate are gone. They were the glue that held the place together.'[5]

As the 'glue' became dilated so more and more senators began to question the Senate's ability to function. Typical was the complaint by Senator Mark Andrews (R – ND) about the amount of time it took to resolve simple issues: 'We spent 75 per cent of our time going through some fandango out here, and all this monkey business undermines confidence in the institution.'[6] In response to such complaints the Senate adopted S.Res 392 on 11 May 1982 authorising a wide-ranging examination of Senate rules and procedures by two 'wise men', former Senators James B. Pearson (R – Kan) and Abraham D. Ribicoff (D – Conn). Under the terms of S.Res 392 Pearson and Ribicoff were to carry out 'a full and complete study of the practices and procedures' of the Senate and to recommend 'such revisions . . . as may be necessary or appropriate to preserve and enhance the traditions, customs, functions, forms and spirit of the United States Senate while enabling the Senate to conduct debate which is focused on major issues of national policy'.

The Pearson–Ribicoff Report was unveiled on 5 April 1983, and its recommendations discussed as a hearing of the Senate's Rules and Administration Committee on 9 May 1983. These recommendations included establishing an annual agenda for the Senate, creating a permanent presiding officer, making procedural changes to expedite floor action, strengthening germaneness requirements for amendments, tightening rules governing debates after cloture is invoked, permitting limited television broadcast of Senate debates, revising the budget process, abolishing several committees, and placing new limitations on senators' committee assignments.[7]

Many of the recommendations of the Pearson–Ribicoff Report were repeated in the report of the Temporary Select Committee to Study the Senate Committee System, chaired by Senator Quayle, in 1984. Created as a response to concern over the state of the Senate's committees the Quayle Committee's recommendations emphasised assignment limits, membership levels, and subcommittee numbers. Specifically, the Committee proposed eliminating exceptions to the assignment limits which had been granted to Senators; reducing the number of seats on 'A' and 'B' committees; limiting to five the number of sub-committees that could be created by any standing committee (with the exception of Appropriations); and limiting senators to a total of nine assignments on committees and subcommittees.[8]

Underlying the recommendations of both the Pearson–Ribicoff Report and the Quayle Committee Report was the belief that the Senate should serve as a national forum of public education and policy clarification. Indeed, the Quayle Committee concluded that 'if senators will agree to reduce their committee assignments, our committees will be better able to perform their duties and the senate as a whole will be taken *more seriously as a reliable and informed national policymaker*'.[9] As such they raised profound questions about the Senate's role in the Federal Government. For example, should senators be law-makers, or should they be concerned with providing a service for their constituents? Should the Senate articulate the major national issues of the day, or refine policy details in committees or subcommittees? To a certain extent, however, such questions are misleading. Institutional change in the Senate is related to changes in the chamber's membership. The problems experienced in the Senate during the late 1970s and early 1980s were largely the result of an electoral climate which rewarded certain behaviour. Reform of the Senate procedures in the way suggested by the Pearson–Ribicoff Report and the Quayle Committee, therefore, would be unlikely to succeed. Firstly, it is unlikely that senators would agree to changes which threatened their independence; and secondly, such reforms merely addressed the *symptoms* of the problem, not its *cause*.

The fragmentation of power that occurred within the Senate in the late 1970s and early 1980s was a consequence of forces generated by developments in the electoral environment which forced senators to become highly independent. In this climate, the Senate's traditional norms of behaviour were generally forgotten as senators put their own interests first and foremost. The breakdown of these norms, however, effected almost every aspect of the Senate's operations: from the ability of the leadership to control the legislative agenda to individual senators' relationships with each other, with their constituents and with interest groups.

Notes

Chapter One—Introduction

1 Kenneth J. Shepsle and David W. Rohde, *Taking Stock of Congressional Research: The New Institutionalism* (St Louis, Center for the Study of American Business, Washington University, 1978), pp. 11-12.
2 For the purpose of this study Senator James L. Buckley (Conservative - NY) is classified as a Republican.
3 *Congressional Quarterly Weekly Report*, 14 September 1974, p. 2459.
4 William A. Rusher, *The Making of the New Majority Party* (New York, Steed and Ward, 1975), p. 177.
5 *Roe* v. *Wade*, 410 US 113 (1973); *Doe* v. *Bolton*, 410 US 179 (1973).
6 *Planned Parenthood of Missouri* v. *Danforth*, 428 US 52 (1976); *Maher* v. *Roe* 432 US 464 (1977); *Bellotti* v. *Baird* 443 US 622 (1979); and *Harris* v. *McRae*, 448 US 297 (1980). For the background to these cases see Carl E. Schneider and Morris A. Uinovstis eds., *The Law and Politics of Abortion* (Lexington, Lexington Books, 1980); and Robert A. Burt, 'The Burger Court and the Family' in Vincent Blasi ed., *The Burger Court* (New Haven, Yale University Press, 1983), pp. 92-112. For a discussion of the legitimacy of the abortion decisions see Lawrence M. Friedman, 'The Conflict over Constitutional Legitimacy' in Gilbert Y. Steiner ed., *The Abortion Issue and the American System* (Washington D.C., Brookings, 1983), pp. 13-29.
7 *New York Times*, 18 August 1980, p. B7.
8 For an examination of the New Right and the Christian Right see Gillian Peele, *Revival and Reaction* (Oxford, Oxford University Press, 1984), chapters 2 and 3.
9 The Republicans showed a net gain of twelve seats in the 1980 elections. This was one seat less than they won in the congressional elections of 1946.
10 See Gillian Peele, 'Campaign Consultants', *Electoral Studies*, December 1982, p. 355.
11 See Barbara Hinckley, *Congressional Elections* (Washington D.C., Congressional Quarterly Press, 1981), chapter 4.
12 *New York Times*, 8 February 1981, VI, p. 25.
13 For a pessimistic view of the future of the Republican Party see Everett Carll Ladd, *Where Have All the Voters Gone?* (New York, W. W. Norton and Co., 1982), chapter 1.
14 The classification of regions used throughout this book are those found in Norman J. Ornstein, Thomas E. Mann, Michael J. Malbin, John F. Bibby, *Vital Statistics on Congress 1982* (Washington D.C., American Enterprise Institute, 1982), pp. 6-7. The regions are classified as follows:
   South: Alabama, Arkansas, Florida, Georgia, Louisiana, Mississippi, North Carolina, South Carolina, Tennessee, Texas, Virginia.
   Border: Kentucky, Maryland, Missouri, Oklahoma, West Virginia.
   New England: Connecticut, Maine, Massachusetts, New Hampshire, Rhode Island, Vermont.
   Mid-Atlantic: Delaware, New Jersey, New York, Pennsylvania.
   Midwest: Illinois, Indiana, Michigan, Ohio, Wisconsin.
   Plains: Iowa, Kansas, Minnesota, Nebraska, North Dakota, South Dakota.
   Rocky Mountains: Arizona, Colorado, Idaho, Montana, Nevada, New

Mexico, Utah, Wyoming.

Pacific Coast: California, Hawaii, Oregon, Washington.

15 Kevin P. Phillips, *The Emerging Republican Majority* (New Rochelle, Arlington House, 1969).

16 Kirkpatrick Sale, *Power Shift* (New York, Random House, 1975), p. 109.

17 See Jerrold S. Schneider, *Ideological Coalitions in Congress* (Westport, Greenwood Press, 1979), pp. 11–12.

18 James Reichley, *Conservatives in an Age of Change* (Washington D.C., Brookings, 1981), p. 22.

19 Gary C. Jacobson, *The Politics of Congressional Elections* (Boston, Little, Brown and Co., 1983), p. 8.

20 The most comprehensive examination of these developments is by Larry J. Sabato, *The Rise of Political Consultants* (New York, Basic Books, 1981).

21 A senator who has served more than one term of office in the Senate is deemed to have had experience of elected office.

22 See Stanley Kelley, *Professional Public Relations and Political Power* (Baltimore, Johns Hopkins University Press, 1956), pp. 109–15.

23 See Thomas E. Mann, 'Elections and Change in Congress' in Thomas E. Mann and Norman J. Ornstein eds., *The New Congress* (Washington D.C., American Enterprise Institute, 1981), p. 38.

24 *Congressional Quarterly Weekly Report*, 4 September 1982, p. 2177.

25 In 1949 northern Democrats tried to obtain a new rule from Vice-President Barkley overruling Vandenburg's original ruling. Barkley overruled Russell's point of order, but then in a vote of the entire chamber, the Senate rejected Barkley's ruling. For an account of this episode see Robert J. Donovan, *Tumultuous Years* (New York, W. W. Norton, 1982), pp. 118–19.

26 *US News and World Report*, 7 June 1960, p. 88.

27 For a description of 'The Treatment' see Rowland Evans and Robert Novak, *Lyndon B. Johnson: the Exercise of Power* (New York, New American Library, 1966), p. 104.

28 James Madison, 'Federalist Paper No. 62' in Alexander Hamilton, James Madison, John Jay, *The Federalist Papers* (New York, New American Library, 1961), p. 378.

29 Thomas E. Mann, 'Elections and Change in Congress', *op. cit.*, p. 38.

30 *New York Times*, 21 March 1983, p. B6.

31 *Congressional Quarterly Weekly Report*, 5 August 1978, p. 2023.

32 Barbara Sinclair, 'Senate Styles and Senate Decision-Making, 1955–1980'. Paper presented to the annual meeting of the American Political Science Association, New Orleans, Louisiana, 1985.

33 *Congressional Quarterly Weekly Report*, 4 September 1982, p. 2178.

34 Roger H. Davidson and Thomas Kephart, *Indicators of Senate Activity and Workload* (Washington D.C., CRS, 1985), p. 24.

35 *Congressional Record*, 98th Congress, 2nd sess., September 28, 1984, p. S12271.

36 *New York Times*, 25 November 1985, I, p. 1.

Chapter Two—The interaction between party and institution

1 Austin Ranney, *Curing the Mischiefs of Faction* (Berkeley, University of California Press, 1975), p. 179.

2 For a comprehensive account of the reforms carried out in the selection of delegates to the Democratic Party Convention see Byron E. Shafer, *Quiet Revolution* (New York, Russell Sage Foundation, 1983). For an account of the reforms carried out within the Republican Party by the DO Committee (1969–72) and the Rule 29 Committee (1972–9) see Charles H. Longley, 'National Party Renewal' in Gerald M. Pomper ed., *Party Renewal in America* (New York, Praeger, 1980), pp. 69–77. The supremacy of national party rules over state

party rules were upheld by the Supreme Court in *Cousins* v. *Wigoda*, 419 US 477 (1975).

3 V. O. Key, *Politics, Parties and Pressure Groups* (New York, Thomas Y. Crowell, 1958), p. 347.

4 Samuel J. Eldersveld, *Political Parties in American Society* (New York, Basic Books, 1982), p. 99.

5 George H. Meyer, *The Republican Party 1854–1964* (New York, Oxford University Press, 1964), Malcolm Moos, *The Republicans: A History of Their Party* (New York, Random House, 1956).

6 James Madison, *Notes of Debate in the Federal Convention of 1787* (New York, W. W. Norton, 1969), pp. 38–9.

7 *Ibid.*, p. 158.

8 George C. Haynes, *The Senate of the United States*, 2 vols. (Boston, Houghton Mifflin, 1935), vol. 1, p. 3.

9 James Madison, 'Federalist Paper No. 62', p. 377.

10 George Haynes, *op. cit.*, vol. II, p. 1037.

11 James Madison, 'Federalist Paper No. 62', p. 377.

12 James Madison, 'Federalist Paper No. 63', p. 384.

13 James Madison, 'Federalist Paper No. 52', p. 322.

14 James Madison, *Notes, op. cit.*, p. 193.

15 Richard F. Fenno, *The United States Senate: A Bicameral Perspective* (Washington D.C., American Enterprise Institute, 1982), p. 4.

16 James Madison, 'Federalist Paper No. 62', p. 378.

17 For an interesting discussion of the Senate's role in the federal system see William H. Riker, 'The Senate and American Federalism', *American Political Science Review*, June 1955, pp. 452–69.

18 See Robert Keith, 'The Use of Unanimous Consent in the Senate' in US Senate, Commission on the Operation of the Senate, *Committees and Senate Procedures*, 94th Congress, 2nd sess., pp. 140–68.

19 See Stanley Bach, 'Germaness Rules and Bicameral Relations in the U.S. Congress', *Legislative Studies Quarterly*, August 1982, pp. 341–57.

20 See Richard S. Beth, 'Senate Organisation and Operations: Proposals for Changes in the 98th Congress', *Issue Brief* (Washington D.C., Congressional Research Service, 1983), p. 7.

21 *Constitution, Jefferson: Manual and Rules of the House of Representatives*, 97th Congress, 2nd sess., H. Doc. No. 97–271, p. 235.

22 Richard R. Beeman, 'Unlimited Debate in the Senate: The First Phase', *Political Science Quarterly*, September 1968, pp. 419–59.

23 For a history of the filibuster see Franklin L. Burdette, *Filibusting in the Senate* (Princeton, Princeton University Press, 1940).

24 *Congressional Quarterly Weekly Report*, 22 February 1975, p. 412.

25 Rule 32 is now Rule 5.

26 Randall B. Ripley, *Power in the Senate* (New York, St Martin's Press, 1969), p. 16.

27 James Madison, 'Federalist Paper No. 62', p. 372.

28 David R. Mayhew, *Congress: The Electoral Connection* (New Haven, Yale University Press, 1974); Richard Fenno, *Congressmen in Comittees* (Boston, Little, Brown and Co., 1973); Morris Fiorina, *Congress: Keystone of the Washington Establishment* (New Haven, Yale University Press, 1977).

29 H. Douglas Price, 'Congress and the Evolution of Legislative "Professionalism" ' in Norman Ornstein ed., *Congress in Change* (New York, Praeger, 1975), p. 5.

30 See Rochelle Jones and Peter Woll, *The Private World of Congress* (New York, The Free Press, 1979), p. 5.

31 William H. Riker, *op. cit.*, pp. 462–63.

32 H. Douglas Price, 'The Electoral Arena' in David B. Truman ed., *The Congress and America's Future* (Englewood Cliffs, Prentice-Hall, 1965), p. 32.

33 John Bibby and Roger Davidson, *On Capitol Hill* (New York, Hall Rinehart and Winston, 1967), p. 15.

34 David J. Rothman, *Politics and Power: The US Senate 1869-1901* (Cambridge, Harvard University Press, 1968), p. 111.
35 *Ibid.,* p. 128.
36 *Ibid.,* pp. 135-6.
37 See Nathaniel W. Stephenson, *Nelson W. Aldrich* (New York, Scribners, 1930); Leland L. Saye, *William Boyd Allison* (Iowa City, University of Iowa Press, 1956); and John R. Lambert, *Arthur P. Gorman* (Baton Rouge, Louisiana State University Press, 1963).
38 See Randall B. Ripley, *op. cit.,* p. 26.
39 See Xandra Kayden and Eddie Mahe, *The Party Goes On* (New York, Basic Books, 1985), pp. 44-5.
40 Milton Rakove, *Don't Make No Waves, Don't Back No Losers* (Bloomington, Indiana University Press, 1975), p. 42.
41 Austin Ranney, *op. cit.,* p. 130.
42 George Rothwell Brown, *The Leadership of Congress* (Indianapolis, Bobbs-Merrill, 1922), pp. 195-7.
43 James Madison, 'Federalist Paper No. 62', p. 378.
44 See John R. Hibbing and John R. Alford, 'Economic Conditions and the Forgotten Side of Congress: A Foray into US Senate Elections', *British Journal of Political Science,* October 1982, pp. 505-12.
45 See James Holt, *Congressional Insurgents and the Party System 1909-1916* (Cambridge, Harvard University Press, 1967); and James M. Clubb and Howard M. Allen, 'Party Loyalty in the Progressive Years: The Senate 1909-1915', *Journal of Politics,* August 1967, pp. 567-84.
46 See Donald R. Matthews, *US Senators and their World* (Chapel Hill, University of North Carolina Press, 1960) especially chapter 5; and William S. White, *Citadel* (New York, Harper and Brothers, 1957), especially chapters 5-10.
47 *Congressional Record,* 88th Congress, 1st sess., 19 February 1965, pp. S2554-5.
48 Joseph S. Clark, *Congress: The Sapless Branch* (New York, Harper and Row, 1964), p. 5.
49 For an interesting account of the problems that John F. Kennedy had in getting his legislation through the Senate, see Herbert S. Parmet, *JFK: The Presidency of John F. Kennedy* (Harmondsworth, Penguin, 1984), pp. 205-9.
50 George B. Galloway, *The Legislative Process in Congress* (New York, Thomas Y. Crowell, 1953), p. 289.
51 The career of Senator Wayne Morse is examined in Ralph K. Huitt, 'The Outsider in the Senate: An Alternative View', *American Political Science Review,* September 1961, pp. 566-75.
52 James Q. Wilson, *The Amateur Democrat* (Chicago, University of Chicago Press, 1962).
53 See Roger Davidson, 'Subcommittee Government' in Thomas Mann and Norman Ornstein eds., *The New Congress* (Washington D.C., American Enterprise Institute, 1981), p. 107.
54 The best account of the changes which occurred in the Senate between 1958 and 1972 is Michael Foley, *The New Senate* (New Haven, Yale University Press, 1980).
55 See Judy Schneider, 'Senate Rules and Practices on Committees, Subcommittees and Chairmanship Assignments', *Issue Brief* (Washington D.C., Congressional Research Service, 1982), p. 2.
56 *Congressional Quarterly Weekly Report,* 14 June 1975, p. 1236.
57 *Congressional Quarterly Weekly Report,* 10 April 1976, p. 837.
58 See Judith H. Parris, 'The Senate Reorganises its Committees', *Political Science Quarterly,* Summer 1979, pp. 319-34.
59 The standing committees abolished by S. Res 4 (1977) were: District of Columbia, Post Office, and Space Sciences. The joint committees abolished were: Atomic Energy, Congressional Operations, and Defense Production.
60 In 1975 this threshhold was raised from fifteen to twenty members by the House

Democratic Caucus.

61 *Congressional Quarterly Weekly Report*, 12 February 1977, p. 280.

62 Roger H. Davidson, 'Congressional Committees as Moving Targets', *Legislative Studies Quarterly*, February 1986, pp. 19-34.

63 Steven S. Smith and Christopher J. Deering, *Committees in Congress* (Washington D.C., Congressional Quarterly Press, 1984), p. 54.

64 Norman J. Ornstein, Thomas E. Mann, Michael J. Malbin, John F. Bibby, *Vital Statistics on Congress, 1982* (Washington D.C., American Enterprise Institute, 1982), p. 110.

65 Susan Webb Hammond, 'The Operation of Senator's Offices', US Senate, Commission on the Operation of the Senate, *Senators, Offices, Ethics, and Pressures*, 95th Congress, 2nd sess., 1976, p. 4.

66 See Michael J. Malbin, *Unelected Representatives* (New York, Basic Books, 1980).

67 *Congressional Quarterly Weekly Report*, 4 September 1982, p. 2176.

Chapter Three—The electoral environment

1 See Jeanne J. Kirkpatrick, 'Changing Patterns of Electoral Competition' in Anthony King ed., *The New American Political System* (Washington D.C., American Enterprise Institute, 1979), pp. 276-80.

2 See James Sundquist, *Dynamics of the Party System* (Washington D.C., Brookings, 1983), chapter 17.

3 See Colin Francombe, 'Abortion Politics in the US', *Political Studies*, December 1980, p. 616.

4 David McKay, *American Politics and Society* (Oxford, Basil Blackwell, 1985), p. 111.

5 Norman J. Ornstein, Thomas E. Mann, Michael J. Malbin, John F. Bibby, *Vital Statistics on Congress 1982* (Washington D.C., American Enterprise Institute, 1982), p. 53.

6 For a lengthy discussion of dealignment theory see Everett Carll Ladd and Charles D. Hadley, *Transformations of the American Party System* (New York, W. W. Norton, 1978).

7 See Warren L. Kostroski, 'Party and Incumbency in Postwar Senate Elections: Trends, Patterns and Models', *American Political Science Review*, December 1973, pp. 1213-34.

8 Barbara Hinckley, *Congressional Elections* (Washington D.C., Congressional Quarterly Press, 1981), p. 39.

9 Candice Nelson, 'The Effects of Incumbency on Voting in Congressional Elections 1964-1974', *Political Science Quarterly*, winter 1978, pp. 665-78.

10 Thomas Mann and Norman Ornstein, eds., *The American Elections of 1982* (Washington D.C., American Enterprise Institute, 1983), p. 160.

11 See, for example, Barbara Hinckley, 'House Reelections and Senate Defeats: The Role of the Challenger', *British Journal of Political Science*, October 1980, pp. 441-60; and Thomas Mann and Raymond E. Wolfinger, 'Candidates and Parties in Congressional Elections', *American Political Science Review*, September 1980, pp. 622-6.

12 Martin P. Wattenberg, 'From Parties to Candidates: Examining the Role of the Media', *Public Opinion Quarterly*, summer 1982, p. 216.

13 See Stanley Kelly, *Professional Public Relations and Political Power* (Baltimore, Johns Hopkins University Press, 1956), p. 141.

14 For an extensive examination of the use of television in political campaigns see Larry Sabato, *The Rise of Political Consultants* (New York, Basic Books, 1981), chapter 3. For a more general examination of the role of television in American politics, see Austin Ranney, *Channels of Power* (New York, Basic Books, 1983).

15 See Doris A. Graber, *Mass Media and American Politics* (Washington D.C., Congressional Quarterly Press, 1980), p. 161.

16 Michael J. Robinson and Kevin R. Appel, 'Network News Coverage of Congress', *Political Science Quarterly*, fall 1979, p. 409.

17 See William J. Crotty and Gary C. Jacobson, *American Parties in Decline* (Boston, Little, Brown and Co., 1980), p. 83.

18 V. Lance Tarrance, *Negative Campaigns and Negative Votes: The 1980 Elections* (Washington D.C., The Free Congress Research and Education Foundation, 1982), p. 1.

19 *New York Times*, 17 August 1980, I, p. 1.

20 Larry Sabato, *op. cit.*, p. 281.

21 *Buckley* v. *Valeo*, 424 US 1 (1976).

22 FEC, *Campaign Guide for Presidential Candidates and their Committees* (Washington D.C., FEC, 1979), pp. 9, 36–7.

23 US Senate, Committee on Rules and Administration, 'Application and Administration of the Federal Election Campaign Act of 1971, As Amended', *Hearings*, 97th Congress, 1st sess., 24 November 1981, p. 190.

24 For a good account of the anti-abortion movements' impact in Senate campaigns see Marjorie Randon Hershey and Darrell M. West, 'Single Issue Politics: Prolife Groups and the 1980 Senate Campaign' in Allan J. Cigler and Burdette A. Loomis eds., *Interest Group Politics* (Washington D.C., Congressional Quarterly Press, 1983), pp. 31–59.

25 *Congressional Quarterly Weekly Report*, 23 November 1980, pp. 3405–9.

26 Interview, Stuart Rothenberg, Director of the Political Division The Free Congress Research and Education Foundation, Washington D.C., 19 October 1983.

27 *New York Times*, 24 March 1980, p. B6.

28 *Ibid.*

29 *New York Times*, 21 January 1980, p. A21.

30 See James L. Guth, 'Politics of the Christian Right', in Cigler and Loomis eds., p. 69.

31 *Ibid.*, p. 75.

32 *New York Times*, 24 March 1980, p. B6.

33 Ornstein, Mann, Malbin, Bibby, *op. cit.*, p. 91.

34 *Ibid.*, p. 90.

35 Philip Williams and Graham Wilson, 'The American Mid-Term Elections', *Political Studies*, December 1979, p. 606.

36 *Congressional Quarterly Weekly Report*, 28 July 1979, p. 1540.

37 *Ibid.*

38 *Congressional Quarterly Weekly Report*, 15 November 1980, p. 3372.

39 *Ibid.*

40 P. M. Williams and S. J. Reilly, 'The 1980 Elections and After', *Political Studies*, September 1983, p. 381.

41 *Congressional Quarterly Weekly Report*, 15 November 1980, p. 3372.

42 The expenditure figures for the 1982 elections have been calculated from data given by Gary C. Jacobson, 'Money in the 1980 and 1982 Congressional Elections' in Michael Malbin ed., *Money and Politics in the United States* (New Jersey, Chatham House, 1984), p. 52.

43 *Congressional Quarterly Weekly Report*, 4 September 1982, p. 2177.

44 Michael J. Malbin and Thomas W. Skladony, 'Selected Campaign Finance Data, 1974–1982' in Michael J. Malbin ed., *op. cit.*, p. 282.

45 *Ibid.*, p. 295.

46 Austin Ranney, 'The Political Parties: Reform and Decline', in Anthony King, ed., *op. cit.*, p. 243.

47 *Congressional Quarterly Weekly Report*, 17 May 1980, p. 1356.

48 Michael J. Malbin and Thomas W. Sklodony, *op. cit.*, pp. 288–9. In 1982 the proportion of funds contributed to candidates for the Senate by nonparty PACs fell to 13 per cent.

49 This percentage fell to 17 per cent in the 1982 elections.

50 SUNPAC: FEC Advisory Opinion 1975–23 (24 November 1975).

51 *Congressional Quarterly Weekly Report*, 10 January 1976, p. 47.
52 See Larry Sabato, *PAC Power* (New York, W. W. Norton, 1984), pp. 142–3.
53 Ornstein, Mann, Malbin, Bibby, *op. cit.*, p. 83.
54 *Ibid.*
55 H. E. Alexander, *Financing the 1980 Election* (Lexington, Lexington Books, 1983), p. 83.
56 See John A. Crittenden, *Parties and Elections in the United States* (Englewood Cliffs, Prentice-Hall, 1982), p. 233.
57 Quoted in Alan Crawford, *Thunder On the Right* (New York, Pantheon, 1980), p. 51.
58 *Congressional Quarterly Weekly Report*, 24 December 1977, p. 2651.
59 See William Crotty and Gary Jacobson, *op. cit.*, p. 146.
60 *New York Times*, 20 July 1980, p. A14.
61 Robert Pitchell, 'The Influence of Professional Campaign Management Firms in Partisan Elections in California', *Western Political Quarterly*, June 1958, pp. 281–2.
62 *National Journal*, 26 September 1970, pp. 2084–5.
63 Gary C. Jacobson, *The Politics of Congressional Elections* (Boston, Little, Brown and Co., 1983), p. 8.
64 Nelson W. Polsby, *The Consequences of Party Reform* (New York, Oxford University Press, 1983), p. 133.
65 See Robert Agranoff, 'The New Style of Campaigning: The Decline of Party and the Rise of a Candidate-Centered Technology', in Jeff Fishel ed., *Parties and Elections in an Anti-Party Age* (Bloomington, Indiana University Press, 1978).
66 *Congressional Quarterly Weekly Report*, 6 March 1982, p. 449.
67 Quoted in Wayne Greenhaw, *Elephants in the Cotton Fields* (New York, Macmillan, 1983), p. 163.
68 H. E. Alexander, *Financing Politics* (Washington D.C., Congressional Quarterly Press, 1980), p. 123.
69 *Washington Post*, 27 January 1981, p. A4.
70 Wayne Greenhaw, *op. cit.*, p. 167.
71 *Ibid.*, cited p. 168.
72 *Los Angeles Times*, 16 May 1978, p. A16.
73 *New York Times*, 23 September 1980, p. B11.
74 Edie N. Goldenberg and Michael W. Traugott, *Campaigning For Congress* (Washington D.C., Congressional Quarterly Press, 1984), p. 74.
75 Thomas Mann and Norman Ornstein, 'The Republican Surge in Congress' in Austin Ranney ed., *The American Elections of 1980* (Washington D.C., American Enterprise Institute, 1981), p. 265.
76 See Cornelius Cotter and John Bibby, 'Institutional Development and the Thesis of Party Decline', *Political Science Quarterly*, spring 1980, p. 12.
77 See John F. Bibby, 'Party Renewal in the National Republican Party', in Gerald M. Pomper ed., *Party Renewal in America* (New York, Praeger, 1980), p. 107.
78 Bliss quoted by A. James Reichley, 'The Rise of National Parties' in John E. Chubb and Paul E. Peterson eds., *The New Direction in American Politics* (Washington D.C., Brookings, 1985), pp. 186–7. For details of the reforms carried out by Ray Bliss see Bernard Cosman and Robert Hochschom eds., *Republican Parties: The 1964 Campaign and its Aftermath for the Party* (New York, Praeger, 1968), pp. 205–33.
79 *New York Times*, 30 May 1977, p. A31.
80 See Larry Sabato, *The Rise of Political Consultants, op. cit.*, p. 291.
81 The RNC had been codifying and categorising newspaper clippings for some time; if a candidate required current information on a topic a computerised retrieval system supplied it without delay. For further details see Dan Nimmo, *The Political Persuaders* (Englewood Cliffs, Prentice-Hall, 1970), p. 72.
82 *New York Times*, 30 May 1977, p. A31.
83 *National Journal*, 11 April 1981, p. 600.
84 Xandra Kayden and Eddie Mahe, *The Party Goes On* (New York, Basic Books,

1985), p. 76.
85 *New York Times*, 26 January 1975, p. 1.
86 This phenomenon is often known as 'Fenno's Paradox'. See Richard Fenno, 'If As Ralph Nader Says, Congress Is "The Broken Branch" How Come We Love Our Congressmen So Much?' in Norman Ornstein, ed., *Congress in Change* (New York, Praeger, 1975), pp. 277–87; and Glen Parker and Roger Davidson, 'Why Do Americans Love Their Congressmen So Much More Than Their Congress?' *Legislative Studies Quarterly*, February 1979, pp. 53–62.
87 See Barbara Hinckley, *Stability and Change in Congress* (New York, Harper and Row, 1983), pp. 28–9.
88 *New York Times*, 19 January 1980, p. A14.
89 *Ibid.*
90 *New York Times*, 31 January 1980, p. A18.
91 Martin P. Wattenberg, *The Decline of American Political Parties* (Cambridge, Harvard University Press, 1984), p. 52.
92 Figures given by Gary C. Jacobson, 'Money in the 1980 and 1982 Congressional Elections' in Michael Malbin ed., *op. cit.*, pp. 46–7.
93 Michael J. Malbin and Thomas W. Skladony, *op. cit.*, pp. 288–9.
94 *Ibid.*, pp. 292–3.
95 For a list of those candidates for whom the National Party Committees spent more than $200,000 in 1980 and 1982 see Gary Jacobson, 'Money in the 1980 and 1982 Congressional Elections', *op. cit.*, pp. 47–8.
96 Gary C. Jacobson, 'The Effect of Campaign Spending in Congressional Elections', *American Political Science Review*, June 1978, p. 482.
97 See Ornstein, Mann, Malbin, Bibby, *op. cit.*, pp. 67–8.
98 See David Adamany, 'Political Parties in the 1980s', in Michael Malbin ed., *Money and Politics in the United States, op. cit.*, p. 76.
99 Interview, M. E. Lewis, director Lewis and Associates, Washington D.C., 17 October 1983.
100 *National Journal*, 20 Octyber 1979, p. 1765.
101 Ornstein, Mann, Malbin, Bibby, *op. cit.*, pp. 72–3.
102 For an interesting discussion of this point see Alan Ware, 'The 1980 US Elections: Party Renewal or Continuing Party Decline?' *Parliamentary Affairs*, spring 1981, pp. 174–90.
103 See Gary C. Jacobson, *The Politics of Congressional Elections, op. cit.*, p. 150.
104 See Margaret M. Conway, 'Republican Political Party Nationalisation, Campaign Activities, And Their Implications for the Party System', *Publius*, winter 1983, pp. 1–17.
105 Thomas E. Mann and Norman J. Ornstein, 'The Republican Surge in Congress', *op. cit.*, p. 293.

Chapter Four—The new party

1 See Thomas E. Mann, 'Elections and Changes in Congress' in Thomas E. Mann and Norman J. Ornstein eds., *The New Congress* (Washington D.C., American Enterprise Institute, 1981), p. 32; and David W. Brady, 'Critical Elections, Congressional Politics, and Clusters of Policy Changes', *British Journal of Political Science*, January 1978, pp. 79–100.
2 See Kevin Phillips, *The Emerging Republican Majority* (New Rochelle, Arlington House, 1969); Patrick Buchanan, *Conservative Votes–Liberal Victories* (New York, New York Times Books, 1975); and William Rusher, *The Making of the New Majority Party* (New York, Steed and Ward, 1975).
3 The exact definition of the term 'sunbelt' is unclear. See John W. House, 'Regional and Area Development' in John W. House ed., *United States Public Policy* (Oxford, Clarendon Press, 1983), p. 43. For the purpose of this book the sunbelt is regarded as including the eleven states of the Confederacy, the Border state of

Oklahoma, and the Desert states of Arizona, Nevada, New Mexico and California.

4 Everett Carll Ladd, *Where Have All the Voters Gone?* (New York, W. W. Norton, 1982), chapter 1.

5 Henry Fairlie, *The Parties* (New York, St Martin's Press, 1978), p. 11.

6 Following the 1980 elections the Democrats held eleven seats in the South, the Independent Harry Byrd Jr. was treated as a Democrat for organisational purposes, but on most measures voted with the Republicans.

7 Thomas E. Mann and Norman J. Ornstein, 'The Republican Surge in Congress' in Austin Ranney ed., *The American Elections of 1980* (Washington D.C., American Enterprise Institute, 1981), p. 293.

8 See Norman J. Ornstein, Thomas E. Mann, Michael J. Malbin, John Bibby, *Vital Statistics on Congress 1982* (Washington D.C., American Enterprise Institute, 1982), pp. 14–15.

9 In the 68th Congress the GOP held sixteen seats in the Northeast while in the 80th Congress it held only thirteen seats in that region.

10 Ornstein, Mann, Malbin, Bibby, *op. cit.,* pp. 10–11.

11 For an account of the political environment in these states see Neal R. Peirce and John Keefe, *The Great Lake States of America* (New York, W. W. Norton, 1980), p. 16.

12 See Norman H. Nie, Sidney Verba and John Petrocik, *The Changing American Voter* (Cambridge, Harvard University Press, 1976), p. 234.

13 See US Bureau of the Census, *Statistical Abstract of the United States 1980* (Washington D.C., GPO, 1981).

14 See Gillian Peele, *Revival and Reaction* (Oxford, Oxford University Press, 1984), p. 127.

15 John R. Petrocik, *Party Coalitions* (Chicago, University of Chicago Press, 1981), p. 47.

16 See William Schneider, 'Democrats and Republicans; Liberals and Conservatives' in Seymour Martin Lipset ed., *Party Coalitions in the 1980s* (San Francisco, The Institute for Contemporary Studies, 1981), pp. 224–5.

17 See Alan Crawford, *Thunder on the Right* (New York, Pantheon, 1980), p. 279.

18 *New York Times*, 8 November 1977, p. 12.

19 Ornstein, Mann, Malbin, Bibby, *op. cit.,* pp. 10–11.

20 For an account of the party system in the Plains states see Neal R. Peirce, *The Great Plains States* (New York, W. W. Norton, 1973), p. 23.

21 See Louis M. Seagull, *Southern Republicanism* (New York, John Wiley, 1975), p. 5; Allan P. Sindles, 'The South in Political Transition' in John C. McKenney and Edgar T. Thompson, eds., *The South in Continuity and Change* (Durham, NC, Duke University Press, 1965), p. 299.

22 Quoted in Monroe Lee Billington, *The Political South in the Twentieth Century* (New York, Charles Scribner's, 1975), p. 161.

23 See Malcolm E. Jewell, 'Participation in Southern Poliics' in Lawrence W. Moreland, Tod A. Barker and Robert P. Steed eds., *Contemporary Southern Political Attitudes and Behaviour* (New York, Praeger, 1982), p. 82.

24 See Merle Black and Earl Black, 'The Growth of Contested Republican Primaries in the American South' in Moreland, Baker and Steed, *op. cit.,* p. 122.

25 Quoted in David S. Broder and Stephen Hess, *The Republican Establishment* (New York, Harper and Row, 1967), p. 346.

26 The phenomenon of Presidential Republicanism in the South has been examined in some detail. See, for example, Donald S. Strong, 'Durable Republicanism in the South' in Allan Sindler ed., *Change in the Contemporary South* (Durham, NC, Duke University Press, 1963), pp. 174–86; Donald S. Strong, 'The Presidential Election in the South, 1952', *Journal of Politics*, August 1955; Bruce A. Campbell, 'Patterns of Change in the Partisan Loyalties of Native Southerners', *Journal of Politics*, August 1977, pp. 730–61; and Monroe Lee Billington, *op. cit.,* pp. 131–47.

27 See John H. Kessel, *The Goldwater Coalition* (New York, Bobbs-Merrill, 1965),

pp. 39-40.

28 See Stanley P. Brun, *Geography and Politics in America* (New York, Harper and Row, 1974), p. 21; and Gordon B. McKenney, *Southern Mountain Republicans 1865-1900* (Chapel Hill, University of North Carolina Press, 1978).

29 Jack Bass and Walter DeVries, *The Transformation of Southern Politics* (New York, Basic Books, 1970), pp. 24-5.

30 Numan V. Bartley, 'The South and Sectionalism in American Politics', *Journal of Politics*, August 1970, p. 256.

31 Quoted in Donald S. Strong, *Issue-Voting and Party Realignment* (University, University of Alabama Press, 1977), p. 48.

32 Walter DeVries and Jack Bass, 'Cross Pressures in the White South' in Seymour Martin Lipsett ed., *Emerging Coalitions in American Politics* (San Francisco, Institute for Contemporary Studies, 1978), p. 308.

33 Monroe Lee Billington, *op. cit.*, p. 169.

34 See Kirkpatrick Sale, *Power Shift* (New York, Random House, 1975), p. 109.

35 Quoted in DeVries and Bass, 'Cross-Pressures in the White South', *op. cit.*, p. 309.

36 *Ibid.*, p. 310.

37 See Jody Carlson, *George Wallace and the Politics of Powerlessness* (New Brunswick, Transaction Books, 1981), p. 40.

38 Quoted in Kessel, *op. cit.*, p. 195.

39 *National Review*, 12 February 1963, pp. 109-12.

40 See Seymour Martin Lipsett and Earl Raab, *The Politics of Unreason* (Chicago, University of Chicago Press, 1978), pp. 421-2.

41 See Benjamin I. Page, *Choices and Echoes in Presidential Elections* (Chicago, University of Chicago Press, 1978), p. 143.

42 Quoted in Reg Murphy and Hal Gulliver, *The Southern Strategy* (New York, Charles Scribners', 1971), p. 1.

43 See James Sundquist, *op. cit.*, p. 365.

44 Steven J. Rosenstone, Roy L. Behr, Edward H. Lazarus, *Third Parties in America* (Princeton, Princeton University Press, 1984), p. 113.

45 Quoted in Rowland Evans and Robert D. Novak, *Nixon in the White House* (New York, Vintage Books, 1971), p. 145.

46 See Paul Allen Beck, 'Partisan Dealignment in the Postwar South', *American Political Science Review*, June 1977, pp. 477-8.

47 For an account of this process see John Egerton, *The Americanization of Dixie* (New York, Harpers Magazine Press, 1979).

48 See Robert Estall, 'The Changing Balance of the Northern and Southern Regions of the United States', *Journal of American Studies*, December 1980, p. 365.

49 See Susan W. Hammond, Daniel P. Mulhollan, Arthur G. Stevens, 'Informal Congressional Caucuses and Agenda Setting', *Western Political Quarterly*, December 1985, pp. 583-605.

50 The Northeast-Midwest Congressional Coalition is examined by Robert J. Dilger, *The Sunbelt/Snowbelt Controversy* (New York, New York University Press, 1982).

51 *Congressional Quarterly Weekly Report*, 6 December 1975, p. 2625.

52 Lance LeLoup, 'The Impact of Domestic Spending Patterns on Senate Support: An Examination of Three Policy Areas', *American Politics Quarterly* (5), 1977, pp. 219-36.

53 Wayne Greenhaw, *Elephants in the Cottonfields* (New York, Macmillan, 1982), p. 158.

54 *Congressional Quarterly Weekly Report*, 28 June 1980, p. 1749.

55 For an excellent study of 'Western Progressivism' see Ronald L. Feinman, *Twilight of Progressivism* (Baltimore, Johns Hopkins University Press, 1981).

56 Michael W. Miles, *The Odyssey of the American Right* (New York, Oxford University Press, 1980), p. 4.

57 Edward Kennedy and Mark Hatfield, *Freeze! How You Can Help Prevent Nuclear War* (New York, Bantam Books, 1982).

58 See Conrad Joyner, *The Republican Dilemma* (Tucson, University of Arizona Press, 1963), p. 5.

59 Karl Hess, *In a Cause That Will Triumph* (Garden City, Doubleday, 1967), p. 16.

60 Jacob Javits, *Order of Battle* (New York, Atheneum, 1969), p. 46.

61 *New York Times*, 12 June 1977, XI, p. 7.

62 Richard Schweiker tended to become more conservative in the late 1970s. For example, he voted against school busing and the Panama Canal Treaties.

63 *National Journal*, 8 May 1982.

64 For Jacob Javits's role in the formulation of the War Powers Resolution see Robert F. Turner, *The War Powers Resolution* (Philadelphia, Foreign Policy Research Institute, 1983), pp. 10-12. See also Jacob Javits, *Who Makes War? The President Versus the Congress* (New York, Morrow, 1973).

65 See William R. Shaffer, *Party and Ideology in the US Congress* (Washington D.C., University Press of America, 1980), p. 114.

66 *New York Times*, 22 March 1984, p. 134.

67 Ornstein, Mann, Malbin, Bibby, *op. cit.*, pp. 226-33.

68 *Ibid.*, pp. 234-41.

69 Nelson W. Polsby, 'Coalitions and Factions in American Politics: An Institutional View' in Lipsett ed., *Emerging Coalitions, op. cit.*, p. 117.

70 See Raymond Moley, *The Republican Opportunity* (New York, Duell, Sloan and Pearce, 1962), p. 160.

71 Polsby, 'Coalitions and Factions', *op. cit.*, p. 161.

72 Cited in James T. Patterson, *Mr Republican* (Boston, Houghton Mifflin, 1972), p. 329.

73 Gary W. Reichard, *Reaffirmation of Republicanism* (Knoxsville, University of Tennessee Press, 1975), p. 39.

74 *Ibid.*, p. 60.

75 See Marquis Childs, *Eisenhower: The Captive Hero* (New York, Harcourt, 1958), p. 142.

76 Cited in Clinton Rossiter, *Conservatism in America* (London, Heineman, 1955), p. 189.

77 See Larry N. Rieselbach, *The Roots of Isolationism* (Indianapolis, Bobbs-Merrill, 1966), chapter 5; and Larry Pressler, *US Senators From the Prairie* (Vermillion, Dakota Press, 1982), p. 11.

78 Mainstream Republicans dominated the Party Leadership from 1959 when Senator Everett Dirksen (R – Ill) was elected leader. Hugh Scott replaced him in 1969 and had Robert Griffin as his whip. Howard Baker and Ted Stevens took over from Scott and Griffin in 1977.

79 *National Journal*, 10 September 1983, p. 1826.

80 Cited by Henry Fairlie, *op. cit.*, p. 68.

81 Cited in Richard Hofstadter, *The Paranoid Style in American Politics* (New York, Alfred Knopf, 1965), p. 97.

82 Robert E. Hartley, *Charles H. Percy* (New York, Rand McNally, 1975), p. 112.

83 Barry Goldwater, *Conscience of a Conservative* (Shepardsville, Victor Publishing, 1960).

84 *Ibid.*, p. 43.

85 James Reichley, *Conservatives in an Age of Change* (Washington D.C., Brookings, 1981), p. 27.

86 See Neal R. Peirce, *The Mountain States of America* (New York, W. W. Norton, 1972), pp. 25-7.

87 See Richard Viguerie, *The New Right: We're Ready to Lead* (Falls Church, The Viguerie Co., 1981), p. 56.

88 Neal R. Peirce, *The New England States of America* (New York, W. W. Norton, 1976), pp. 49-50.

89 Walter Dean Burnham, 'American Politics in the 1980s', in *The Current Crisis in American Politics* (Oxford, Oxford University Press, 1982), pp. 251-2.

90 See Paul Weyrich, 'Blue Collar or Blue Blood', in Robert W. Whitaker ed., *The

New Right Papers (New York, St Martin's Press, 1982), p. 49.

91 Quoted by Kevin Phillips, *Post-Conservative America* (New York, Random House, 1981), p. 47.

92 *Ibid.*, pp. 49–50.

93 *Congressional Quarterly Weekly Report*, 5 August 1978, p. 2022.

94 *Ibid.*, p. 2023.

95 Much of the material in this section was first published in Christopher J. Bailey, 'The US Senate: The New Individualism and the New Right', *Parliamentary Affairs*, July 1986, pp. 354–67.

96 *Congressional Quarterly Weekly Report*, 12 May 1979, p. 903.

97 *New York Times*, 26 June 1979, p. A13.

98 Senator Allen's career is discussed in David J. Barling, 'The Role of the Individual Senator and Adaptive Change in the U.S. Senate, 1969 to 1978', Ph.D. Thesis, The University of Keele, 1982, pp. 178–211.

99 Once cloture had been invoked further debate was limited to 100 hours. Prior to 1979 quorum calls and votes on amendments were not counted against the 100 hours.

100 At the outset of the 51st Congress (1889–90) when Read assumed office, filibustering by the minority in the House had reached such proportions that it had become difficult for the majority to transact business. The minority was able to paralyse the House by introducing a series of dilatory motions, such as motions to recess or adjourn, or by demanding time-consuming roll-call votes on other motions.

101 *Congressional Quarterly Weekly Report*, 2 September 1982, p. 2180.

102 Interview, Gregory Butler, director of operations, Coalitions for America, 19 October 1983.

103 *New York Times*, 4 October 1984, p. 1318.

104 *National Journal*, 21 January 1984, p. 24.

105 See Neal R. Peirce, *The Pacific States of America* (New York, W. W. Norton, 1972), p. 18.

Chapter Five—The party leadership

1 For an account of the early development of the floor leadership posts see Margaret Munk, 'Origin and Development of the Party Floor Leadership in the US Senate', *Capitol Studies*, winter 1974, pp. 23–41.

2 *Congressional Record*, 96th Congress, 2nd sess., 9 May 1980, p. S5059.

3 David B. Truman, *The Congressional Party* (New York, John Wiley, 1959), p. 96.

4 Woodrow Wilson, *Congressional Government* (London, Constable, 1914), p. 213.

5 Quoted in the Introduction to Frank H. Mackaman ed., *Understanding Congressional Leadership* (Washington D.C., Congressional Quarterly Press, 1981), p. 2.

6 *Congressional Quarterly Weekly Report*, 12 September 1981, p. 1743.

7 Roger H. Davidson and Walter J. Oleszek, *Congress and its Members* (Washington D.C., Congressional Quarterly Press, 1981), p. 184.

8 William J. Crotty and Gary C. Jacobson, *American Parties in Decline* (Boston, Little, Brown and Co., 1980), p. 184.

9 See Barbara Hinckley, *Stability and Change in Congress* (New York, Harper and Row, 1983), p. 165.

10 Roger Davidson and Walter Oleszek, *op. cit.*, p. 184.

11 Walter J. Oleszek, *Congressional Procedures and the Policy Process* (Washington D.C., Congressional Quarterly Press, 1984), p. 26.

12 For an interesting discussion of this episode see Howard Baker, *No Margin for Error* (New York, Times Books, 1980), pp. 24–32.

13 *Congressional Record*, 96th Congress, 2nd sess., 18 April 1980, p. S3924.

14 See Robert L. Peabody, *Leadership in Congress* (Boston, Little, Brown and Co.,

1976), p. 325.

15 See Norman J. Ornstein, Robert L. Peabody, and David W. Rohde, 'The Contemporary Senate: Into the 1980s', in Lawrence C. Dodd and Bruce Oppenheimer eds., *Congress Reconsidered* (Washington D.C., Congressional Quarterly Press, 1981), p. 20.

16 Quoted in Roger Davidson and Walter Oleszek, *op. cit.*, p. 178.

17 Quoted in David M. Abshire and Ralph D. Nunberger, *The Growing Power of Congress* (Beverley Hills, Sage, 1981), p. 161.

18 See Randall B. Ripley, *Congress: Process and Policy* (New York, W. W. Norton, 1978), p. 210; and Charles O. Jones, *The Republican Party in American Politics* (London, Macmillan, 1965), chapter 5.

19 Donald A. Gross, 'Changing Patterns of Voting Agreement Among Senatorial Leadership 1947–1976', *Western Political Quarterly*, March 1984, p. 124.

20 *Congressional Quarterly Weekly Report*, 4 December 1982, p. 2973.

21 See Michael Malbin, *Unelected Representatives* (New York, Basic Books, 1980), pp. 12–13.

22 See Susan Schjelderup and Judy Schneider, 'Congressional Committee Staffs and Funding', *Issue Brief* (Washington D.C., CRS, 1983), p. 2.

23 Hugh A. Bone, 'An Introduction to the Senate Policy Committees', *American Political Science Review*, June 1956, p. 352. See also Hugh A. Bone, *Party Committees and National Politics* (Seattle, University of Washington Press, 1958); and Malcolm E. Jewell, 'The Senate Republican Party Committee and Foreign Policy', *Western Political Quarterly*, December 1959, pp. 966–80.

24 *National Journal*, 21 May 1977, p. 780.

25 Cited by Joshua Muravchik, 'The Senate and National Security' in David M. Abshire and Ralph D. Nurnberger, *op. cit.*, p. 249.

26 *Ibid.*, p. 250.

27 See Charles O. Jones, *The United States Congress* (Homewood, Ill., The Dorsey Press, 1982), p. 304.

28 Rule changes adopted by the Democratic Caucus in 1973 left it to the Caucus rather than the Rules Committee to decide whether a particular amendment should be considered on the House floor, thereby effectively terminating the Rule Committee's power to send bills unilaterally to the House floor with closed rules—rules banning floor amendments.

29 For a discussion of the relationship between the Rules Committee and the leadership of the House see Bruce I. Oppenheimer, 'The Changing Relationship Between House Leadership and the Rules Committee' in Frank H. Mackaman ed., *op. cit.*, pp. 218–24.

30 The Senate Committee on Rules and Administration plays an administrative rather than a legislative role in the Senate's proceedings. See US Senate, Committee on Rules and Administration, *History of the Committee on Rules and Administration*, 96th Congress, 1st sess., 2 August 1979.

31 US Senate, Committee on Rules and Administration, *Senate Manual*, 97th Congress, 1st sess., 1981, Rule VII, p. 7.

32 See William J. Keefe and Morris S. Ogul, *The American Legislative Process* (Englewood Cliffs, Prentice-Hall, 1981), pp. 271–2; and Ralph K. Huitt, 'The Internal Distribution of Influence, The Senate', in Ralph K. Huitt and Robert L. Peabody eds., *Congress: Two Decades of Analysis* (New York, Harper and Row, 1969), p. 191.

33 US Senate, Temporary Select Committee to Study the Senate Committee System, 'Operation of the Senate Committee System', *Appendix to the Second Report*, John G. Stewart, 'Committee System Management: Getting the Act Together—the Senate Leadership's Role in the Policy Process', 1977, p. 7.

34 See Wayne Greenhaw, *Elephants in the Cottonfields* (New York, Macmillan, 1982), pp. 208–9.

35 For an examination of Dirksen's leadership style and philosophy see Neil MacNeil, *Dirksen: Portrait of a Public Man* (New York, World Publications, 1970).

36 See Randall B. Ripley, *Power in the Senate* (New York, St Martin's Press, 1969), p. 712.

37 *National Journal*, 11 April 1981, p. 597.

38 See, for example, the exchange between Baker and Byrd over changing the date for the second concurrent budget resolution from 15 September 1980 to 25 August 1980. *Congressional Record*, 96th Congress, 2nd sess., 9 May 1980, p. S5064.

39 Quoted in Robert Peabody, 'Senate Party Leadership: From the 1950s to the 1980s' in Frank Mackaman ed., *op. cit.*, p. 86.

40 See Jimmy Carter, *Keeping Faith* (London, Collins, 1982), pp. 87–8.

41 *New York Times*, 5 January 1977, p. A14.

42 *New York Times*, 25 March 1982, VI, p. 17.

43 *Washington Post*, 18 February 1982, p. A1.

44 *National Journal*, 11 April 1981, p. 596.

45 *New York Times*, 2 October 1981, p. A24.

46 *Washington Post*, 18 February 1982, p. A8.

47 *Congressional Quarterly Weekly Report*, 12 September 1981, p. 1742.

48 Roger H. Davidson and Thomas Kephart, *Indicators of Senate Activity and Workload* (Washington D.C., CRS, 1985), p. 31.

49 Senator Baker's proposals on televising the Senate were incorporated in S.Res 20 (1981).

50 US Senate, Committee on Rules and Administration, 'Television and Radio Coverage of Proceedings in the Senate Chamber', *Committee Print*, 97th Congress, 1st sess., 1981, pp. 4–5.

51 *Ibid.*, p. 6.

52 *New York Times*, 3 December 1980, p. A22.

53 See Richard Beth, 'Senate Organisation and Operations: Proposals for Change in the 98th Congress', *Issue Brief* (Washington D.C., CRS, 1983), pp. 3–6.

54 *Congressional Quarterly Almanac 1984*, p. 209.

55 See Walter J. Oleszek, *op. cit.*, p. 152.

56 *Congressional Record*, 95th Congress, 1st sess., 21 January 1977, p. S928.

57 See Stephen K. Bailey, *Congress in the Seventies* (New York, St Martin's Press, 1976), p. 44.

58 See Ted Siff and Alan Weil, *Ruling Congress* (New York, Grossman, 1975), p. 80.

59 *New York Times*, 10 January 1983, p. A16.

60 *National Journal*, 10 September 1983, p. 1825.

61 *New York Times*, 2 October 1981, p. A24.

62 See Christopher J. Bailey, 'The United States Senate: The New Individualism and the New Right', *Parliamentary Affairs*, July 1986, pp. 354–67.

63 *New York Times*, 25 April 1981, p. A2.

64 US Senate, Committee on the Judiciary, Subcommittee on the Separation of Powers, *Hearings*, 'The Human Life Bill', 97th Congress, 1st sess., vol. 1, p. 51.

65 *Ibid.*, p. 37.

66 *New York Times*, 28 March 1982, VI, p. 74.

67 *New York Times*, 7 May 1983, p. A7.

68 *New York Times*, 28 March 1982, VI, p. 74.

69 See Michael Barone and Grant Ujifusa, *The Almanac of American Politics 1984* (Washington D.C., National Journal, 1983), p. xxxi.

70 Roger H. Davidson, Walter J. Oleszek, Edward M. Davis, 'Changing the Guard in the United States Senate, 1981', Paper presented to the 1982 annual meeting of the American Political Science Association, Denver, Colorado, 1–4 September 1981, p. 24.

71 *New York Times*, 27 March 1981, p. A14.

72 Paul Weyrich quoted in the *Washington Post*, 18 February 1982, p. A8.

73 US Senate, Committee on the Judiciary, Subcommittee on the Constitution, *Hearings*, 'Balancing the Budget', 97th Congress, 1st sess., 29 May 1981, p. 2.

74 For President Carter's view of his relationship with Congress see Jimmy Carter, *op. cit.*, chapter 3.

75 *Congressional Quarterly Weekly Report*, 12 September 1981, p. 1747.

76 *National Journal*, 11 April 1981, pp. 597-8.

77 *Ibid.*, p. 598.

78 *New York Times*, 28 March 1982, VI, p. 19.

79 See I. M. Destler, 'The Evolution of Reagan's Foreign Policy', in Fred I. Greenstein, ed., *The Reagan Presidency* (Baltimore, Johns Hopkins University Press, 1983), pp. 122-3.

80 Cited by Alexander M. Haig, *Caveat* (London, Weidenfeld and Nicolson, 1984), p. 185.

81 *Time*, 9 November 1981, pp. 12-13.

82 Anthony King, 'A Mile And a Half Is a Long Way' in Anthony King ed., *Both Ends of the Avenue* (Washington D.C., American Enterprise Institute, 1983), p. 264.

83 *New York Times*, 28 March 1982, VI, p. 17.

84 *National Journal*, 10 September 1983, p. 1824.

85 See Norman J. Ornstein, Thomas E. Mann, Michael J. Malbin, John F. Bibby, *Vital Statistics on Congress 1982* (Washington D.C., American Enterprise Institute, 1982), pp. 166-7.

86 Figures from *Congressional Quarterly Almancas 1981-1984*.

87 The six belonging to the moderate wing of the party were: Arlen Specter (R - Penn), John Heinz (R - Penn), Bob Packwood (R - Ore), John Chafee (R - Mo), William Cohen (R - Me) and Lowell Weicker (R - Conn). The three belonging to the conservative wing of the party were: Barry Goldwater (R - Ariz), John East (R - NC), and Jesse Helms (R - NC). See *Congressional Quarterly Weekly Report*, 16 July 1983, p. 1429.

88 *Time*, 3 January 1983, p. 36.

89 *National Journal*, 10 September 1983, p. 1825.

90 Roger H. Davidson, Walter J. Oleszek, and Edward M. Davis, *op. cit.*, pp. 32-3.

91 *Congressional Record*, 97th Congress, 2nd sess., 21 July 1982, p. S8752.

92 *Congressional Quarterly Weekly Report*, 16 July 1983, p. 1429.

93 *National Journal*, 12 April 1986, p. 867.

Chapter Six—Presidential-senatorial relations

1 See Ronald C. Mose and Steven C. Teel, 'Congress as Policy-Maker: A Necessary Reappraisal', *Political Science Quarterly*, September 1970, p. 443.

2 Samuel P. Huntington, 'Congressional Responses to the Twentieth Century', in David B. Truman ed., *The Congress and America's Future* (Englewood Cliffs, Prentice-Hall, 1965), p. 23.

3 See Charles O. Jones, 'Congress and the Presidency' in Thomas E. Mann and Norman J. Ornstein eds., *The New Congress* (Washington D.C., American Enterprise Institute, 1981), p. 225.

4 William J. Keefe, *Congress and the American People* (Englewood Cliffs, Prentice-Hall, 1980), p. 120.

5 Ben W. Heineman and Curtis A. Hessles, *Memorandum For the President* (New York, Random House, 1980), p. 91.

6 See James Reichley, *Conservatives in an Age of Change* (Washington D.C., Brookings, 1981), p. 323.

7 James Madison, 'Federalist Papers No. 46' in Alexander Hamilton, James Madison, and John Jay, *The Federalist Papers* (New York, New American Library, 1961), p. 296.

8 Gerald R. Ford, *A Time to Heal* (New York, Harper and Row, 1979), p. 150.

9 Jimmy Carter, *Public Papers 1978*, vol. 1, p. 1414.

10 See Richard A. Watson and Norman C. Thomas, *The Politics of the Presidency* (New York, John Wiley, 1983), pp. 296-7.

11 See Aaron Wildavsky, 'The Two Presidencies', *Trans-Action*, December 1966, pp. 7–14; and Lance LeLoup and Steven A. Schull, 'Congress versus the Executive: The "Two Presidencies" Reconsidered', *Social Science Quarterly*, March 1979, p. 712.

12 For an examination of the Senate's opposition to the Versailles Treaty see Arthur S. Link, *Woodrow Wilson: Revolution, War and Peace* (Arlington Heights, AHM Publishing, 1979), pp. 105–8. The opposition to America's entry into the World Court is examined in Robert Dallek, *Franklin D. Roosevelt and American Foreign Policy* (New York, Oxford University Press, 1979), p. 95.

13 Quoted by Richard F. Fenno, *Congressmen in Committees* (Boston, Little, Brown and Co., 1973), p. 141.

14 *Congressional Record*, 95th Congress, 2nd sess., 15 May 1978, p. S7378.

15 The only member to be re-elected was Senator John Glenn (D – Ohio).

16 The figures being compared are the President's percentage of the presidential vote in each state, and each senator's poll on the last occasion on which he stood for election.

17 President Reagan's success rate in the Senate in 1981 was eleven percentage points higher than that achieved by Carter in 1977. Their respective success rates were 87·3 per cent and 76·1 per cent.

18 *Congressional Quarterly Almanac 1981*, p. 19C.

19 *New York Times*, 4 December 1980, p. D22.

20 Jimmy Carter, *Keeping Faith* (London, Collins, 1982), p. 80.

21 See Eric L. Davis, 'Legislative Reform and the Decline of Presidential Influence on Capitol Hill', *British Journal of Political Science*, October 1979, pp. 466–7.

22 Nelson W. Polsby, *Consequences of Party Reform* (New York, Oxford University Press, 1980), pp. 106–7.

23 See Eric L. Davis, 'Legislative Liaison in the Carter Administration', *Political Science Quarterly*, summer 1979, pp. 287–301.

24 James Fallows, 'The Passionless Presidency', *Atlantic*, May 1979, p. 41.

25 *Congressional Quarterly Weekly Report*, 3 February 1979, p. 195.

26 *New York Times*, 13 March 1977, IV, p. 23.

27 See Haynes Johnson, *In the Absence of Power* (New York, The Viking Press, 1980), p. 22.

28 *New York Times*, 8 January 1978, VI, p. 32.

29 See Austin Ranney, 'The Carter Administration' in Austin Ranney ed., *The American Elections of 1980* (Washington D.C., American Enterprise Institute, 1981), pp. 18–19.

30 *New York Times*, 13 August 1978, p. 107.

31 *New York Times*, 8 January 1978, VI, p. 33.

32 Jimmy Carter, *Keeping Faith, op. cit.*, p. 67. For comments on Carter's radical nominations see Betty Glad, *Jimmy Carter* (New York, W. W. Norton, 1980), p. 418.

33 See Richard Cohen, 'The President's Problems' in Thomas E. Cronin ed., *The Carter Presidency Under Pressure* (Washington D.C., National Journal Reprint Series, 1979), p. 35.

34 *New York Times*, 27 January 1977, p. A1.

35 *Ibid.*

36 *Congressional Quarterly Almanac 1977*, p. 654.

37 George C. Edwards, *Presidential Influence in Congress* (San Francisco, W. H. Freeman, 1980), p. 175.

38 Eric L. Davis, 'Legislative Liaison in the Carter Administration', *op. cit.*, p. 289.

39 *Congressional Quarterly Weekly Report*, 3 February 1979, p. 197.

40 *New York Times*, 4 December 1980, p. D22.

41 *Congressional Quarterly Weekly Report*, 3 February 1979, p. 197.

42 Betty Glad, *op. cit.*, p. 425.

43 The Senate deemed that these conditions had been fulfilled with the election of Bishop Abel Mazorewa as Prime Minister. Senator Sam Hayakawa (R – Calif),

summing up the feelings of most senators argued that 'It seems to me that the Administration's refusal to lift the sanctions does represent a *de facto* support of the guerillas'. US Senate, Committee on Foreign Relations, 'Trade Sanctions Against Rhodesia', *Hearings*, 96th Congress, 1st sess., 12 June 1979, p. 22. The Senate promptly passed an amendment to the Fiscal 1980 Defense Department Authorisation Bill (S.428) which required Carter to lift sanctions against Rhodesia immediately.

44 Lawrencel H. Shoup, *The Carter Presidency and Beyond* (Palo Alto, Ramparts Press, 1980), p. 183.

45 *New York Times*, 6 January 1981, p. B8.

46 *Congressional Quarterly Weekly Report*, 1 February 1975, pp. 226–8.

47 Ronald Reagan, *Public Papers 1982*, vol. 2, p. 257.

48 *Ibid.*, p. 949.

49 For example, see Ronald Reagan, *Public Papers 1981*, pp. 896, 626, 1071; and Ronald Reagan, *Public Papers 1982*, p. 949.

50 Quoted in Randall B. Ripley and Grace A. Franklin, *Congress, The Bureaucracy and Public Policy* (Homewood, The Dorsey Press, 1984), p. 62.

51 For an early appraisal of the legislative possibilities of central clearance see Richard E. Neustadt, 'Presidency and Legislation: The Growth of Central Clearance', *American Political Science Review* (48) 1954, pp. 641–71. A more recent account of the OMB is Larry Berman, *The Office of Management and Budget* (Princeton, Princeton University Press, 1974).

52 Fred I. Greenstein, 'The Need for an Early Appraisal of the Reagan Presidency' in Fred I. Greenstein ed., *The Reagan Presidency* (Baltimore, Johns Hopkins University Press, 1983), p. 16.

53 See Allen Schick, 'How The Budget Was Won And Lost' in Norman J. Ornstein ed., *President and Congress: Assessing Reagan's First Years* (Washington D.C., American Enterprise Institute, 1982), pp. 14–43.

54 Randall B. Ripley and Grace A. Franklin, *op. cit.*, p. 170.

55 The figures quoted show the percentage of votes on which senators from specific regions supported the President's position on legislation.

56 Thomas M. Franck and Edward Weisband, *Foreign Policy By Congress* (New York, Oxford University Press, 1979), p. 92.

57 *Congressional Quarterly Almanac 1977*, p. 374.

58 US Senate, Committee on Foreign Relations, 'Rhodesia', *Hearings*, 96th Congress, 1st sess., 27 November 1979, p. 9.

59 *Congressional Quarterly Almanac 1981*, p. 250.

60 *New York Times*, 28 November 1984, p. A24.

61 *New York Times*, 7 May 1983, p. A7.

62 *New York Times*, 20 May 1983, p. A15.

63 See *Congressional Quarterly Almanac 1978*, p. 410.

64 US Senate, Committee on Banking, Housing, and Urban Affairs, 'The President's New Anti-Inflation Program', *Hearings*, 95th Congress, 2nd sess., 3 November 1978, p. 7.

65 See Austin Ranney, 'The Carter Administration', *op. cit.*, p. 26.

66 *New York Times*, 16 February 1982, p. A16.

67 Cited by James Reichley, *op. cit.*, p. 326.

68 The Senate *completed* consideration of the reconciliation legislation on 2 April, a full two weeks before the House Budget Committee *began* dealing with the legislation on 16 April.

69 John W. Ellwood, 'Inter-Chamber Relations in the US Congress and the Congressional Budget Process'. Paper presented for the Conference on the Congressional Budget Process, Carl Albert Center for the Study of Legislative Affairs, University of Oklahoma, 12–13 February 1982, p. 5.

70 *Los Angeles Times*, 29 July 1982, Part 1, p. 8.

71 Charles H. Percy, 'The Partisan Gap', *Foreign Policy* (45), 1981–2, p. 9.

72 John G. Tower, 'Congress Versus the President: The Formulation and Imple-

mentation of American Foreign Policy', *Foreign Affairs* (60:2) 1981/1982, p. 230.

73 *Congressional Quarterly Weekly Report*, 14 March 1981, p. 477.

74 *New York Times*, 1 October 1981, p. A9.

75 John G. Tower, 'Congress Versus the President', p. 233.

76 See Joshua Muravchik, 'The Senate and National Security: A New Mood' in David M. Abshire and Ralph D. Nurnberger eds., *The Growing Power of Congress* (Beverley Hills, Sage, 1981), pp. 235-6.

77 See Christopher J. Bailey, 'President Reagan, The US Senate, and American Foreign Policy, 1981-1986'. Paper presented to the Annual Conference of the American Politics Group (Political Studies Association of the United Kingdom), Birkbeck College, University of London, 3-5 January 1987.

Chapter Seven—The new individualism

1 *New York Times*, 26 November 1984, p. A1.

2 *Congressional Record*, 97th Congress, 2nd sess., 22 September 1982, pp. S11939-S11940.

3 *New York Times*, 26 November 1984, p. A1.

4 *New York Times*, 21 March 1983, p. B6.

5 *New York Times*, 8 April 1983, p. D15.

6 *New York Times*, 21 March 1983, p. B6.

7 See Richard S. Beth, 'Senate Organisation and Operations: Proposals For Change in the 98th Congress', *Issue Brief* (Washington D.C., Congressional Research Service, 1983), p. 2.

8 See Roger H. Davidson and Thomas Kephart, *Indicators of Senate Activity and Workload* (Washington D.C., Congressional Research Service, 1985), p. 9.

9 US Senate, Temporary Select Committee to Study the Senate Committee System, *Report Together With Prepared Resolution*, 98th Congress, 2nd sess., p. 5 (my italics).

Select bibliography

Abramson, Paul R., *Political Attitudes in America* (San Francisco, W. H. Freeman & Co., 1983).

Abshire, David M. and Nurnberger, Ralph D. eds. *The Growing Power of Congress* (Beverley Hills, Sage, 1981).

Agranoff, Robert, *The Management of Electoral Campaigns* (Boston, Holbrook, 1976).

Alexander, Herbert E. *Financing the 1976 Election* (Washington D.C., Congressional Quarterly Press, 1979).

——— *Financing Politics* (Washington D.C., Congressional Quarterly Press, 1980).

——— *Financing the 1980 Elections* (Lexington, Mass., Lexington Books, 1983).

Arico, Susan M. *Trends in the 1980 Congressional Elections* (Washington D.C., The Free Congress Research and Education Foundation, 1981).

Asher, Herbert A. 'The Learning of Legislative Norms', *American Political Science Review*, June 1973, pp. 449–513.

Bach, Stanley, 'Germaneness Rules and Bicameral Relations in the U.S. Congress', *Legislative Studies Quarterly*, August 1982, pp. 341–57.

Bailey, Christopher J. 'The U.S. Senate: The New Individualism and the New Right', *Parliamentary Affairs*, July 1986, pp. 354–67.

Bailey, Stephen K. *Congress in the Seventies* (New York, St Martin's Press, 1970).

Baker, Howard H. *No Margin For Error* (New York, Times Books, 1980).

Baker, R. *The United States Senate: A Historical Bibliography* (Washington D.C., GOP, 1977).

Barone, Michael and Ujifusa, Grant, *The Almanac of American Politics 1982* (Washington D.C., Barone & Co. 1981).

——— *The Almanac of American Politics 1984* (Washington D.C., National Journal, 1983).

Bartley, Numan V. and Graham, Hugh D. *Southern Politics and the Second Reconstruction* (Baltimore, Johns Hopkins University Press, 1975).

Bartley, Numan V. 'The South and Sectionalism in American Politics', *Journal of Politics*, August 1976, pp. 234–57.

Bass, Jack and Devries, Walter, *The Transformation of Southern Politics* (New York, Basic Books, 1976).

Beck, Paul A. 'Partisan Dealignment in the Postwar South', *American Political Science Review*, June 1977, pp. 477–96.

Beeman, Richard R. 'Unlimited Debate in the Senate: The First Phase', *Political Science Quarterly*, September 1968, pp. 419–59.

Berman, Larry, *The Office Management and Budget 1921–1979* (Princeton, Princeton University Press, 1979).

Bibby, John nd Davidson, Roger, *On Capital Hill* (New York, Rinehart and Winston, 1967).

Billington, Monroe L. *The Political South int he Twentieth Century* (New York, Charles Scribner's, 1975).

Blasi, Vincent ed. *The Burger Court* (New Haven, Yale University Press, 1983).

Bolling, Richard, *House Out of Order* (New York, Dutton, 1965).

Bone, Hugh A. 'An Introduction to the Senate Policy Committees', *American Political Science Review*, June 1956, pp. 339–59.

_____ *Party Committees and National Politics* (Seattle, University of Washington Press, 1958).

Brady, David W. 'Critical Elections, Congressional Parties, and Clusters of Policy Changes', *British Journal of Political Science*, January 1978, pp. 79-100.

Broder, David S. and Hess, Stephen, *The Republican Establishment* (New York, Harper and Row, 1967).

Brown, George R. *The Leadership of Congress* (Indianapolis, Bobbs-Merrill, 1922).

Brun, Stanley P. *Geography and Politics in America* (New York, Harper and Row, 1974).

Buchanan, Patrick J. *Conservative Votes–Liberal Victories* (New York, New York Times Books, 1975).

Burdette, Franklin L. *Filibustering in the Senate* (Princeton, Princeton University Press, 1940).

Burnham, Walter D. *Critical Elections and the Mainsprings of American Politics* (New York, W. W. Norton, 1970).

_____ *The Current Crisis in American Politics* (Oxford, Oxford University Press, 1982).

Campbell, Bruce A. 'Patterns of Change in the Partisan Loyalties of Native Southerners: 1952-1972', *Journal of Politics*, August 1977, pp. 730-61.

Carlson, Jody, *George Wallace and the Politics of Powerlessness* (New Brunswick, Transaction Books, 1981).

Carter, Jimmy, *Keeping Faith* (London, Collins, 1982).

Chamberlain, Lawrence H. *The President, Congress, and Legislation* (New York, Oxford University Press, 1946).

Childs, Marquis, *Eisenhower: Captive Hero* (New York, Harcourt, 1958).

Chubb, John E. and Peterson, Paul e. eds., *The New Direction in American Politics* (Washington D.C., Brookings, 1985).

Cigler, Allan J. and Loomis, Burdette A. eds., *Interest Group Politics* (Washington D.C., Congressional Quarterly Press, 1983).

Clark, Joseph S. *Congress: The Sapless Branch* (New York, Harper and Row, 1964).

Clubb, Jerome M. and Allen, Howard W., 'Party Loyalty in the Progressive Years: The Senate 1909-1915', *Journal of Politics*, August 1967, pp. 567-84.

Conway, Margaret M., 'Republican Political Party Nationalisation, Campaign Activities, And Their Implications for the Party System', *Publius*, winter 1983, pp. 1-17.

Cosman, Bernard and Hochshom, Robert eds., *Republican Politics: The 1964 Campaign and its Aftermath for the Party* (New York, Praeger, 1968).

Cotter, Cornelius P. and Bibby, John F. 'Institutional Development of Parties, and the Thesis of Party Decline', *Political Science Quarterly*, spring 1980, pp. 1-28.

Cotton, Norris, *In the Senate: Amidst the Conflict and Turmoil* (New York, Dodd, Mead & Co., 1978).

Crabb, Cecil V. and Holt, Pat M. *Invitation to Struggle: Congress, the President and Foreign Policy* (Washington D.C., Congressional Quarterly Press, 1980).

Crawford, Alan, *Thunder on the Right* (New York, Pantheon, 1980).

Crittenden, John A. *Parties and Elections in the U.S.* (Englewood Cliffs, Prentice Hall, 1982).

Cronin, Thomas E. *The Carter Presidency Under Pressure* (Washington D.C., National Journal Reprint Series, 1979).

Crotty, William J. and Jacobson, Gary C. *American Parties in Decline* (Boston, Little, Brown and Co., 1980).

Dallek, Robert, *Franklin D. Roosevelt and American Foreign Policy* (New York, Oxford University Press, 1979).

Davidson, Roger H., Kovenock, David M., O'Leary, Michael, *Congress in Crisis* (New York, Hawthorn Books, 1969).

Davidson, Roger H. and Oleszek, Walter J. *Congress and its Members* (Washington D.C., Congressional Quarterly Press, 1981).

Davidson Roger H. 'Congressional Committees As Moving Targets', *Legislative Studies Quarterly*, February 1986, pp. 19-39.

Davis, Eric L. 'Legislative Liaison in the Carter Administration', *Political Science*

Quarterly, summer 1979, pp. 287-301.

———— 'Legislative Reform and the Decline of Presidential Influence on Capitol Hill', *British Journal of Political Science*, October 1979, pp. 465-79.

Dilger, Robert J. *The Sunbelt/Snowbelt Controversy* (New York, New York University Press, 1982).

Dodd, Lawrence C. and Oppenheimer, Bruce I. *Congress Reconsidered* (Washington D.C., Congressional Quarterly Press, 1985).

Dodd, Lawrence C. and Schott, Richard L. *Congress and the Administrative State* (New York, John Wiley, 1979).

Donovan, Robert J. *Tumultuous Years* (New York, W. W. Norton, 1982).

Drew, Elizabeth, *Senator* (New York, Touchstone, 1980).

Edwards, George C. *Presidential Influence in Congress* (San Francisco, W. H. Freeman, 1980).

Egerton, John, *The Americanisation of Dixie* (New York, Harper's Magazine Press, 1979).

Eidelberg, Paul, *The Philosophy of the American Constitution* (New York, The Free Press, 1968).

Eldersveld, Samuel J. *Political Parties in American Society* (New York, Basic Books, 1982).

Estall, Robert, 'The Changing Balance of the Northern and Southern Regions Of the U.S.', *Journal of American Studies*, December 1980, pp. 365-86.

Evans, Rowland and Novak, Robert D. *Lyndon B. Johnson: The Exercise of Power* (London, George Allen and Unwin, 1967).

———— *Nixon in the White House: The Frustration of Power* (New York, Vintage Books, 1971).

———— *The Reagan Revolution* (New York, E. P. Dutton, 1981).

Fairlie, Henry, *The Parties* (New York, St Martin's Press, 1978).

Federal Election Commission, *Campaign Guide for Presidential Candidates and their Committees* (Washington D.C., FEC, 1979).

Feinman, Ronald L. *Twilight of Progressivism* (Baltimore, Johns Hopkins University Press, 1981).

Fenno, Richard F. *Congressmen in Committees* (Boston, Little, Brown and Co., 1973).

———— *Home Style* (Boston, Little, Brown and Co., 1978).

———— *The U.S. Senate: A Bicameral Perspective* (Washington D.C., American Enterprise Institute, 1982).

Feulner, Edwin J. *Conservatives Stalk the House* (Ottawa, Ill., Green Hill, 1983).

Fiorina, Morris P. *Congress: Keystone of the Washington Establishment* (New Haven, Yale University Press, 1977).

———— *Retrospective Voting in American National Elections* (New Haven, Yale University Press, 1981).

Fishel, Jeff ed., *Parties and Elections in an Anti-Party Age* (Bloomington, Indiana University Press, 1978).

Foley, Michael, *The New Senate* (New Haven, Yale University Press, 1980).

Follett, Mary P. *The Speaker of the House of Representatives* (New York, Burt Franklin Reprint, 1974).

Ford, Gerald R. *A Time to Heal* (New York, Harper and Row, 1979).

Fox, Harrison W. and Hammond, Susan W. *Congressional Staffs* (New York, The Free Press, 1977).

Franck, Thomas M. and Weisband, Edward, *Foreign Policy By Congress* (Oxford, Oxford University Press, 1979).

Francombe, Colin, 'Abortion Politics in the U.S.', *Political Studies*, December 1980, pp. 613-21.

Fribourg, Marjorie G. *The U.S. Congress: Men Who Steered its Course 1787-1867* (Philadelphia, Macrae Smith, 1972).

Fuller, Hubert B. *The Speaker of the House* (Boston, Little, Brown and Co., 1909).

Glad, Betty, *Jimmy Carter* (New York, W. W. Norton, 1980).

Goldenberg, Edie N. and Traugott, Michael W. *Campaigning for Congress* (Washington

D.C., Congressional Quarterly Press, 1984).

Goldwater, Barry, *Conscience of a Conservative* (Shepardsville, Ky., Victor Publishing, 1960).

—— *With No Apologies* (New York, William Morrow, 1979).

Goldwin, Robert A. and Schambra, William A. eds., *How Democratic is the Constitution?* (Washington D.C., American Enterprise Institute, 1980).

Goodman, William, *The Two Party System in the U.S.* (New Jersey, D. Van Nostrand, 1965).

Greeley, Andrew M. 'How Conservative Are American Catholics?' *Political Science Quarterly*, summer 1977, pp. 199–218.

Greenhaw, Wayne, *Elephants in the Cottonfields* (New York, Macmillan, 1983).

Greenstein, Fred I. ed., *The Reagan Presidency* (Baltimore, Johns Hopkins University Press, 1983).

Griffith, Ernest S. *Congress: Its Contemporary Role* (New York, New York University Press, 1961).

Haig, Alexander, *Caveat* (London, Weidenfeld and Nicolson, 1984).

Hamilton, Alexander; Madison, James; Jay, John, *The Federalist Papers* (New York, New American Library, 1961).

Hammond, Susan W., Mulhollan, Daniel P., Stevens, Arthur G., 'Informal Congressional Caucuses and Agenda Setting', *Western Political Quarterly*, December 1985, pp. 583–605.

Harris, Joseph P. *Congress and the Legislative Process* (New York, McGraw-Hill, 1972).

Hartley, Robert E. *Charles H. Percy* (New York, Rand McNally, 1975).

Haynes, George H. *The Senate of the United States*, 2 vols. (Boston, Houghton Mifflin, 1938).

Heineman, Ben W. and Hessles, Curtis A. *Memorandum For the President* (New York, Random House, 1980).

Hess, Karl, *In a Cause that Will Triumph* (Green City, N.Y., Doubleday, 1967).

Hibbing, John R. and Alford, John R. 'Economic Conditions and the Forgotten Side of Congress: A Foray into U.S. Senate Elections', *British Journal of Political Science*, October 1982.

Hinckley, Barbara, 'Seniority 1975: Old Conflicts Confront New Facts', *British Journal of Political Science*, October 1977, pp. 383–400.

—— 'House Re-election and Senate Defeats: The Role of the Challenger', *British Journal of Political Science*, October 1980.

—— *Congressional Elections* (Washington D.C., Congressional Quarterly Press, 1981).

—— *Stability and Change in Congress* (New York, Harper and Row, 1983).

Hofstadter, Richard, *The Paranoid Style in American Politics* (New York, Alfred Knopf, 1965).

Holt, James, *Congressional Insurgents and the Party System 1909–1916* (Cambridge, Harvard University Press, 1967).

House, John W. ed., *United States Public Policy* (Oxford, Clarendon Press, 1983).

Huitt, Ralph K. 'The Outsider in the Senate: An Alternative Role', *American Political Science Review*, September 1961, pp. 566–75.

Huitt, Ralph K. and Peabody, Robert L. *Congress: Two Decades of Analysis* (New York, Harper and Row, 1969).

Jacobson, Gary C. 'The Effects of Campaign Spending in Congressional Elections', *American Political Science Review*, June 1978, pp. 469–91.

—— *Money in Congressional Elections* (New Haven, Yale University Press, 1980).

—— *The Politics of Congressional Elections* (Boston, Little, Brown and Co., 1983).

Javits, Jacob K. *Order of Battle* (New York, Atheneum, 1964).

—— *Who Makes War? The President Versus the Congress* (New York, Morrow, 1973).

Jewell, Malcolm E. 'The Senate Republican Policy Committee and Foreign Policy', *Western Political Quarterly*, December 1959.

Jewell, Malcolm E. and Patterson, Samuel C. *The Legislative Process in the United States* (New York, Random House, 1966).

Jewell, Malcolm E. and Olson, David M. *American State Parties and Elections* (Homewood, Ill., The Dorsey Press, 1982).

Johnson, Haynes, *In the Absence of Power* (New York, The Viking Press, 1980).

Jones, Charles O. *The Republican Party in American Politics* (London, Macmillan, 1965).

────── *The United States Congress* (Homewood, Ill., The Dorsey Press, 1982).

Jones Rochelle and Woll, Peter, *The Private World of Congress* (New York, The Free Press, 1979).

Joyner, Conrad, *The Republican Dilemma* (Tuscon, The University of Arizona Press, 1963).

Kayden, Xandra and Mahe, Eddie, *The Party Goes On* (New York, Basic Books, 1985).

Keefe, William J. *Congress and the American People* (Englewood Cliffs, Prentice Hall, 1980).

Keefe, William J. and Ogul, Morris S. *The American Legislative Process* (Englewood Cliffs, Prentice Hall, 1981).

Kelley, Stanley Professional, *Public Relations and Political Power* (Baltimore, Johns Hopkins University Press, 1956).

Kennedy, Edward M. and Hatfield, Mark O. *Freeze! How You Can Help Prevent Nuclear War* (New York, Bantam Books, 1982).

Kessel, John H. *The Goldwater Coalition* (New York, Bobbs Merrill, 1968).

Key, V. O. *Politics, Parties, and Pressure Groups* (New York, Thomas Crowell, 1952).

King, Anthony ed., *The New American Political System* (Washington D.C., American Enterprise Institute, 1978).

────── ed., *Both Ends of the Avenue* (Washington D.C., American Enterprise Institute, 1983).

Kostroski, Warren L. 'Party and Incumbency in Postwar Senate Elections: Trends, Patterns and Models', *American Political Science Review*, December 1973, pp. 1213–34.

Ladd, Everett C. and Hadley, Charles D. *Transformation of the Party System* (New York, W. W. Norton, 1978).

Ladd, Everett C. *Where Have All the Voters Gone?* (New York, W. W. Norton, 1982).

Lambert, John R. *Arthur P. Gorman* (Baton Rouge, Louisiana State University Press, 1963).

Lamis, Alexander P. *The Two-Party South* (New York, Oxford University Press, 1984).

LeLoup, Lance, 'The Impact of Domestic Spending Patterns on Senate Support: An Examination of Three Policy Areas', *American Politics Quarterly* (5), 1977, pp. 291–36.

Liebman, Robert C. and Wuthnow, Robert, eds., *The New Christian Right* (New York, Aldine Publishing, 1984).

Link, Arthur S. *Woodrow Wilson: Revolution, War and Peace* (Arlington Heights, Ill., AHM Publishing, 1979).

Lipset, Seymour M. *Emerging Coalitions in American Politics* (San Francisco, Institute for Contemporary Studies, 1978).

────── ed. *Party Coalitions in the 1980s* (San Francisco, Institute for Contemporary Studies, 1981).

────── and Raab, Earl, *The Politics of Unreason* (Chicago, The University of Chicago Press, 1978).

Mackaman, Frank H. ed., *Understanding Congressional Leadership* (Washington D.C., Congressional Quarterly Press, 1981).

McIntyre, Thomas, *The Fear Brokers* (New York, The Pilgrim Press, 1979).

McKinney, Gordon B. *Southern Mountain Republicans 1865-1900* (Chapel Hill, University of North Carolina Press, 1978).

McKenney, John C. and Thompson, Edgar T. *The South in Continuity and Change* (Durham, Duke University Press, 1965).

MacNeil, Neil, *Dirksen: Portrait of a Public Man* (New York, World Publications, 1970).

MacNeil, Robert, *The People Machine* (London, Eyre and Spottiswoode, 1970).

Madison, James, *Notes of Debate in the Federal Convention of 1787* (New York, W. W. Norton, 1964).

Malbin, Michael J. *Parties, Interest Groups and Campaign Finance Laws* (Washington D.C., American Enterprise Institute, 1980).

—— *Unelected Representatives* (New York, Basic Books, 1980).

—— ed. *Money and Politics in the United States* (Chatham, N.J., Chatham House, 1984).

Mann, Thomas and Ornstein, Norman J. eds., *The New Congress* (Washington D.C., American Enterprise Institute, 1981).

Mann, Thomas and Wolfinger, Raymond E. 'Candidates and Parties in Congressional Elections', *American Political Science Review*, September 1980, pp. 617-32.

Marcus, Robert D. *Grand Old Party: Political Structure in the Guilded Age 1880-1896* (New York, Oxford University Press, 1971).

Matthews, Donald R. *U.S. Senators and their World* (Chapel Hill, University of North Carolina Press, 1960).

Mayer, George H. *The Republican Party 1854-1964* (New York, Oxford University Press, 1964).

Mayhew, David R. *Congress: The Electoral Connection* (New Haven, Yale University Press, 1974).

Miles, Michael W. *The Odyssey of the American Right* (New York, Oxford University Press, 1980).

Molley, Raymond, *The Republican Opportunity* (New York, Duell, Sloan, and Pearce, 1962).

Moos, Malcolm, *The Republicans: A History of their Party* (New York, Random House, 1956).

Moreland, Lawrence W., Baker, Tod A., and Steed, Robert P. eds., *Contemporary Southern Political Attitudes and Behaviour* (New York, Praeger, 1982).

Mose, Ronald C. and Teel, Steven C. 'Congress as Policy Maker: A Necessary Reappraisal', *Political Science Quarterly*, September 1970, pp. 443-70.

Munk, Margaret, 'Origin and Development of the Party Floor Leadership in the U.S. Senate', *Capitol Studies*, winter 1974, pp. 23-41.

Murphy, Roy and Gulliver, Hal, *The Southern Strategy* (New York, Charles Scribner's Sons, 1971).

Nelson, Candice, 'The Effects of Incumbency on Voting in Congressional Elections 1964-1974', *Political Science Quarterly*, winter 1978, pp. 665-78.

Neustadt, Richard E. 'Presidency and Legislation: The Growth of Central Clearance', *American Political Science Review* (48), 1954, pp. 641-71.

Nie, Norman; Verba, Sidney; Petrocik, John R. *The Changing American Voter* (Cambridge, Harvard University Press, 1976).

Niemi, Richard G. and Weisberg, Herbert F. eds., *Controversies in American Voting Behaviour* (San Francisco, W. H. Freeman, 1976).

Nimmo, Dan, *The Political Persuaders* (Englewood Cliffs, Prentice Hall, 1970).

Orfield, Gary, *Congressional Power: Congress and Social Change* (New York, Harcourt Bruce Jovanovich, 1975).

Ornstein, Norman J. ed., *Congress in Change: Evolution and Reform* (New York, Praeger, 1975).

—— ed. *President and Congress: Assessing Reagan's First Year* (Washington D.C., American Enterprise Institute, 1982).

—— Mann, Thomas; Malbin, Michael; Bibby, John, *Vital Statistics on Congress 1982* (Washington D.C., American Enterprise Institute, 1982).

Page, Benjamin I. *Choices and Echoes in Presidential Elections* (Chicago, University of Chicago Press, 1978).

Palmer, J. L. and Sawhill, I. V. *The Reagan Experiment* (Washington D.C., The Urban Institute, 1982).

Parker, Glen and Davidson, Roger, 'Why Do Americans Love Their Congressmen So Much More Than Their Congress?' *Legislative Studies Quarterly*, February 1979, pp. 53-62.

Parmet, Herbert S. *JFK: The Presidency of John F. Kenendy* (Harmondsworth, Penguin, 1984).

Parris, Judith H. 'The Senate Reorganises its Committees, 1977', *Political Science Quarterly*, summer 1979.

Patterson, James T. *Congressional Conservatism and the New Deal* (Lexington, University of Kentucky Press, 1967).

—— *Mr Republican* (Boston, Houghton Mifflin, 1972).

Peabody, Robert L. *Leadership in Congress* (Boston, Little Brown and Co., 1976).

—— and Polsby, Nelson, eds., *New Perspectives on the House of Representatives* (Chicago, Rand McNally, 1977).

Peele, Gillian, 'Campaign Consultants', *Electoral Studies*, December 1982, pp. 355–62.

—— *Revival and Reaction* (Oxford, Oxford University Press, 1984).

Petit, Lawrence K. and Keynes, Edward, eds., *The Legislative Process in the U.S. Senate* (Chicago, Rand McNally, 1964).

Petrocik, John R. *Party Coalitions* (Chicago, University of Chicago Press, 1981).

Phillips, Kevin P. *The Emerging Republican Majority* (New Rochelle, Arlington House, 1969).

—— *Post-Conservative America* (New York, Random House, 1982).

Pitchell, Robert, 'The Influence of Professional Campaign Management Firms in Partisan Elections in California', *Western Political Quarterly*, June 1958.

Polsby, Nelson W. ed. *Congressional Behaviour* (New York, Random House, 1971).

—— *Consequences of Party Reform* (New York, Oxford University Press, 1983).

Pomper, Gerald M. ed. *The Election fo 1976: Reports and Interpretations* (New York, Longman, 1977).

—— ed. *Party Renewal in America* (New York, Praeger, 1980).

—— ed. *The Elections of 1980: Reports and Interpretations* (Chatham, Chatham House, 1981).

Prewitt, Kenneth and Nowlin, William, 'Political Ambition and the Behaviour of Incumbent Politicians', *Western Political Quarterly*, June 1964, pp. 298–308.

Pressler, Larry, *U.S. Senators from the Prairie* (Vermillion, Dakota Press, 1982).

Rakove, Milton, *Don't Make No Waves, Don't Back No Losers* (Bloomington, Indiana University Press, 1975).

Ranney, Austin, *Curing the Mischiefs of Faction* (Berkeley, University of California Press, 1975).

—— ed. *The American Elections of 1980* (Washington D.C., American Enterprise Institute, 1981).

—— *Channels of Power* (New York, Basic Books, 1983).

Reichard, Gary W. *Reaffirmation of Republicanism* (Knoxville, University of Tennessee Press, 1975).

Reichley, James A. *Conservatism in an Age of Change* (Washington D.C., Brookings, 1981).

Reinhard, David W. *The Republican Right Since 1945* (Lexington, University Press of Kentucky, 1983).

Rieselbach, Leroy N. *Legislative Reform* (Lexington, Lexington Books, 1979).

Riker, William H. 'The Senate and American Federalism', *American Political Science Review*, June 1955, pp. 452–69.

Ripley, Randall B. *Party Leaders in the House of Representatives* (Washington D.C., Brookings, 1967).

—— *Power in the Senate* (New York, St Martin's Press, 1969).

—— *Majority Party Leadership in Congress* (Boston, Little, Brown and Co., 1969).

—— *Congress: Process and Policy* (New York, W. W. Norton, 1978).

—— and Franklin, Grace A. *Congress, the Bureaucracy, and Public Policy* (Homewood, Ill., The Dorsey Press, 1984).

Roberts, James C. *The Conservative Decade* (Westport, Conn., Arlington House, 1980).

Robinson, Michael J. and Appel, Kevin R. 'Network News Coverage of Congress', *Political Science Quarterly*, fall, 1979.

Rogers, Lindsay, *The American Senate* (New York, Alfred Knopf, 1926).

Rossiter, Clinton, *Conservatism in America* (London, William Heineman, 1955).

—— *1787: The Grand Convention* (New York, Macmillan, 1966).

Rothenberg, Stuart, *Campaign Regulation and Public Policy* (Washington D.C., The Free Congress Research and Education Foundation, 1981).

Rothman, David J. *Politics and Power: The U.S. Senate 1869-1901* (Cambridge, Harvard University Press, 1966).

Rusher, William A. *The Making of the New Majority Party* (New York, Steed and Ward, 1975).

Sabato, Larry J. *The Rise of Political Consultants* (New York, Basic Books, 1981).

_____ *PAC Power* (New York, W. W. Norton, 1984).

Sage, Leland L. *William Boyd Allison* (Iowa City, University of Iowa Press, 1956).

Sale, Kirkpatrick, *Power Shift* (New York, Random House, 1975).

Saloma, John S. *Congress and the New Politics* (Boston, Little Bronw and Co., 1964).

Scammon, Richard and Wattenberg, Ben, *The Real Majority* (New York, Coward-McCann, 1970).

Schattschneider, E. E. *Party Government* (New York, Farrar and Rinehart, 1940).

Schneider, Carl E. and Vinovskis, Morris A. eds., *The Law and the Politics of Abortion* (Lexington, Lexington Books, 1980).

Schneider, Jerrold E. *Ideological Coalitions in Congress* (Westport, Conn., Greenwood Press, 1979).

Seagull, Louis M. *Southern Republicanism* (New York, John Wiley, 1975).

Shafer, Byron E. *Quiet Revolution* (New York, Russell Sage, 1983).

Shaffer, William R. *Party and Ideology in the U.S. Congress* (Washington D.C., University Press of America, 1980).

Shelley, Mack C. *The Permanent Majority* (University, Ala., The University of Alabama Press, 1983).

Shepsle, Kenneth J. and Rohde, David W. *Taking Stock of Congressional Research: The New Institutionalism* (St Louis, Washington University, 1978).

Shoup, Lawrence H. *The Carter Presidency and Beyond* (Palo Alto, Ramparts Press, 1980).

Sindler, Allan ed. *Changein the Contemporary South* (Durham, Duke University Press, 1963).

Smith, Steven S. and Deering, Christopher J. *Committees in Congress* (Washington D.C., Congressional Quarterly Press, 1984).

Spanier, John and Nogee, Joseph, *Congress, The Presidency, and American Foreign Policy* (Oxford, Pergamon Press, 1981).

Spanier, John and Uslaner, Eric M. *Foreign Policy and the Democratic Dilemma* (New York, CBS College Publishing, 1982).

Steiner, Gilbert Y. ed. *The Abortion Issue and the American System* (Washington D.C., Brookings, 1983).

Strong, Donald S. 'The Presidential Election in the South, 1952', *Journal of Politics*, August 1955.

_____ *Issue-Voting and Party Realignment* (University, Ala., The University of Alabama Press, 1977).

Sundquist, James L. *The Decline and Resurgence of Congress* (Washington D.C., Brookings, 1981).

_____ *Dynamics of the Party System* (Washington D.C., Brookings, 1983).

Swanstrom, Roy, *The United States Senate 1787-1801* (Washington D.C., GPO, 1962).

Tarrance, Lance V. *Negative Campaigns and Negative Votes: The 1980 Elections* (Washington D.C., The Free Congress Research and Education Foundation, 1982).

Truman, David B. *The Congressional Party* (New York, John Wiley, 1959).

_____ ed. *The Congress and America's Future* (Englewood Cliffs, Prentice Hall, 1965).

Tuchel, Peter S. and Tejera, Felipe, 'Changing Patterns in American Voting Behaviour 1914-1980', *Public Opinion Quarterly*, summer 1983, pp. 230-47.

Turner, Julius and Schneier, Edward V. *Party and Constituency* (Baltimore, Johns Hopkins University Press, 1970).

Turner, Robert F. *The War Powers Resolution* (Philadelphia, Foreign Policy Research Institute, 1983).

US Bureau of the Census, *Statistical Abstract of the U.S. 1980*.

US Congress, Joint Commission on the Organisation of the Congress, *Final Report*, 89th Congress, 2nd sess., 28 July 1966.

US Senate, Commission on the Operation of the Senate, *Committees and Senate Procedures*, 94th Congress, 2nd sess., 1976.

—— Commission on the Operation of the Senate, *Senators, Offices, Ethics, and Pressures*, 95th Congress, 2nd sess., 1978.

—— Committee on Banking, Housing and Urban Affairs, *Hearings*, 'The President's New Anti-Inflation Program', 95th Congress, 2nd sess., 1978.

—— Committee on Foreign Relations, *Hearings*, 'The Panama Canal Treaties', 95th Congress, 2nd sess., 1978.

—— Committee on Foreign Relations, *Hearings*, 'Trade Sanctions Against Rhodesia', 96th Congress, 1st sess., 1979.

—— Committee on the Judiciary, Subcommittee on the Constitution, *Hearings*, 'Affirmative Action and Equal Protection', 97th Congress, 1st sess., 1981.

—— Committee on the Judiciary, Subcommittee on the Constitution, *Hearings*, 'The 14th Amendment and School Busing', 97th Congress, 1st sess., 1981.

—— Committee on the Judiciary, Subcommittee on the Constitution, *Hearings*, 'Constitutional Restraints Upon the Judiciary', 97th Congress, 1st sess., 1981.

—— Committee on the Judiciary, Subcommittee on the Constitution, *Hearings*, 'Balancing the Budget', 97th Congress, 1st sess., 1981.

—— Committee on the Judiciary, Subcommittee on the Separation of Powers, *Hearings*, 'The Human Life Bill', 97th Congress, 1st sess., 1981.

—— Committee on Rules and Administration, *Hearings*, 'Federal Election Proposals of 1977', 95th Congress, 1st sess., 1977.

—— Committee on Rules and Administration, *Report*, 'Public Financing of Senate General Elections Act', 95th Congress, 1st sess., 1977.

—— Committee on Rules and Administration, *History of the Committee On Rules and Administration*, 96th Congress, 1st sess., 1979.

—— Committee on Rules and Administration, *Hearings*, 'Application and Administration of the Federal Election Campaign Act of 1971, As Amended', 97th Congress, 1st sess., 1981.

—— Committee on Rules and Administration, *Committee Print*, 'Television and Radio Coverage of Proceedings in the Senate Chamber', 97th Congress, 1st sess., 1981.

—— Committee on Rules and Administration, *Senate Manual*, 97th Congress, 1st sess., 1981.

—— Temporary Select Committee to Study the Senate Committee System, *First Staff Report*, 'The Senate Committee System, Jurisdictions, Referrals, Numbers and Sizes, and Limitations on Membership', 94th Congress, 2nd sess., 1976.

—— Temporary Select Committee to Study the Senate Committee System, *Second Report*, 'The Operation of the Senate Committee System', 94th Congress, 2nd sess., 1976.

—— Temporary Select Committee to Study the Senate Commitee System, *Report Together With Prepared Resolutions*, 98th Congress, 2nd sess., 1984.

Viguerie, Richard, *The New Right: We're Ready to Lead* (Falls Church, Va., The Viguerie Co., 1981).

Ware, Alan, 'The 1980 Elections; Party Renewal or Continuing Party Decline?' *Parliamentary Affairs*, spring 1981, pp. 174–90.

Wattenberg, Martin P. 'From Parties to Candidates: Examining the Role of the Media', *Public Opinion Quarterly*, summer 1982, pp. 216–27.

—— *The Decline of American Political Parties* (Cambridge, Harvard University Press, 1984).

Whitaker, Robert W. ed. *The New Right Papers* (New York, St Martin's Press, 1982).

White, William S. *Citadel* (New York, Harper and Row, 1957).

Wildavsky, Aaron, 'The Two Presidencies', *Trans-Action*, December 1966, pp. 7–14.

Williams, Philip M. and Wilson, Graham, 'The American Mid-Term Elections', *Political Studies*, December 1979, pp. 603–9.

Williams, Philip M. and Reilly, S. J. 'The 1980 U.S. Election and After', *Political Studies*, September 1982, pp. 371–92.

Wilson, James Q. *The Amateur Democrat* (Chicago, University of Chicago Press, 1962).

Wilson, Woodrow, *Congressional Government* (London, Constable, 1914).

Young, James S. *The Washington Community 1800–1928* (New York, Columbia University Press, 1966).

Index